Educating New Americans

Immigrant Lives and Learning

Sociocultural, Political, and Historical Studies in Education
Joel Spring, Editor

Educating New Americans

Immigrant Lives and Learning

Donald F. Hones

Cher Shou Cha

LAWRENCE ERLBAUM ASSOCIATES, PUBLISHERS
1999   Mahwah, New Jersey   London

Lawrence Erlbaum Associates, Inc., Publishers
10 Industrial Avenue
Mahwah, NJ 07430

Cover design by Kathryn Houghtaling Lacey

Library of Congress Cataloging-in-Publication Data

Hones, Donald F.
Educating new Americans : immigrants lives and learning / by Donald F. Hones and Cher Shou Cha.
   p.   cm. — (Sociocultural, political, and historical
   studies in education)
Includes bibliographical references and index.
ISBN 0-8058-3133-9 (cloth : alk. paper). —
   ISBN 0-8058-3134-7 (pbk. : alk. paper.)
1. Immigrants—Education—United States—Case
   studies.   2. Immigrants—United States—Social life
   and customs—Case studies.   3. Cha, Cher Shou.
   4. Hmong Americans—Biography.   5. Americanization.   6. Multicultural education—United
   States.   I. Cha, Cher Shou.   II. Title.   III. Series.
LC3731.H635   1998
371.86'91'0973—dc21   98-24514
                                                    CIP

Books published by Lawrence Erlbaum Associates are
printed on acid-free paper, and their bindings are chosen
for strength and durability.

Printed in the United States of America
10 9 8 7 6 5 4 3 2

Dedicated
to elders, who keep the memories;
to children, who carry the dreams;
to parents and teachers, who provide the bridge.

৪০ ✳ ಐ

Contents

A Note on Authorship
and Ownership

This book began as a research project about what it means to be an American with Shou Cha's story at its center. Much of this text is in Shou Cha's words, and his reflections and viewpoints have helped to shape both individual chapters and the overall theme of the work.

The nature of our collaboration, and the value that we derived from sharing our stories and our thoughts about children, school, culture, and society, has led to our shared authorship of this book. We share ownership for its contents, although Don Hones, as the writer, accepts ultimate responsibility for the shape our words have taken on the pages that follow.

Preface

This book examines what it means to be an American through the life history of a refugee from Laos. Shou Cha is a community liaison for an elementary school, an evangelical preacher, a community leader, a husband, and a father. His lifetime of learning, presented mostly in his own voice, is framed by various historical and sociological contexts that have shaped his life, the lives of other Hmong refugees, and the lives of other Americans, old and new: These contexts include the history of immigrant education policies in the United States as seen through the lives of immigrant children, the historical and sociological impact of warfare as well as missionary work in the lives of the Hmong people, and the sociology of generational conflict, especially as it is felt among immigrant groups. Finally, *Educating New Americans* suggests that immigrant parents such as Shou Cha can contribute to the process of teaching peace to children, and making peace among diverse groups in America, the land of *e pluribus unum*.

Part I opens with "Prelude to a Life: The Shooting," concerning a pivotal moment in Shou Cha's American experience—his brush with death. Chapter 1 introduces the major questions that concern this book: How can we understand the educational lives of immigrants within broader societal and historical contexts? What kinds of education take place outside the school, in immigrant homes and communities, and how can schools acknowledge and benefit from this learning? How can the study of the educational life of an immigrant help address the needs of immigrants themselves, and increase our understanding of how best to further the education of all Americans?

Chapter 2 uses the methods of narrative inquiry to provide a new reading of the educational lives presented in the immigrant autobiographies of Richard Rodriguez and Leonard Covello. The lives of Rodriguez and Covello illustrate the value of educational narratives for grappling with questions of immigrant education and what it means to be an American. Woven into these educational narratives is a discussion of the larger social and historical context of immigrant education in the United States.

Conflicting societal goals regarding the education of immigrants have problematized the following questions: How can a unified culture be developed within a nation made up largely of immigrants and their descendants? How can the children of cultural minorities best be prepared for participation within the dominant culture? This new reading of the lives of Rodriguez and Covello serves as a reminder of the importance of creating educational narratives of new Americans such as Shou Cha.

Part II forms the narrative body of this study. Chapter 3 develops Shou Cha's educational experiences from his youth in Laotian villages to his arrival in the United States. The history of the Hmong is a history of movement and struggle, and Shou's understanding of the present is shaped by his knowledge of the Hmong's long road from the Yellow River in China ages ago, through the Laotian villages and Thai refugee camps, to the urban landscapes of the United States in the 1990s. Significantly, the history of the Hmong in the last 40 years is intimately entwined with the history of U.S. military, political, and economic involvement in Indochina. The Chas, as new immigrants, are part of the latest chapter in American social history. This chapter suggests the significant learning that often takes place in the lives of persons, such as Shou, who have little formal education, and that their resourcefulness is an educational value for all Americans.

Chapter 4 has two interconnected strands. On the one hand, it develops Shou Cha's experiences with religion, especially recounting his conversion and work within an evangelical ministry. The Chas spend much of their time with the Hmong Christian community in Windigo. Shou Cha ministers to this Christian community, his children are active in its youth group, and his house is a common meeting place for its members. This ministry is perhaps one of the most significant aspects of Shou's adult life. On the other hand, this chapter explores the powerful association between the "word" of religion and literacy, especially for the Hmong. This chapter considers the troubling issues that accompany evangelization, as well as assessing the significant teacher preparation and literacy education that takes place in the church.

Chapter 5 focuses specifically on the parent–children relationship in the Cha family. Special attention is paid to the way in which the young generation of Hmong Americans faces its world, and how its world is shaped by crosscurrents of home culture and the dominant culture. The role of generativity, the handing down of important life information from one generation to the next, is discussed within the context of Shou's family life: Proud to recall his own family past, Shou is yet a problematic mediator between the traditional world of his forefathers, his own fundamentalist beliefs, and the new, "Americanized" ways of his children. Recent work by Bruner (1990) has suggested the value of studying the lives of individuals within the family context, as the family represents the microcosm of the culture. Hmong culture has been described as group-focused, and in comparison to the dominant American culture, the Hmong place little emphasis on individuality or self-identity (Walker-Moffat, 1995). By focusing on an individual's life in the family context, I seek to better capture Hmong cultural nuances. Moreover, analysis of family interactions can help to uncover the intergenerational learning that takes place in a context where immigrant elders pass many values to the young, but where the young often take on many responsibilities for the family due to their greater facility with the language and cultural norms of the adopted country.

Chapter 6 examines Shou Cha's efforts to "make peace" between and within Hmong families, between families and the school, between children of various cultural backgrounds, and with himself and his own changing Hmong American identity. Three of the Cha children attend the Horace Kallen school, in Windigo, Michigan, where their father works as a bilingual aide and community liaison. Community liaisons such as Shou Cha play an extremely important role in this multicultural school. More than cultural border guides, they play the role of peacemaker for children from various fractious communities, preparing in this way the next generation of multiethnic Americans. The perspectives of the director, assistant director, the classroom teacher with whom Shou works, his fellow community liaisons, and Shou are brought into an overall discussion about "making peace" as an important aspect of educating children for a diverse society. Finally, Shou Cha provides his own reflections of how working at this multicultural school has helped him to make peace with America, and has served as an antidote to the feelings of homelessness and helplessness he felt after being shot near his home.

Part III reflects on what can be learned from the life history of a Hmong American, and returns to the educational policy issues raised in Chapter 1, and the concerns of narrative inquiry raised in Chapter 2. Chapter 7 examines the major themes in this life history and discusses their implications for a variety of readers. I examine three themes of resourcefulness, relationship, and respect that emerge from the life history narrative: The value of resourcefulness is explored through Shou Cha's tremendous ability to adapt to changing circumstances, a quality that seems also to be present in many refugee and immigrant communities. The value of relationship is seen in the high value Shou Cha places on ties with family, clan, and community. Respect, at all levels, is what makes these relationships work. I suggest that these three values are not only of fundamental importance for the Hmong, but for all Americans. Therefore, these "3 R's" are also needed as part of anyone's education.

Chapter 8 continues the exploration of the theme of what it means to be an American for individuals of widespread roots and experiences. The autobiographies of Eva Hoffman, Maxine Hong Kingston, and Jesus Colon are highlighted as works wherein individual lives can provide lenses onto broader social, cultural, and historical contexts. These autobiographies, like the life history of Shou Cha, offer all Americans a place to begin new dialogues about who we are as a rainbow people and how we would prepare for the world of our children.

ACKNOWLEDGMENTS

I thank the AERA Spencer Foundation Fellowship program for both funding and facilitating my contact with a national community of scholars during the initial stages of this work, and the many colleagues who offered helpful suggestions at the two AERA Spencer institutes, and the AERA Annual Meeting in 1996.

Yvonne Caamal Canul, Sharon Peck, and the staff and students of the Center for Language, Culture and Communication Arts in Lansing, Michigan, welcomed me into their community, where I was able to spend time getting to know the school and its people. Lao Lo was especially helpful in providing me with initial contacts and insights into the Hmong community.

I express my gratitude to my many friends and colleagues at Michigan State University. I was fortunate to receive useful criticism of an early draft of this work from David Labaree, and Cathy Reischl and Susan Melnick offered insightful suggestions as this work neared its completion. My special thanks goes to Lynn Paine, Susan Florio-Ruane, James Gavelek, Brian Delany, and Jay Featherstone, members of my dissertation committee, for the care and thoughtfulness of their responses to hundreds of pages of my writings and rewritings, and to Steve Weiland, my advisor, for encouraging me to begin writing and to keep writing, and to organize this work in three parts, like a *book*. His humor, understanding, and camaraderie were a blessing to me and kept me focused on the end of the road.

Naomi Silverman of Lawrence Erlbaum Associates and Joel Spring, editor of the Sociocultural, Political, and Historical Studies in Education Series, offered valuable suggestions and encouragement, helping me to refine this text for a wider audience.

I am thankful for the support of my family: my mother and father, brothers and sisters, who have been my role models; Margaret McClear, whose honest and critical perspectives on language and culture inspired me to enter a doctoral program; and Kathleen, Orion, and Ariana, who have helped me through this story with playfulness, tolerance, and love.

Finally, I thank Shou Cher Cha and his family for sharing a year of their lives with me. You have taught me that by sharing our stories from the heart we can begin to break down the walls that separate us, and to heal ourselves and our world.

It is a beginning.

—Donald F. Hones

I

Immigrant Identity
in School and Society

Prelude to a Life History:
The Shooting

My days are swifter than a runner;
They flee away, they see no good.
They go by like skiffs of reed,
Like an eagle swooping on the prey.
                              —The Book of Job, 9:25–26

*On a cold November night in 1994 Shou Cha, a Hmong refugee from Laos,
finishes his shift as a pizza delivery driver, picks up his wife and daughter,
and drives to the convenience store around the corner from his home. The
store is on Michigan Avenue, a busy one-way street that cuts through a tough
northside neighborhood in Windigo, Michigan. There are no windows in the
store. Outside, on the grim brick exterior, is a sign posted, "No loitering. Ten
minute parking only. Violators will be towed." Across the side street is a rib
joint. On the opposite corner, across Michigan, is a gas station. Next to the
convenience store is a block of apartments whose narrow, dark windows remind one of a prison. Inside, the store contains the limited selection of over-
priced food items one customarily finds in inner city neighborhoods. Save
for the unsmiling clerk and two teenage girls, Shou is alone in the store. He
pays for his milk and heads back to the car. As he prepares to get in, four
shots ring out behind him. Shou Cha, who has survived a war that annihi-
lated one third of his people and years spent in a dangerous, squalid camp in
Thailand, has been gunned down in the "land of opportunity." He describes
this pivotal incident of his American experience, and his thoughts and feelings at that time.*

I remember that the time was 8:30 p.m., and I put my two sons into their
room because they were stubborn. So I said, "You stay in your room until I
come back!" Then I and my wife and the little girl went to the store. In the
parking lot there wasn't any car except mine. There were not many people in the store, just two girls who were before me, so they paid for what
they wanted and they came out fast. So I paid for my bottle of milk and I
came out. I opened my door, and I lifted up my seat, and I put the gallon of

milk behind the seat, and I pushed it back. And as I was turning to sit down, I heard the gunshots, four times, from behind me. And my mind told me to sit down fast, in case the bullet came straight. So I did. And when I sat down, I already had gotten shot, in the soft spot in my upper hip, and the bullet almost came through the skin in front, in the upper part of the stomach. So I fell down, sort of sitting and sort of falling down.

I told my wife, "Somebody shot me."

She said, "You're kidding."

"No, I'm not kidding."

My hands were holding the place where the bullets came through, and I showed her my hands, and there was blood in my hands, so she believed, and she yelled, and she went to the store and called for help.

The police came about 2 minutes after I got shot. And they asked me questions, and I was not able to answer them. I did not use my mouth, because it was too weak to say the words, I just made motions.

About 2 minutes after that the ambulance came.

They asked me, "Are you all right?"

"No, I am not all right. No. No."

Then they hurried up and put me on the stretcher. You know, when they stretched me straight, I almost passed out. Because in a sitting position I felt better, and they stretched me laying down, and it got worse. About that time I said to myself, suppose I do not make it. I was not able to tell my two sons, whom I put in the bedroom, that they could come out. You know, because I put the two in there and said stay here until I come back. Suppose that I did not have the time to tell them to come out? I might never have the chance to talk to them again.

At that time, I promised to God: "Dear God. If I made some mistake that caused this to happen to me, forgive me."

I said, "Dear God, if you want me to live on, I will live on. And whatever you want me to do, I'll do it. But I need your help to recover from this."

And I said, "Dear God, if I do not make it, receive my spirit into your hands."

That's how I prayed. And everything happened at the same time, one thing after another. So they put me in the ambulance, and I asked for a pillow, and they said, "No, you are OK with this."

"You're OK."

They told the driver to drive west on Michigan—the wrong way. Because that was the fastest way to the hospital. And it took about 2 minutes to arrive there. And then the men took me inside the emergency room and there was the nurse who I used to be a translator for. So she screamed, "Oh, he's one of our translators!" She screamed, and then everyone came right away! And they just tore me apart, someone held my hand, someone held my head, someone held my legs, someone tore my clothes. And it got worse. And I almost was killed by that time, too. They were putting the tube into my nostrils, it was terrible. Everything was terrible. And my strength was reduced. And they asked me if I was OK, and I said, "No."

"I'm not OK."

Then my wife said, "I'm such a simple person—what can I do?"

I said, "Go and talk to Pastor Lor," who was one of my friends, and who lives in Detroit. "Go and make a phone call and so you guys can pray for me."

And she said, 'Suppose that I do not get back?'

I had no answer for her.

So she left, and immediately the surgeon came, and they demanded that I go, because I heard the nurse say, 'Hurry up! Go!' And they just rushed me through and went to the surgery room.

I asked the doctor, "Doctor, I would like to pray my last prayer." Then I prayed again.

I said, "Doctor. Suppose that I do not make it. Tell my wife to love the children."

He said, "Don't worry. You'll make it."

Then he said, "Are you ready?"

I said, "Yes, I am ready." And that is all I heard.

The next thing I heard, one of the pastors who was my friend called my name. And he said, "Can you hear what I say?" I could not answer, because I was so weak. So I made the motion, "Yes." Someone told me that I was unconscious for 4 or 5 hours.

At that time I was still in intensive care so just two people could see me at any one time. I had so many friends see me that I could not sleep at all! Which is good, but I could not sleep. Yeah. So the nurse said, "You go! And he can sleep!" I'd love them to stay, but I could not sleep! There was very much support. Many of the pastors from around the country called me and supported me in a lot of things. The district superintendent for my area called and he supported me and sent a representative to visit me. So everything went well at that time. I had a lot of help from my family, too. My mother was in St. Paul, Minnesota at that time, where my youngest sister lives, and my brother-in-law, too. They heard about the shooting immediately, because my wife called. So they even wanted to go to the airport and fly to see me right away if they had the chance. They supported me so much. They came and they stayed the whole week, and my mother stayed for the whole 2 months.

The people in the neighborhood supported me so much, too. I didn't know them very well. But they know me quite well, just because I am the one with the family with the most children, and of course, my children and their children go to the same school, and when they talk to me, I talk to them, and when they ask me questions, I answer them. Besides, the police officer who works in this area, he mentioned the shooting to the neighborhood. Also, the sergeant-major of the police department came to visit me a couple of times. He came to talk to me, too. He mentioned that if I would like help, they would ask the neighborhood to help, and they helped a lot. Some of them brought mattresses, couches, food and Christmas items. I should say, talking about Christmas presents, that year was the most that we have seen. In these things you need someone to encourage you. And the encouragement really helps.

I believe it was the first day, because I was still in the intensive care room. Someone was calling me, and I just opened my eyes, and someone was holding me, and said, "Mr. Cha?"

And then I saw Rachel, and another person, Diana. And they introduced themselves. Diana was the principal, and Rachel, who I knew better. They were working in the school that my children go to. And they visited me.

So, I said, "Oh, I forgot to fill out the application for a job as bilingual aide in the school."

They said, "No! Don't worry! We'll save the job for you! That job is yours!"

So, I think that they had mercy in that, too.

You know, by that time, so many terrible things had happened to my family. Before I got shot, I and my wife already made a decision to resign as pastors. We just did not have the paper to resign, but we already made the decision. Because our income, our way, our encouragement, everything was low. So we said, that's the bottom. We'll stop. Maybe God does not choose us for this. So we were ready to stop. But for the shooting, I put my hope in God, only, and some of the church helpers, too, they helped me a lot. And I could not stop, so I had to go on.

But after I came from the hospital, the first week, I'm gonna tell you what I thought.

I said:

> *There isn't any solid place,*
> *any place of peace on Earth.*
> *There isn't.*
> *I stayed in the hospital for two weeks.*
> *I disown that place.*
> *The hospital is not my place.*
> *They said:*
> *You can go home.*
> *And I don't have a home to go to.*
> *This house I live in is not my house.*
> *Not my home.*

I live by the money.
This place belongs to someone else.
It's not my house.
I don't belong to this Earth.

Besides, I am scared.
I do not know if
the next day I will get shot again.
I don't trust going outside.
I do not know how I should live.
I do not want to stay by the window.
I don't want to live in this area.
I don't want to live anywhere.
I don't belong to this Earth.

Five days after I got shot,
My mother fell on the cement sidewalk.
And all her face got bruised and scratched.
She does not know why.
And that even brought me lower.
I said,
Why did that happen?
And when I came back
her mouth was still kind of swollen,
her face was still bruised and scratched.
And I said,
Oh no.
Why me?
Why me?
My mother also said,
This Earth does not belong to us.
We do not belong to this Earth.

The only good thing we experienced at that time
is when we said,
We don't belong to the Earth.
We belong to Heaven,
where we should go.
And we should keep going until we are there.

Since that time my thoughts have changed. The only thing is that I cannot resign the ministry because of this: I got shot. I should say, I got killed, and God saved me because he might have that purpose for me to go on, and he helps me a lot, and the neighborhood helped me, I do not know why. I cannot give up the ministry, no matter how much I suffer. I cannot give up. The only thing that is still in my mind is that *you should not give up*. So that is why I am still here today.

1

On Being
and Becoming American

Shou Cha remembers. He sees the young boy, walking quietly through the jungle, hunting squirrels and monkeys with a crossbow. He sees the red, the yellow, the purple flowers blooming on the mountain walls of Laos. He listens: Far off are the sounds of war, a land mine exploding, killing a brother, American bombs dropping along the Ho Chi Minh Trail, then a silence. He sees quiet figures of refugees moving through the shadows of night, heading for the Mekong River and an unknown future. He remembers the faces of Hmong warriors, America's "secret army" in Laos, now unwilling captives inside Thai refugee camps. He hears the sound of the shaman's prayer, now challenged by the preaching of the missionaries, and the strange sounds of a new language he must learn: "Good morning. Please take a seat." He remembers getting on the "bus to America," and the "plane to America," and eventually, getting to America. He sees the young father working three jobs, trying desperately to keep a growing family and extended relatives together in a new land. He sees the father holding a baby and watching six other children while the mother works at a factory. He sees himself and his wife, tired from their various jobs, yet encouraging their children to learn English, to study hard, and to never forget the important traditions of their family, clan and people.

He is Hmong from Laos, and that is an essential aspect of Shou Cha's identity. Yet, over the course of 15 years of life in the Midwest, he is also becoming an American. For Shou Cha, being Hmong *and* American is both possible and desirable: It means a sense of communal support for himself and his family, and an important addition to the American cultural landscape. Shou Cha speaks:

Many different peoples live in the
same town
black, brown, yellow.
If they look a certain way, they have
their own community.
I don't deny it.
It is good to serve your own
community.
Please do your best for them.
But then you should
treat others nicely, too.
Black, white, brown, yellow:
We are the same people.
We are different in skin only,
but we are all human.
We are the same, created by God,
one creator,
and it is very beautiful.
Different colors, and very beautiful.

WHAT IT MEANS TO BE AN AMERICAN

Two essays by imminent scholars have appeared in the pages of the *New Republic* in recent years addressing the question of what it means to be an American at the close of the century. In an essay entitled "Against Identity: An Idea Whose Time Has Gone," Wieseltier (1994) writes "In America, we are choking on identity" (p. 24). For Wieseltier, "the American achievement is not the multicultural society, it is the multicultural individual," that focusing on group differences ignores the diverse roots and group ties that each American possesses (p. 30).[1] He concludes that if the differences between individuals and groups were really as great as some multiculturalists claim, dialogue would be impossible, and "There would be only total silence or total war" (p. 30). In "For Identity," Walzer

---

[1]In much of his essay Wieseltier refers to the work of psychologist Erik Erikson, who popularized the term identity in the social sciences in the 1950s. For Erikson (1950), identity was a process located in the core of the individual and also in the core of communal culture, and this process of linking the individual to the community was fundamental for the adolescent stage of human development. Sociologists of the symbolic-interactionist school differed from Erikson by suggesting that identity was socially constructed, sustained, and ever-changing. These two ways of conceptualizing identity contribute to two distinctive ways of viewing ethnicity, as either primordially given or optionally cultivated. For a useful discussion of the historical roots of debates over identity and ethnicity (see Philip Gleason, 1983).

(1996) wrote that the current debate over multiculturalism must be understood in the context of an American history in which deep differences have led to nearly genocidal wars against the native population of the continent, slavery and systematic subordination of African Americans, anti-Catholicism and anti-Semitism, and "hostility to 'Orientals' that culminated in the concentration camps of World War II." Wulzer suggested that, in spite this history of conflict between diverse elements of American society, some Americans continue to "cling to the vision of a singular America, arguing that multiculturalism is the great divisive force. But perhaps their love of singularity also divides us" (p. 39).

Concern over who is, and who ought to be, considered an American is not only expressed in scholarly debates, but at the level of public policy. This is exemplified in recent legislation aimed at both legal and illegal immigrants, as well as speakers of languages other than English. Immigration reform legislation signed into law in 1996 limits the numbers of legal immigrants and denies them welfare benefits; state laws such as Proposition 187 in California preclude basic services, including education, to *illegal* workers, and English Only initiatives in several states seek to limit the use of other languages. Such efforts to control immigration and the use of languages other than English follow on 30 years in which the United States has experienced the largest influx of immigrants in its history. Since the passage of the Immigration Act of 1965, 20 million people have emigrated to the United States (Kennedy, 1996). These newcomers, many of whom are refugees from wars, revolutions, and drastic economic change, differ from previous generations of immigrants in that most come from Latin America and Asia, and relatively few come from Europe (see Table 1.1).[2] By 1976 there were more than twice as many immigrant nationalities represented in the United States than there had been in 1920 (Fuchs, 1990).

This latest wave of newcomers to the United States has helped to fuel continuing debate about who we are as Americans. Proponents of cultural pluralism believe that America's strength lies in its ability to draw from and honor many traditions, many languages, and many roots. Conservative scholars, however, have blamed cultural pluralists for the "disuniting of America," and have called for a renewed focus on "American" cultural literacy and "traditional American values" (Hirsch, 1987; Schlesinger, 1991). Okihiro (1994) summarizes this conservative critique as follows:

---

[2]Refugee status has generally be conferred on people fleeing communist regimes (Cuba, Laos, Vietnam), but not those fleeing regimes deemed "friendly" to the United States (e.g., El Salvador, Guatemala). Nor is official refugee status granted to persons fleeing the chaos caused by rapid economic change and accompanying underemployment and impoverishment of millions in places such as Mexico.

TABLE 1.1
New Americans
Regions/Countries of Origin and Size of Foreign-Born Population
(Based on 1990 Census Data)

Region	Population (N)	% of Total Immigrants
Africa	363,819	1.8
Asia	4,979,030	25.2
Latin America/Caribbean	8,416,924	42.6
Europe & Canada	5,095,233	25.8
*SE Asian Countries of Origin**		
Cambodia	118,833	0.6
Laos	171,577	0.9
Vietnam	543,262	2.7

Speakers of Languages Other Than English in Schools

6.3 million children ages 5–17 speak languages other than English[**];
2.31 million children classified as Limited English Proficient (LEP)[***].

[*]Figures for Southeast Asian countries are pulled out of the general category for Asia in order to give readers an idea of the numbers of people, such as Shou Cher and his family, who have come as refugees as a direct result of the Vietnam War and its aftermath.

[**]Based on the 1990 census.

[***]Figures for 1992 from U.S. Department of Education (1993).

In its stress on racial, gender, class and sexual inequality, in its insistence on identity and self-definition, the *margin* has led the nation astray, far from the original formulations that made the Republic great, has created instead balkanized enclaves—ghettos—and even worse, has stirred up social conflict and "culture wars." Without a center, things have fallen apart. (pp. 149–150)

Who are we, as Americans? Can we find a common identity within a diverse society? Are the diverse groups that make up American society to be considered weaknesses or strengths? Has our plurality of cultures, languages and traditions become so many loose threads unraveling the national fabric? Or can we acknowledge the contributions of all people to the growing and changing nature of the American nation? Rather than unraveling the existing fabric of society, can immigrants be seen as colorful new threads who add life and vitality to the weaving?[3]

CHALLENGED MEMORIES

Historically, public education, with its role of assimilating the masses into the American republic, has been a battleground between forces of uniformity and pluralism. How we define what it means to be an American has many implications for the education of immigrants and others.[4] In his comprehensive history of American education, Cremin (1988) notes that immigrants to the United States have often experienced *discordant* education, as school, society and home have tried to inculcate conflicting sets of values and attitudes, often in different languages. *Discordant* can be defined as "lacking in agreement," yet, as Cremin seems to indicate, discordant notes can be rearranged to create harmony. In spite of these discordant notes in their lives, many immigrants have sought ways to contribute to American society without losing their own particularities. Cremin suggests that immigrants have transformed American life and thought, creating "through their efforts alternative American *paideias*[5] both for themselves and for the American community as a whole" (p. 150).

In an essay entitled "What Does It Mean to Be an American," Walzer (1990) examines the paradoxes present in a nation made up of people who came largely from elsewhere:

> It never happened that a group called Americans came together to form a political society called America. The people are Americans only by virtue of having come together. And whatever identity they have before becoming Americans they retain (or better, they are free to retain) afterward. There is, to be sure, another view of Americanization, which holds that the process requires for its success the mental erasure of all previous identities—forgetfulness, or even, as one enthusiast wrote in 1918, "absolute forgetfulness." But on the pluralist view, Americans are allowed to remem-

---

[3]The metaphor of the American *tapestry* has been overused of late. Nevertheless, since *pandau* storycloths or tapestries play an important part in the retelling of Hmong history and traditions, I feel the metaphor of tapestry represents well the Hmong addition to American culture.

[4]These others include all the diverse cultures represented in the United States, but especially those that have been marginalized by the dominant culture, such as Native Americans, African Americans, Asian Americans, and Latino Americans.

[5]*Paideia* is defined by *Webster's Third New International Dictionary* (1976) as training, the purpose of which is to "produce a broad, enlightened, mature outlook harmoniously combined with maximum cultural development."

ber who they were and to insist, also, on *what else they are*. (p. 595; italics in original)

From many lands, from many cultures we have come together, and for Americans concerned about who they are, the dilemma would seem to be how much should one remember, how much should one forget.

Forgetfulness of one's past, often encouraged by the schools, has made an impact on the lives of immigrants and on social relationships in the nation. Immigrant children in the past have probably often felt what Rich (1986) describes as the "psychic disequilibrium" when a teacher describes our society, and "you're not in it ... as if you looked into the mirror and saw nothing" (p. 199). For the historian Takaki (1993), the sharing of our different ethnic stories allows us to recognize ourselves in the mirror, and also to recognize our commonality. In the aftermath of the 1992 riots in Los Angeles, Takaki asked:

> Will Americans of diverse races and ethnicities be able to connect themselves to a larger narrative? ... America does not belong to one race or one group ... and Americans have been constantly redefining their national identity from the moment of first contact on the Virginia shore. By sharing their stories, they invite us to see ourselves in a different mirror. (p. 17)

E pluribus unum, "out of many, one." This motto on our national seal symbolizes for me the central paradox of American identity, and a pivotal purpose for American schools. To what extent should our schools support a plurality of cultures, languages, and ways of knowing the world? To what extent must they prepare all students with academic and civic skills to participate in a democratic nation? By sharing our many stories we come to grips with our changing sense of what it means to be and become Americans at the close of the twentieth century.

A LIFE HISTORY OF A NEW AMERICAN[6]

The debate over identity has come to Windigo, Michigan, where the Michigan Bilingual Education Conference has invited Ray Suarez of *National Public Radio* to host a panel on the topic of what it means to be an American. Suarez and panelists such as R. Richard West of the Smithsonian's National Museum of the American Indian and John Ogbu, professor of anthropology at Berkeley, discussed the problems with the "melting pot" metaphor, and why it was particularly difficult for darker-skinned,

---

[6]Throughout this text *American* and *America* refer to the people and political entity of the United States.

non-European Americans just to blend in. The panelists contended that rather than seek to "melt down" or eliminate the cultures and languages of American minority groups, the cultural contributions of these groups to the enrichment of American society should be acknowledged. I sat in the back of the ballroom with Shou Cha and Pao Xiong, Hmong refugees who work as bilingual assistants for an elementary school. As I listened to the discussion from the panel, I pondered the words Shou had spoken to me a few weeks earlier, when I asked him to define his own place in American culture:

> I think the teacher and the school where I work teach one major culture, and that it is American culture. But that does not mean "white" culture. America, even though I am not a citizen yet, America is this country, is my country!

This book presents the life history of Shou Cha, a refugee from Laos and a new American. Within this story of a particular life, I wish to explore the educational implications of who we have been as Americans, who we are, and who we are becoming. The life and learning of a new American, shaped by his relationships with his family, the school where he works and three of his children study, and his community, provides the context for a larger discussion of what it means to be an American.

The following questions guide this work:

- How can we understand the educational lives of immigrants within the broader societal and historical contexts of immigrant education policies?
- What kinds of education take place outside the school, in immigrant homes and communities, and how can schools acknowledge and benefit from this learning?
- How can the study of the educational life of an immigrant help address the educational needs of immigrants themselves, and increase our understanding of how best to further the education of all Americans?

Shou Cha's life history is unique, shaped by his personal choices and the exigencies of family, community, and sociohistorical contexts. Nevertheless, as an immigrant, a nonnative speaker of English, and a person of modest income, he shares much in common with many Americans whose histories are seldom told. For teachers, policymakers, researchers, and all Americans concerned with the education of the next generation, such histories must be remembered, and lessons from such lives must be learned, in order to foster unity in a diverse society.

Educating New Americans, the main title of this study, has two mean-ings: On the one hand, it refers to the education of recent immigrants and their children who are actively engaged in the adaptation to, and trans-formation of, America. *New Americans*, in this sense, is an inclusive term that recognizes members of diverse cultural and linguistic groups as sharing certain common features as Americans. On the other hand, *Edu-cating New Americans* suggests that American identity is not static, and that infusions of diverse peoples into our society changes and renews America and continues the education of all American people.

This life history explores the role of history, culture, spirituality, and language in learning, and follows important periods of Shou Cha's life, framed by social and historical crises that have forced changes on the Hmong in their long journey from Laos to America. Shou's learning expe-riences are charted through his youth that was spent in mountain farm-ing villages in Laos, experiences of war and refugee camps, adaptation to the new life in the United States; his conversion to fundamentalist Chris-tianity, his ministerial training and the spiritual rifts caused in his family and community; generational issues arising between Shou, his wife, and their Hmong children, who have grown up in the United States; the spe-cial mission of the Horace Kallen School, and Shou's role therein as an ed-ucator for all children; and Shou's role as a member of the Hmong community and American society.

Shou Cha is a member of the Hmong refugee community, whose pres-ence in the United States is a direct result of their past efforts in support of American personnel engaged in the war in Southeast Asia in the 1960s and 1970s. After years of protecting American airbases in Laos and tying up North Vietnamese troops on the Ho Chi Minh Trail, the Hmong were left alone after 1975 to face the wrath of the communist victors. The American government, which did not even acknowledge the "secret war" in Laos until 1970, had no evacuation plans for its former allies, and thou-sands of Hmong were forced to flee their mountain villages on foot and seek refuge in neighboring Thailand. It is estimated that one third of the Hmong in Laos were killed during the war and its aftermath. Those that escaped endured years of confinement in Thai refugee camps. Many have since arrived in the United States as political refugees, where approxi-mately 125,000 Hmong now live.[7] Many of the Hmong live in America's dangerous, decaying urban centers. Hidden away in pockets of poverty, the older generation tries to keep memories alive, while the younger gen-eration of Hmong cross the many borders that separate their home cul-ture from that of the school and larger society.

---

[7]This figure is according to the 1990 census. Due to undercounting, a high birth rate, and continued emigration from the camps in Thailand, the actual number of Hmong now in the United States is probably closer to 250,000.

PERSONAL NARRATIVE AND IDENTITY[8]

I read about Shou Cha long before I actually met him.[9] A newspaper story in November, 1994, reported the shooting of a Laotian immigrant on the northside of Windigo. The story quoted police who suggested that Mr. Cha had been shot "by accident," as the bullets had been intended for another party at the gas station across the street. The paper also mentioned that Mr. Cha had undergone emergency surgery and was in critical condition at a local hospital.

What the paper did not mention is that a few days later, after he had regained consciousness, Mr. Cha received a visit from Diana Canek, director of the Horace Kallen School, a public elementary school of choice with a large immigrant population. Mr. Cha had been told about a job at the school by a friend, but, because he felt unqualified due to his lack of formal schooling, Shou had never applied. Ms. Canek had been hesitant to hire an evangelical minister to work in a public school with children of diverse spiritual beliefs. However, as Cha lay there in the hospital bed, Canek told him that there would be a job waiting for him when he recovered. That is how Shou Cha came to be a bilingual assistant and community liaison for Kallen School.

I eventually made contact with Shou Cha with the help of another Hmong community liaison at Kallen. My work with a different Hmong family had ended, for a time, with their departure to a smaller town in the north, and I was seeking another family with which to continue my narrative research of immigrant lives. When I talked with him over the phone, Mr. Cha was eager to participate, and he invited me to his home. Shou Cha lives with his family in a brown, aging two-story rental on the northwest side. Living at this home are his wife, Mai Cha, their children, Sammy, Mai Jia, Paj Huab, Jesse, Joshua, Rebecca, and Gong Wendy, and Jerry Lee, whose family has moved north, and who wishes to finish high school in Windigo.

His articulateness in English, his charisma, the multiple roles he plays in life, and his receptiveness to the inquiries of a stranger made Shou Cha an ideal protagonist for life history research. With some of my previous Hmong informants my inability to communicate in Hmong or Lao limited our conversations to minimal questions and responses in English. Shou and I were able to have long discussions about a variety of issues,

[8] For an extended review of narrative research and the methods used in creating this life history, refer to Appendix A.

[9] Shou Cha and the members of his family are given their real names in this text. All other personal names, the names of schools, and the names of some cities have been replaced with pseudonyms in order to protect confidentiality.

and this facilitated the greater representation of his "voice" in the text. Shou's charismatic presence in the local Hmong community facilitated my meeting with other Hmong adults and children, many of whom could be found visiting the Chas in their home in the evenings. I became aware of the variety of roles that Shou Cha played: He is a husband and father of seven school-age children; he is an active member of his clan council, working specifically on ways to heal the generational rifts in the Hmong community; he is a bilingual assistant and community liaison for a local elementary school; and he is an evangelical minister. Finally, like the various members of the Hmong community, I was always made to feel welcome in Shou's home, his church, and his workplace. Coming from our disparate linguistic and cultural backgrounds, we were able to form a friendship and converse about the new America that is coming into being.

The form of the text for Shou Cha's life history varies. Some sections contain longer vignettes and little interpretive commentary, such as where Shou Cha relates episodes in his life history In other sections, the dialogue that took place between myself, Shou Cha, and other informants is represented. Representation of this dialogue seemed especially important when our interactions were leading us both to deeper reflection, or when we attempted to interpret parts of the text together. Finally, at several points the narrative text is represented as a poem. Several anthropologists and folklorists have argued that the rhythmic repetitions and formulaic language present in traditional oral cultures such as the Hmong should be represented in the form of poetry instead of prose (Clifford & Marcus, 1986; Conquergood, 1989; Fine, 1984; Tedlock, 1983). The emotive power of Shou Cha's oral account of his life is often best represented through poetry.

Although I wished to allow important themes to emerge from Shou's narrative, as I began the interviewing process, I had certain important questions in mind. As a Hmong refugee from Laos, what insights could Shou Cha provide me on the question of being a new American? Through shared stories and dialogue, could Shou and I make some sense of what it means to be an American, of American identity? Since the concept of *identity* has come to have many different meanings (Gleason, 1983), I began my analysis by using a framework provided by Eriksonian (1950) as well as Vygotskian (1978) concepts that combines the self identity of the individual personality with the social, cultural, historical and ideological contexts of individual lives. An alternative version of the self that reflects years of work among various cultural groups in the schools is put forward by Spindler and Spindler (1994). They conceptualize an *enduring* self that reflects one's past and cultural heritage, and a *situated* self that responds to the exigencies of everyday interaction within a dominant cultural context.[10] However, in analyzing the remarkable adaptations that Shou Cha has made in his long journey from the mountains of Laos to life in the United States, I began to realize that, as the work of Freeman (1993) suggests, Shou was *rewriting* his *self* over time. Moreover, Lifton's (1993) concept of *protean* identity, wherein the postmodern self can adapt to a variety of shapes and forms, seemed particularly relevant to the lived experience of this refugee from Laos. As will be illustrated in later chapters, Shou Cha's life history may well illustrate the complexities of a Hmong American identity that draws from fundamentalist Christian values, Hmong cultural traditions, and a protean ability to adapt to new conditions.[11]

IDENTITY AND THE RESEARCHER

To better understand the Hmong experience as new Americans I need to go back four or five generations to envision, again, my ancestors' arrival to the United States. My mother's great-grandfather left Ireland in the 1830s, after various years of hiding from the British authorities. He settled in one of the mill towns of Connecticut, and soon was able to save enough to send passage money to his wife and children. With the whole family working long hours in the mills, and by taking on lodgers in their cramped company house, they were able to gather the resources for the next move, to the Michigan frontier, where they would carve out a farm in the woodlands. My father's grandmother worked as a cook for the railroad gangs, and various members of her family mixed union organizing with their labor, from the hills of Pennsylvania to the broad streets of Chicago.

In the 19th century over one million Irish left behind a land devastated by famine and foreign oppression, bound for America, only to be greeted by the ubiquitous signs advertising "No Irish Need Apply." One place where they found welcome was in the army. Like the Hmong, the Irish often began their relationship with the United States as soldiers. They were recruited to fight against Mexicans, against the indigenous population, and against each other in the U.S. Civil War.

Their war experiences have left an indelible imprint on American history: In the war in Mexico the Irish made up a good portion of the invad-

---

[10]A more extensive description of the Spindlers' analysis of how members of minority cultures negotiate their identities in school contexts is provided in chapter six.

[11]This work is influenced by various concepts of the self, including those put forward by Erikson, Vygotsky, the Spindlers, and Lifton. A comprehensive review of the many traditional and postmodern metaphors of the self is found in Hoskins and Leseho (1996). The development and change in identity over the life span is explored through the perspectives of psychology, history and literature in Bosma, Graafsma, Grotevant, and de Levita (1994).

ing forces. Not all were to remain committed to the cause of manifest destiny: On recognizing that they had more in common with the poor, largely Catholic peasantry of Mexico than with their Yankee commanders, many of the Irish deserted and switched sides. They formed a brigade in the Mexican army called the San Patricios, and fought desperately in defeat. A memorial to the San Patricios can be seen in a public square in Mexico City, not far from where the last remaining members of the brigade were rounded up, branded, and hanged by the invading forces.

Irish participation in the wars on the Great Plains was also in evidence: The Seventh Cavalry had as its theme music "Garryowen," a song commemorating a native Irish uprising against British oppression. It was a bitter irony that such music should follow the unit to defeat at Little Big Horn against an uprising of Native peoples, and later, to the slaughter of women, children and old men at Wounded Knee.

Thousands of Irish fought and died on both sides in the Civil War. My father took me through the cemetery at the Gettysburg Battlefield when I was a boy to show me the mute testimony to their participation. The Irish who occupy that solemn ground were so new to the country that their family names had yet to be Americanized.[12]

Outside the army, the Irish took the backbreaking jobs available building railroads and cities, digging canals and graves. Often they were pitted against Chinese and African American workers, as their employers strove to pit people against each other and keep wages down. Many of the Irish, including some of the cousins of the McClears, were proslavery and antiLincoln, fearing perhaps the loss of their menial jobs to freed slaves coming north (see Takaki, 1993, especially pp. 139–165).

Some Irish immigrants, however, would find common ground with members of other oppressed groups in the country. One of the most beautiful traditional Irish songs of mid-19th century recounts the story of a young Irish immigrant who arrives in New Orleans. He manages to avoid the deadly work in the canals there that would take the lives of so many compatriots, but finds himself alone and destitute on the banks of Lake Ponchartrain. Although other Americans refuse to help him, he is welcomed into the humble home of a Creole girl:

> I said, "Me pretty Creole girl, me money is no good.
> If it weren't for the alligators, I'd sleep out in the wood.
> "You're welcome here, kind stranger, our house is very plain,
> But we never turn the stranger out by the Lakes of Ponchartrain."

---

[12]For accounts of Irish immigrant involvement in the American wars of the 19th century, see Miller (1989), McCaffrey (1992), Brown (1970), and Saum (1990).

To extend a welcome to strangers, whatever their skin color, accent, or state of impoverishment, is a custom common among many peoples the world over. In places such as the Lake Ponchartrain of song, it has also been an *American* custom, a custom without which our national culture would be sadly diminished,

The Irish, through their work in the mines, fields, and factories, their spirituality, their music, and their relationships to people and to the land, have forever changed the United States. So, too, have millions of other sojourners from Asia, Africa, Europe, and all parts of the Americas. The promise of the United States lies in its global roots, and the understanding that you do not have to be born here to be considered an American (Walzer, 1990). Shou Cha and I, then, are both involved in a process of being and becoming Americans. Perhaps together, we can construct a dialogue and reconstruct the dream of America for the children who will come after us.

FROM NARRATIVE TO CULTURAL DIALOGUE

One's culture plays an enormous factor in shaping one's sense of identity. Geertz (1987) defines the culture of a people as "an ensemble of texts, themselves ensembles, that the anthropologist strains to read over the shoulders of those to whom they properly belong" (p. 239). Being an outsider to the Hmong community and unable to speak the Hmong language, I had no pretensions of coming to a full understanding of Hmong culture. However, as an American, I hoped to learn some of the cultural nuances of a fellow American, whose "ensemble of texts," as a new American, were both similar and vastly different from my own. Coming to understand American culture as it is transformed by one of its diverse participants, then, was my goal. Rabinow and Sullivan (1987) suggest such a dialogical approach to understanding culture:

> Culture—the shared meanings, practices, and symbols that constitute the human world—does not present itself neutrally or with one voice. It is always multivocal and overdetermined, and both the observer and the observed are always enmeshed in it. (p. 7)

I wanted to learn what values Cha Shou and members his family found in Hmong culture, and in what they perceived to be *American* culture, and ways in which they saw these cultural values complementing or contradicting one another.

The Spindlers (1990) have argued that at the center of the American *cultural dialogue* are mainstream values, such as individualism, personal achievement, and a belief in progress, yet "various forms of biculturalism ... may constitute viable adaptations to the need to 'get along' in America at the same time that ethnic pride dictates a retention of self-orientation within one's own culture of origin" (p. 37). In what ways are the Chas adapting to the dominant culture, and in what ways are they retaining a separate identity? How have both formal and informal educational experiences influenced their views on what it means to be a "new" American, and what it means to be Hmong? What knowledge and values are the Cha children learning from their parents (and/or other adult family members)? Specifically, what is the role of the adults in passing along cultural information to the next generation—what Kotre (1984) calls "cultural generativity" (see also Erikson, 1950)? What knowledge about the dominant culture are the children passing on to the adults? Such questions regarding informal and formal education and intergenerational learning are thus important elements in coming to understand the lives of new Americans as they are both transformed by, and transform, America.

What makes a person's life history memorable or relevant to the lives of others? To some extent, Shou Cha's differences help shape the *significance* of his story: By presenting the beliefs, traditions and worldview of a member of a minority culture, his story challenges readers to extend their own visions of the world; it challenges educators to reexamine the educational role of immigrant parents; it challenges all Americans to rethink the role of schools as places to bring diverse young people together, not to separate and pit them against one another. However, the search for significance also extends to what Shou Cha and I (and many readers) share in common, and in many ways these commonalities shape the life history itself: We share a concern for histories, of families, peoples and nations; we share a concern for relationships within families and communities and across generations; we share a concern that schools support families and serve to bring children of diverse families together in positive ways. These issues of history, community, family, school, and differing worldviews, which impact on the education of new Americans, guided my search for significance in the analysis of Shou Cha's narrative.

As a society, we rarely stop to consider what new immigrants have contributed, and are able to contribute to our ever-changing America. Despite the often passive portrayal of immigrants in policy circles, this life history will illustrate the many ways in which a particular Hmong immigrant utilizes new and old cultural tools to actively engage in the transformation of himself, his ethnic community, and American society. Particularly relevant to educators is his role as a peacemaker, between his ethnic community and the school, and between children of various ethnicities within the school. In the pages that follow I contend that new Americans like the Hmong have much to contribute to the education of their own children, and to all of our children. They also have much to teach us about the meaning of "America."

IMPLICATIONS OF THIS STUDY

This study combines an interest in larger sociological and historical contexts of immigrant education and experience with the use of narrative inquiry to represent and interpret an immigrant's life. Through the telling, retelling and sharing of the life history of a new American, the problems and possibilities inherent in the education of new generations of Americans will be explored.

This life history research has implications for a variety of readers. Teachers, concerned with the education of diverse American children, may find in these pages that parents and community leaders such as Shou Cha can provide rich educational, cultural and linguistic resources for all their children. Shou Cha's reminds us of the potential benefits of reconnecting schools to varied cultural communities. Socially, all children could benefit from sharing cultures and languages, and learning to respect and value the differences present in our democratic society. Psychologically, immigrant children could benefit whenever efforts are made to reconnect the culture of school with that of the home. Moreover, immigrant parents, who have often been left isolated and alienated from the wider society and their own children, could benefit from the school's recognition that they, too, are important participants in the education of the community's children. Policymakers may find that this narrative account of a current immigrant family challenges rather static images of immigrants associated with previous historical eras with quite different social and historical contexts. Second, through a lens provided by the personal experiences of one family we can reexamine bilingual and multicultural educational policies, and influence educational policies at the local level to better meet the needs of all Americans, new and old. Researchers, especially those interested in finding ways to represent the voices of diverse American informants, may find that this life history of a Hmong immigrant suggests a variety of forms, including poetry and dramatic dialogue, that illustrate the aesthetic quality inherent in the stories of other human beings, and that narrative inquiry can touch the heart as well as the mind of the reader. Moreover, researchers may learn, as I have, the importance of resourcefulness, relationship, and respect when encountering the life of another.

Finally, this is a work of relevance to all Americans, as it focuses on who we have been, who we are, and who we would be as a people. Shou

Cha, the peacemaker from war-torn Laos, may teach us that schools can be made places of peace, places where diverse Americans can find unity, not by turning their backs on rich cultural and linguistic heritages, but by occupying, in gentle ways, a common civic and moral space.

2

Visions of America: Narratives of Immigrants, School, and Society

What visions have immigrants had of America and American schools? What can we learn from the lives of those who have learned to become Americans? Millions of immigrants have participated in American public education, and their reactions to schooling have been, and continue to be, varied. In what follows I examine some of our history of immigrant education policies by comparing and contrasting the experience of two children of immigrants, Richard Rodriguez and Leonard Covello, who have written autobiographies about their educational experiences in America.[1] *Hunger of Memory* (1982) is Rodriguez' story of how he achieved a public American identity through education. The book and its author have been influential since the 1970s as debates over bilingualism and affirmative action have raged. *The Heart is the Teacher* (1958) is less well known. It recounts Covello's life from his days as an immigrant child in America through his years as a principal in the New York City schools. Although Covello and Rodriguez both grew up in immigrant families in the United States, in many ways their stories are quite different: Covello was an Italian American who arrived in New York at the turn of the century, whereas Rodriguez was a Mexican American growing up in Sacramento in the 1950s, Covello's family lived in a tenement building surrounded by fellow countrymen and the Italian language; Rodriguez' family lived in a middle-class Anglo neighborhood

---

[1] I have chosen the autobiographies of Rodriguez and Covello because each deals at length with issues of immigrant education, and because they offer contrasting viewpoints on the relationship between immigrant youths, immigrant communities, and the larger society. However, other immigrant autobiographies that offer perspectives from women and other immigrants of non-European origin would be valuable to bring into this discussion. A short annotated list of immigrant autobiographies can be found in Appendix E. Several review essays on immigrant autobiographies can be found in Holte, 1988.

where the language of the street was English; Covello championed the teaching of immigrant languages in the schools, whereas Rodriguez champions the use of English, the language of public life; Covello's educational life was community-centered; Rodriguez' centered on the individual. Yet, the crossing of linguistic and cultural boundaries between the home and the school held similar consequences for both Covello and Rodriguez in their familial relationships.

Narrative inquiry contributes conceptual tools for readers as well as writers of lives. Through biography and autobiography, readers can come to an understanding of the complex relationship between individual agency and the social and historical contexts that influence lives. The next chapter provides a new reading of the history of immigrant education in the United States as seen through the lives of two immigrant children who lived, and made, part of that history: Rodriguez, whose parents immigrated to Sacramento, California in the 1940s, and Covello, who immigrated with his family to New York City in the 1890s. The lives of Rodriguez and Covello present the reader with different answers to the question of how best to educate new Americans, and whether educational success necessitates a break with one's linguistic and cultural community. Moreover, the history of immigrant education that backgrounds the lives of Rodriguez and Covello provides a fundamental context for understanding the educational life history of immigrants such as Shou Cha, who have arrived in the United States in the last generation.

The lives of Rodriguez and Covello help frame some of the dominant policy themes in immigrant education: Rodriguez' life, filled as it is with the angst of a middle-class American man who forsook his home language and culture to achieve a public identity, intersects with the rise of influential sociological theories ranging from cultural deprivation to cultural capital, theories that in different ways, suggest that immigrants and members of other nondominant groups must embrace the cultural forms of the elite if they wish to succeed as Americans. Based on his own experience, Rodriguez cautions against bilingual programs in schools, arguing that these will slow the achievement of public identities on the part of second language students. Nevertheless, Rodriguez' later work suggests that, in a world of infinite cultural intersections and transformations, schools must acknowledge the cultural contributions of all Americans. Covello's experiences as a student, teacher, and principal intersects with the one of the largest historical efforts to "Americanize" immigrants. Moreover, in his educational career he challenged eugenic explanations of mental deficiency, and worked for the academic achievement of all students, no matter the color of their skin, their accent or their socioeconomic status. Furthermore, Covello's insistence on the importance of home language and culture in the educational process foreshadows contemporary educational concerns with the representation of diverse cultures and languages in the schools. Finally, through his work as a principal in East Harlem, Covello fostered an understanding of the school as a center of the community, where all community members, no matter how poor or how heavy their accent, would be welcomed home.

E pluribus unum: "Out of many, one " I believe that the challenge to American educators for the 21st century remains much the same as it has been since the time of Horace Mann: A place must be found where the *pluribus* can gather as equals, where diverse traditions are respected, and where the *unum* can acknowledge conflict, yet strive for peace. Schools must be such a place.

RICHARD RODRIGUEZ: OF VOICE AND SILENCE

Hunger of Memory is Rodriguez' story of how he gained a public voice in America, and lost the power to communicate with his parents. In the opening pages we learn that this dark-skinned child of Mexican immigrants has become an assimilated, middle-class American. Yet, despite his economic and social success, his sense of loss is palpable:

> What preoccupies me is immediate: The separation I endure with my parents in loss. This is what matters to me: the story of the scholarship boy who returns home one summer from college to discover bewildering silence, facing his parents. This my story. An American story. (p. 5)

Educational achievement would enable Rodriguez' to gain what he calls a *public identity* as an American, and to fully participate in the social and political arenas of an English-speaking dominant culture. It would also distance him from his *private identity* as a happy youth growing up in the warm, Spanish-speaking world of his home.

Interestingly, it was Rodriguez' parents who encouraged their children to speak only English at home, following a visit by his teachers. Physically separated from the Spanish-speaking community in Sacramento, and encouraged to use English by his parents and teachers, Rodriguez embraced the new language. He blossomed in school, and became enamored with the world of books. In later life, he would not defend the use the first language in school, because he felt that it would prevent the adoption of a "public identity":

> Without question, it would have pleased me to hear my teachers address me in Spanish when I entered the classroom. I would have felt much less afraid. I would have trusted them and responded with ease. But I would have delayed—for how long postponed?—having to learn the language of

public society. I would have evaded—and for how long could I have af-
forded to delay?—learning the great lesson of school, that I had a public
identity. (p. 19)

However, for Rodriguez there is no middle ground between the public
identity of society and the private identity of his (formerly) Spanish-speaking home. Acceptance of one entails the rejection of the other.
To be economically and socially successful in America means breaking
with the traditions and language of nondominant cultures.

Nevertheless, Rodriguez illustrates his continuing hunger for the rich
Spanish communication of his childhood home by contrasting this with
the silence that accompanies his assimilation to the dominant culture:

> Matching the silence I started hearing in public was a new quiet at home.
> The family's quiet was partly due to the fact that, as we children learned
> more and more English, we shared fewer and fewer words with our par-
> ents. Sentences needed to be spoken slowly when a child addressed his
> mother or father. (Often the parent wouldn't understand.) The child
> would have to repeat himself. (Still the parent misunderstood.) The young
> voice, frustrated, would end up saying, "never mind"—the subject was
> closed. (p. 23)

Rodriguez began to feel embarrassed by his parents' lack of formal education. "It was not that I thought they were stupid," he writes, "but stupidly I
took for granted their enormous native intelligence" (p. 52). The authority
that had formerly rested in his parents was now transferred by Rodriguez
to his new idols, his teachers. Books became his new source for knowledge,
especially the books his teachers considered important, and "the information gathered from a book was unquestioned" (p. 53).

Culturally Deprived?

In Sacramento, in the 1950s, Rodriguez' working-class family "lived
among *gringos* and only a block from the biggest, whitest houses. It never
occurred to my parents that they couldn't live wherever they chose" (p.
12). From his earliest years Richard identified English as a public language and Spanish as intimate, the language of the home:

> Like those whose lives are bound by a barrio, I was reminded by Spanish of
> my separateness from *los otros, los gringos* in power. But more intensely
> than for most barrio children—because I did not live in a barrio—Spanish
> seemed to me the language of home ...My parents would say something to
> me and I would feel embraced by the sounds of their words. Those sounds
> said: *I am speaking with ease in Spanish. I am addressing you in words I*

never use with los gringos. *I recognize you as someone special, close, like no one outside. You belong with us. In the family. Ricardo.* (p. 16)

Rodriguez' description of how he became a public man, by distancing himself from the private world of his home language and culture, helps to frame theories of cultural deprivation and cultural capital that have influenced educational research and practice. The 1950s saw the rise of cultural deprivation theory. According to this theory, immigrants and other minority groups suffered from environmental factors—families that did not place emphasis on education, lower-class values and lack of English language skills. Therefore, the job of schools was to change the culture of the "culturally inferior," and thus overcome the inherent handicaps of the immigrant background. Much of the "culture of poverty" research in the 1960s accepted this premise, and sought ways to "replace" the impoverished "culture" of the "disadvantaged classes" with tenets of the dominant culture (see, for example Hellmuth, 1967).

Culture deprivation theory influenced many of the Great Society programs, and continues to be influential for many politicians and policymakers today—witness the attention given to "at-risk" students and the problem of "single parent" families (see Baca Zinn, 1989; Swadener & Lubeck, 1995). In a critique of Culture deprivation theory, Di Leonardo (1984) suggested that by focusing on the family as the determining factor in failure or success, one could conveniently overlook racial and class inequalities in America: "[Culture deprivation theory] divorces individuals' economic statuses from the larger economy and its evolutions, and from its entire ethnic/racial infrastructure of institutional racism ...It blames the victim" (p. 21).

"Cultural capital" theory has come into vogue among educational theorists as a new way to explain the environmental factors that contribute to educational failure or success. Rather than place blame on the family, theorists argue that socioeconomic class (as well as racial) distinctions contribute to educational achievement. Bourdieu (1977) argued that members of higher socioeconomic classes had more cultural capital because of their greater exposure to high culture (e.g., the arts, music, literature). Because of their accumulation of cultural capital, their children would have better chances at success in school, where such capital was valued: They were better prepared to master academic material, handle abstract concepts, and receive the favor of teachers. Children of lower socioeconomic classes, on the other hand, had little exposure to "high culture," and in school the often became discouraged, had fewer accomplishments, and little positive recognition from teachers. In studies of cultural capital in the United States, Wells and Serna (1996) have described how elite parents use their cultural and political capital to resist curricular changes that would end the separation of students into academic, general and vocational tracks, thus mixing their young with the children of lower social classes. Kalmijn and Kraakamp (1996) have suggested that ethnic minorities, when given access to what they call "highbrow" culture, may find a means for social mobility. This could certainly be said to be the case with Rodriguez in his transformation into a "middle-class man."

However, caught up in the effort to find ways to provide cultural capital to those who seem to lack it, many educational theorists have failed to question whether there is indeed a hierarchy of "cultures," or the extent to which all socioeconomic and ethnic groups contribute to the arts, music, literature, and other elements of a supposedly "high culture." Our national literature, for example, is imbued with a richness that derives from its multiple roots and subjects, a richness embodied in the poetry of Walt Whitman and Maya Angelou, and the prose of Mark Twain's *Huckleberry Finn* and Louise Erdrich's *Love Medicine*. Walzer (1990) illustrates the multicultural roots of American "high culture" with his description of Gene Kelly's *danse Americaine* in the movie, *American in Paris*:

> "Une danse Americaine," Gene Kelly tells the French children as he begins to tap dance. What else could he call it, this melted-down combination of Northern English clog dancing, the Irish jig and reel, and African rhythmic foot stomping, to which had been added, by Kelly's time, the influence of the French and Russian ballet? Creativity of this sort is both explained and celebrated by those writers and thinkers, heroes of the higher culture, that we are likely to recognize as distinctively American. (p. 607)

All the cultures that influence "American" culture have value, whether or not a price tag can be placed on them; failure to recognize this explicitly is the supreme fallacy of cultural capital theory, just as it is with theories of cultural deprivation and eugenics. In a world where cultures are constantly intermingling and transforming, new theories are necessary that neither seek to promote the domination of one culture over others nor to isolate culturally distinct groups from each other.

In his recent book, *Days of Obligation: An Argument with My Mexican Father* (1992), Rodriguez engages in a process of reexamining the interconnectedness of cultures, especially those of California and Mexico. He looks at the multiple Native American, Mexican and Anglo histories of the mission towns in California; the influence of Mexican, workers who constantly renegotiate national and cultural boundaries; and his own paradoxical role as a writer and researcher of Mexican descent, interviewing in the honky-tonks of Tijuana by day, retreating to San Diego, the land of promise, at night. In illustrating the ongoing process of cultural transformation taking place in Mexico, in the United States, and within himself, Rodriguez is perhaps finding a way to make peace with his heritage, his family and his America.

Language Deficiency and Bilingual Policy

In *Hunger of Memory*, Rodriguez makes a strong argument against bilingual education, suggesting that it could prevent working-class, nonnative speakers of English from achieving a public identity, and the rights and opportunities due all Americans:

> Only when I was able to think of myself as an American, no longer an alien in *gringo* society, could I seek the rights and opportunities necessary for full public individuality ...Those middle-class ethnics who scorn assimilation seem to me filled with decadent self-pity, obsessed by the burden of public life. Dangerously, they romanticize public separateness and they trivialize the dilemma of the socially disadvantaged. (p. 27)

Rodriguez seems to recognize that, to have access to social and political power, members of cultural minorities would have to learn, and conform to, the parameters set by the dominant culture. Referencing Shakespeare's quintessential dispossessed native, he says "I have taken Caliban's advice. I have stolen their books. I will have some run of this isle" (p. 3).

Rodriguez speaks also of the danger of romanticizing public separateness. Clearly, the historical debates over language and cultural issues in the United States are filled with references to the danger of political and social fragmentation that might result if large numbers of people were to continue speaking languages other than English. Benjamin Franklin, who taught himself French, German, Italian, Spanish, and Latin, and in 1732, had published the first German-language newspaper in North America, was one of the first colonists to emphasize the importance of "Anglifying" the general population. In his "Observations Concerning the Increase of Mankind" (1751), Franklin wrote that the increase of the German-speaking population in Pennsylvania was a definite threat: "Why should Pennsylvania, founded by the English, become a Colony of Aliens, who will shortly be so numerous as to Germanize us instead of our Anglifying them, and will never adopt our Language or Customs any more than they can acquire our Complexion?" (quoted in Shell, 1993, p. 109). Although many English colonists of the time may have shared Franklin's sentiments, diversity of languages and bilingualism was a fact of colonial life. Besides numerous Amerindian languages, the African languages of slaves, and the French and Spanish of adjacent colonial territories, one-fourth of the Europeans in the British colonies spoke languages other than English. During the Revolutionary War, the Continental Congress published many official documents in French and German, including the Articles of Confederation. In matters of education, the use of English spread in the early years of the 19th century, but many non-English language schools continued to thrive, and German, French and Spanish were sanctioned by several states as languages of instruction (Crawford, 1989). However, by the early 20th century the arrival of millions of non-English speaking immigrants began to raise worries in some quarters that internal divisions would follow. Theodore Roosevelt, one of the strongest supporters of Americanization programs, summarized this reaction to massive immigration when he said, "We have room for but one language in this country, and that is the English language, for we intend to see that the crucible turns our people out as Americans, of American nationality, and not as dwellers in a polyglot boarding house" (quoted in Crawford, 1989, p. 23). Public policies against the use of diverse languages in schools were not widely implemented, however, until the advent of World War One, when the use of English was increasingly seen as a test of political loyalty.[2]

"Sink or swim" English teaching strategies slowly gave way to language replacement strategies and the rise of specific English as a second language (ESL) instruction in the 1950s. Within such ESL classes, curriculums continued to exclude discussion of minority cultures or present them in stereotypical fashion. In the words of Diego Castellanos, ESL's replacement strategy tended to produce "half-lingual stutterers in thought, stammerers in spirit" (quoted in Crawford, 1989, p. 27).

In response to the advocacy of members of minority language groups and growing awareness of low academic achievement and high dropout rates among minority language students, Congress passed the Bilingual Education Act of 1968. This was the first federal legislation to support the needs of non-English speaking children in the schools. However, the goals of the program seemed unclear: Was it to be a remedial program, overcoming "language deficiency" and working for assimilation—or was it to be bilingual enrichment, developing students' inherent linguistic resources, and preserving pluralistic cultural heritages?

---

[2]For example, in 1915, German was the most widely spoken language in the United States after English, and 24% of all secondary students were enrolled in the study of German. However, anti-German feeling caused by the war would curtail the use and study of German sharply. Several states banned German speech in public places, including schools; the study of German was forbidden at public and private schools in Ohio, German language teachers were either thrown out of work or reassigned to teach "Americanism." By 1922, enrollment of secondary students in German was less than 1% (Crawford, 1989).

Amendments, civil rights guidelines and a key court decision were to help clarify the intent of the Bilingual Education Act. Amendments in 1974 clarified that both English and native languages could be used in bilingual classrooms. Further amendments in 1978 and 1984 would redefine eligible children as "limited English proficient" (LEP), thus reinforcing the deficit approach to teaching minority language children; provide Family

English Literacy programs for adults and youths not in school; and, in a significant move away from the deficit model, provide programs aimed at the achievement of proficiency in English *and a second language* (see Table 2.1).

Title VI of the Civil Rights Act, which prohibits discrimination on the basis of race, color or national origin, influenced federal guidelines regarding equal opportunity for "disadvantaged" minority language students. In 1974, the U.S. Supreme Court ruled in *Lau v. Nichols* schools were obligated to prepare non-English speaking students for a meaningful education. Justice Douglas, author of the court's decision, wrote: "There is no equality of treatment merely by providing students with the same facilities, textbooks, teachers, and curriculum; for students who do not understand English are effectively foreclosed from any meaningful education" (quoted in Lyons, 1990, p. 71).

Rodriguez, however, sees contradictory impulses driving bilingual education that could endanger the education of those it is meant to serve: "(Advocates) propose bilingual schooling as a way of helping students acquire the skills of the classroom crucial for public success. But they likewise insist that bilingual instruction will give students a sense of their identity apart from the public" (p. 34).

Rodriguez argues that bilingual education, in fact, is a disservice to students, as it will slow the nonnative speakers acquisition of a public identity in an English-speaking society. Like Rodriguez, many supporters of an English language amendment feel that students participating in bilingual education classes are unfairly segregated from the dominant culture and its opportunities. Thernstrom (1990) contends that bilingual programs have led to low student academic achievement, inability to pass employer English tests, and *de facto* segregation of minority language students:

Those who monitor desegregation plans count ethnic and racial heads in a school and pretend that the presence of Hispanic and other language-minority children counts toward integration. Yet there is little that is integrated about the education of these students. The students may dabble in paints and dribble a ball together, but, for most of the day, a bilingual classroom is a school within a school—a world apart. (p. 48)

TABLE 2.1
Some Important Events in Immigrant Education History

1780s	Articles of Confederation and other official documents of the new United States published in English, French and German.
1840s	Massive immigration to U.S. by Irish, and later Germans. Rise of the common schools to teach a common Anglo-Protestant worldview. In many parts of the country immigrants organize their own schools where immigrant languages are spoken.
1850s	Sometimes violent controversies as immigrant Catholics are forced to read Protestant bibles in public schools. Rise of the Know Nothing anti-immigrant movement.
1882	Chinese Exclusion Act signals racial preference of immigration policy.
1890s	Beginning of massive immigration from Eastern and Southern Europe.
early 1900s	Rise of Americanism movement. Spread of eugenic explanations of immigrant (and other non-Teutonic) inferiority. Expansion of comprehensive high schools with academic and vocational tracks, immigrant children largely occupying the latter.
1917	The United States enters the war against Germany. With the war come efforts to forbid the teaching of German in schools. The teaching of other languages declines.
1924	New laws passed by the U.S. Congress severely restrict immigration.
1950s	Rise in popularity of cultural deprivation theory.
1965	Congress removes barriers to immigration. A new wave of immigrants, largely from Latin America and Asia, begins to arrive in the United States.
1968	Congress passes the Bilingual Education Act.
1974	In *Lau v Nichols*, Supreme Court rules that schools must provide meaningful education to non-English speaking students.
1975	The aftermath of war in Southeast Asia brings hundreds of thousands of refugees from Vietnam, Laos and Cambodia to the United States over the next several years.
1986	California passes Proposition 63, making English the official language of the state. Other states follow this lead with similar legislation.
1995	Passage of Proposition 187 in California. Denial of medical and educational services to illegal immigrants and their children.

continued on next page

1996	Illegal Immigration Reform and Immigrant Responsibility Act signed into law. Removes welfare benefits for immigrants, places limits on extended family who can immigrate, strengthens barriers to illegal immigration.
1997	In California, a proposition entitled "English for the Children" seeks to end bilingual education in the state. In Wisconsin, and other states, organizations such as English First continue working for English Only laws at city, county and state levels of government.

U.S. English spokesperson Gerda Bikales has argued that such segregation leaves minority students "cut off from interaction with their American peers, doomed to remain forever strangers in their new country" (quoted in Imhoff, 1990, p. 57).

In the 1980s efforts to more fully assimilate immigrants have crystallized around the perceived threat to national unity posed by speakers of languages other than English. In 1986, California voters passed Proposition 63, making English the official language of the state. In the following 2 years, ten more states passed similar legislation. In addition, groups such as U.S. English are actively working to pass the English language Amendment, making English the official language of the United States. Imhoff (1990), a consultant for U.S. English, contends that the organization respects diversity of languages and cultures within the United States, but believes that schools must teach students English as quickly as possible, and the government should "foster the similarities that unite us rather than the differences that separate us" (p. 49).

The fact that federal support for bilingual education was initially presented as a program to reduce the language deficit of "disadvantaged" minority-language children has led to much of the controversy surrounding the efficacy of bilingual policy. Opponents of bilingual policy such as Bikales, Thernstrom and Imhoff tend to ignore the fact that minority language children have historically been placed in lower tracks and in special education classes (Oakes, 1986); yet clearly separate bilingual education classes can lead to an unequal education as well. Proponents of bilingual policy tend to stress the importance of proficiency in two (or more) languages, for minority language children as well as all members of American society. Moreover, some see legislation such as the proposed English Language Amendment as a new effort at language restriction, the passage of which could lead to a denial of basic rights to non-English speakers, as well as political and social turmoil. The English Language Amendment, in this view, would represent "exclusionary language policy" and send the following message to minority language groups:

Return to the age of less dignified status—to that time when your children were linguistically excluded from the classroom, to a time when language barred you from voting, to a time when you were unable to understand court proceedings because you could not speak English. To minority language groups, the picture is clear: The English Language Amendment has little to do with language; it has everything to do with oppression. (Duenas, Schott, & Vasquez, 1988, p. 29)

The supporters of English Only legislation claim that they would defend the rights of individual non-English speakers to the achievement of a public identity in an English-speaking nation. Rodriguez' story in *Hunger of Memory* provides them with some ammunition, as it tells the tale of how one man *overcame* his family and his past by embracing English and becoming a player in the larger society. Yet, *Hunger of Memory* is also the story of a youth, a family, and a multiethnic, multilingual society in the throes of fragmentation, that have yet to make peace with themselves.

LEONARD COVELLO: TEACHING FOR COMMUNITY

Leonard Covello was 9 years old when his family immigrated to America from the poverty-stricken village of Avigliano in Southern Italy. The family settled into the Aviglianese colony in East Harlem, New York, a neighborhood that Covello would later describe as "one of the most heterogeneous and congested communities in the United States, with poverty and unemployment as its main characteristics and its atmosphere one of tension and struggle" (p. 179). In this neighborhood Leonard would go to school and later, spend much of his career as a teacher and administrator, as he made a lifelong commitment to improving the lives of East Harlem's residents.

Shortly after his family immigrated to New York City from Southern Italy in 1896, Covello began attending the Soup School, a place characterized by its strict discipline and bowl of soup at lunch, and run for immigrant children by the Female Guardian Society of America. The school assemblies and the singing of songs in an unknown language are vivid memories for Covello:

It was always the same. We stood at attention as the Bible was read and at attention as the flag was waved back and forth, and we sang the same song. I didn't know what the words meant but I sang it loudly with all the rest, in my own way, "Tree Cheers for de Red Whatzam Blu!" But best of all was another song that we used to sing at these assemblies. It was a particular favorite of Mrs. Cutter's, and we sang it with great gusto, "Honest boys who never tread the streets." This was in the days when we not only trod the streets but practically lived in them. (p. 27)

The emphasis on God, country and personal morality symbolized by the Bible reading, the flag, and the song "Honest Boys" reflect the goals of a civic and moral education that extend back to the time of the Common Schools. In their mission to "make Americans" out of immigrants, to forge an *unum* out of children of diverse cultures, schools have sometimes failed to honor the values and traditions of immigrant children and their parents. In this regard schools merely reflect the generations of political and educational leaders who have left large numbers of our diverse people out of their definitions of "American," and out of their visions of America.

Kaestle (1983) has suggested that the Common School reform movement of the mid-19th century contained an ideology of republicanism, Protestantism, and capitalism. At the heart of the ideology was a series of Anglo-American Protestant cultural beliefs and values:

Human beings are born malleable and potentially good but need much careful guidance; all men are equal in some formal ways, but some groups are more able, wise, and refined than others; and therefore it is important that in education, economics, and politics, institutions be shaped to maintain the values and leadership of cultivated, native, Protestant Americans. (p. 95)

Kaestle argues that the arrival of the Irish Catholic, as well as massive immigration by nonEnglish-speaking Germans, reinforced the moral, cultural and civic mission of the schools. These "outsiders" threatened the uniform, Anglo-American Protestant world of the reformers and the native elite, and thus common schools would need to teach "a common English language and a common Protestant morality, much as earlier charity schools had been directed at those qualities of Blacks or poor Whites that educational reformers saw as undesirable or threatening" (p. 71).

By the end of the 19th century children of immigrants were becoming schoolteachers themselves, and the Anglo-American Protestant values presented in schools were transformed to a certain degree. Nevertheless, Handlin (1982) suggests that the new generation of teachers retained the same sense of mission as that propagated by the earlier generation of Common Schoolmen:

To stamp out dialect, to stamp in correct modes of behavior, to define life's goals and prepare all to grasp its opportunities. The men and women who had made it valued their respectability and were no more tolerant of Wops and Sheenies than their predecessors had been of Micks. (p. 14)

On one occasion Coviello brought home his report card to be signed, and his parents discovered that "Leonardo Coviello" had been changed by the school to "Leonard Covello." Angrily, his father asked him why the family name had been changed, and Leonard responded that the principal had changed it to make it easier for her to pronounce. Leonard asked:

"What difference does it make? It's more American. The *i* doesn't help anything." It was one of the very few times that I dared oppose my father. But even at that age I was beginning to feel that anything that made a name less foreign was an improvement.

For a moment my father sat there, bitter rebellion building in him. Then with a shrug of resignation, he signed the report card and shoved it over to me. My mother now suddenly entered the argument. "How is it possible to do this to a name? Why did you sign the card? Narduccio, you will have to tell your teacher that a name cannot be changed just like that ...A person's life and his honor is in his name. He never changes it. A name is not a shirt or a piece of underwear." (p. 30)

A youth such as Covello could see the value of stripping away vestiges of foreignness that might cause him ridicule. This stripping down, and remaking of immigrants into "Americans" would be a goal of the Americanization movement of the early 20th century, and would have a lasting impact on immigrant education policies.

Higham (1971) suggested that the Americanization movement contained both democratic and nativistic impulses. Initially concerned with the social welfare of new immigrants, the National Americanization Committee sponsored a nationwide "Americanization Day" on July 4, as a celebration of new citizenship. However, the Committee's pluralistic slogan, "Many Peoples, but One Nation," would soon give way to "America First." As American involvement in the war in Europe loomed, business and civic organizations and schools embraced Americanization, with new importance placed on being "one hundred percent American." By 1918, the National Americanization Committee was urging "the suppression of unrest and disloyalty, the elimination of conditions under which 'anti-American' influences flourished, and the dissolution of minority cultures" (pp. 248–249).

In the world of business Henry Ford set an example for Americanization programs, compelling his non-English-speaking immigrants to attend a company English school where they would, besides learning English, reenact the theory of the melting pot on stage:

A long column of immigrant students descended into the pot from backstage, clad in outlandish garb and flaunting signs proclaiming their fatherlands. Simultaneously from either side of the pot another stream of men emerged, each prosperously dressed in identical suits of clothes and each carrying a little American flag. (Higham, 1971, pp. 247–248)

Ford's efforts at "Americanizing" his immigrant workers reflected an Americanization movement increasingly threatened by the cultural attachments immigrants maintained with their lands of birth. Americanization, which began as an effort to improve the social conditions of immigrants, and to educate them as democratic citizens, turned into an effort to weed out "divided loyalties" and the dissolution of minority cultures during and after the World War One.

More Americanization legislation was adopted at the state level during the postwar economic recession and "Red Scare," when political and business leaders, citing the threat of communist revolution in the United States, cracked down on trade unions, leftist political parties, and ethnic organizations. The impetus to reform immigrants soon gave way to a renewed effort to exclude them. Immigration laws in 1921 and 1924 severely restricted total immigration, and established a nationality quota system: "While the movement for the redemption of the alien ebbed in 1920, the old drive for the rejection of the immigrant passed all previous bounds" (Higham, 1971, p. 263). Historian Oscar Handlin (1951) writes:

> There was a fundamental ambiguity to the thinking of those who talked about 'assimilation' in these years. They had arrived at their own view that American culture was fixed, formed from its origins, by shutting out the great mass of immigrants who were not English or at least not Teutonic. Now it was expected that those excluded people would alter themselves to earn their portion in Americanism. (p. 274)

Covello's life, of course, was touched by the Americanization movement, yet he found a way to return to the philosophy of "many peoples, but one nation." While a student at Columbia University, Covello became involved in the YMCA's Americanization campaign as an English teacher in his old neighborhood. Covello soon discovered that when he communicated to the older Italian men in their own language, they became more willing, not only to learn English, but to share other concerns with him as well:

> Some of the men brought their children with them, to ask my advice about a school situation or problem concerning them. It was then that I realized how little these parents understood about school conditions and regulations affecting their children. Not knowing the language, they were reluctant to make any attempt to straighten out a child's difficulty outside the home. I came to the conclusion that while it was important to teach English

to immigrant people, it was equally important for me to find out about the problems they were unable to solve in becoming adjusted to a new way of life in a new country. And I could only do this through the use of their native language. (p. 68)

Covello would eventually work to create an Italian language program in the New York City schools, but his efforts would be constricted by larger societal pressures at the time of the World War I to encourage only the use of English.

Quality Education for All

Leonard Covello was not deterred by the difficulties of American schooling, largely because he saw education as a way to avoid the life of toil of his father and so many other members of his Italian immigrant community:

> The constant drilling and pressure of memorizing, the homework, and detention after school raised havoc with many students. For me, this type of discipline seemed merely the continuation of my training in Italy. I wanted to go to school. School meant books and reading and an escape from the world of drudgery which dulled the mind and wore out the body and brought meager returns ... "Nardo," my father repeated again and again. "In me you see a dog's life. Go to school. Even if it kills you. With the pen and with books you have the chance to live like a man and not like a beast of burden. (p. 41)

With hard work and the help of a scholarship, Covello went on to study at Columbia University. Based on his own experience, he knew that children raised in immigrant homes and poor neighborhoods such as East Harlem were capable of academic achievement. Yet, many civic and educational leaders did not share his beliefs about the abilities of poor youths. When a high school was being planned for East Harlem, Covello fought hard to make it a comprehensive, rather than an industrial or trade school: "The stigma attached to an industrial high school! The psychological effect upon the pupils and the community! Sure, people say on the outside, 'the proper school for them dumb immigrants. They don't deserve any better'" (p. 181).

Benjamin Franklin, a comprehensive high school, was established in East Harlem with Covello as principal. Nevertheless, Covello admits that he and his staff "had constantly to be on the alert against those who wanted to lower academic standards" (p. 203).

By maintaining that poor immigrant children could achieve as well as other children Covello was in opposition to beliefs about the inferiority of certain ethnic and racial groups that were firmly entrenched in many educational and policy circles. In his description of the new immigrants from Southern Europe who arrived to the United States in large numbers after 1890, Cubberley (1934), dean of Stanford University's college of education, reveals a great deal about the ethnocentric and racist attitudes that guided much of educational policy in his day:

> Largely illiterate, docile, often lacking in initiative, and almost wholly without the Anglo-Saxon conceptions of righteousness, liberty, law, order, public decency, and government, their coming has served to dilute tremendously our national stock and to weaken and corrupt our political life ...The new peoples, and especially those from the South and East of Europe, have come so fast that we have been unable to absorb and assimilate them, and our national life, for the past quarter century, has been afflicted with a serious case of racial indigestion. (pp. 485–486)

Many Progressive Era educational reformers shared Cubberley's views, and their arguments were bolstered by the results of English-language IQ tests given to immigrants, which suggested strongly that their inferiority was genetic. Not surprisingly, eugenic explanations of immigrant inferiority grew in popularity as the nation's economy contracted. Kallen (1924) observed that in the early part of the century "immigration, formerly more than welcomed as an economic boon, was now scrutinized as a eugenic menace"(p. 24). Terman, one of the early proponents of IQ testing, suggested that the immigrant "dullness seems to be racial ... Children of this group should be segregated in special classes" (quoted in Oakes, 1986, p. 149). The widely accepted view of immigrant cultural inferiority led to a policy of segregation for many immigrant students in "vocational," rather than academic, tracks. As America approaches the year 2000, members of minority linguistic and cultural communities continue to be overrepresented in lower academic tracks (Oakes, 1986).

At Benjamin Franklin High, however, the story was somewhat different. By the 1950s, 40% to 50% of graduates of one of the poorest neighborhood schools in New York were applying to attend college. Covello realized that "a vocational or trade school would have restricted many of these boys in their preparation for higher education" (p. 203). Without question Covello believed that a comprehensive school would better serve the needs of his students, yet at the same time it would serve to support the interests of a socially and economically marginalized East Harlem community.

School, Family, and Community

In writing of his experimental school in Chicago, John Dewey (1900) suggested that a preeminent question guiding progressive education must be how to connect the life of the school with the life of the community:

What can be done, and how can it be done, to bring the school into closer relation with the home and neighborhood life—instead of having the school a place where the child comes solely to learn certain lessons? What can be done to break down the barriers which have unfortunately come to separate the school life from the rest of the everyday life of the child. (p. 166)

Through his work with the New York public schools, Covello would develop a community-centered approach to education. The need for such an approach was apparent from his own school experience as an immigrant whose Italian culture and language were effectively and completely ignored by the educational system. Significantly, Covello saw this as part of the process for Americanizing immigrant youth, and for dividing them from their parents:

The Italian language was completely ignored in the American schools ...I do not recall one mention of Italy or the Italian language or what famous Italians had done in the world, with the possible exception of Christopher Columbus, who was pretty popular in America. We soon got the idea that "Italian" meant something inferior, and a barrier was erected between children of Italian origin and their parents. This was the accepted process of Americanization. We were becoming Americans by learning how to be ashamed of our parents. (p. 43)

As the gulf between the world of school and the world of home became wider, Covello found he had less and less to share with his parents; rather, personal issues were shared with other young Italian immigrants who could better understand what he was going through.

As early as the 1870s, William Torrey Harris, superintendent of St. Louis schools, argued that immigrant culture was an important ingredient in the educational formation of immigrant children and that efforts aimed at breaking the child's bonds to family and culture would have detrimental consequences (Crawford, 1989). A few decades later, Jane Addams, whose close work with immigrant families in the settlement houses had alerted her to the cultural gap between home and school, argued that schools needed to reconnect immigrant children with their families:

The public school too often separates the child from his parents and widens that old gulf between fathers and sons which is never so cruel and so wide as it is between the immigrants who come to this country and their children who have gone to public school and feel that they have learned it all ...Can we not say, perhaps, that the schools ought to do more to connect these children with the best things of the past, to make them realize something of the beauty and charm of the language, the history, and the traditions which their parents represent. (quoted in Lagemann, 1985, pp. 137–138)

Kallen, a contemporary of Addams, took issue with educational leaders such as Cubberley and Terman who argued that the "new immigrants" of the early 20th century weakened America culturally and genetically. Kallen contended rather that the "flowering" of American arts and sciences after a generation of massive immigration was a testament to the immigrants' enrichment of American culture. He asked:

> Can it be that the freshness, the candor, the poignancy and beauty as well as the strangeness of this flowering have no relation to the contrasted doctrines and disciplines of the communities living in the land, nourishing one another's spirits through mutual contagion? (p. 230)

Although the voices of Addams and Kallen were largely lost in a sea of "Americanization," tenets of cultural pluralism and the importance of reconnecting schools with immigrant homes would be put into practice by school leaders such as Covello.

When he became principal at Benjamin Franklin High School in East Harlem, Covello worked to bring parents and community members into the school and take the school to the community. Franklin High was open 24 hours a day, 7 days a week, effectively serving as a center of community life. The school respected the diversity of the East Harlem community, and Covello understood the importance of being able to communicate in the languages of the immigrant students and their families:

> The bilingual teacher is a necessity in our schools. I myself speak English, French, Spanish, and several Italian dialects, and have a working knowledge of German ...We had a dozen other teachers equally at ease with the different languages of our students. The importance of this cannot be overstressed. It helped gain us the confidence of the boys. It set us on an equal footing with the mothers and fathers. We were not separate, off somewhere in a world of our own, unapproachable to the man, woman or child who could not speak English. How often have I seen the lightning joy on the face of a dubious immigrant parent when he hears the sound of a familiar tongue! How many barriers crumble before the shared language! (pp. 266–267)

Covello was determined to bridge the gulf that often separated immigrant families from the life of school. Moreover, he sought to bridge the differences that sometimes gave rise to racial and ethnic strife in East Harlem. With students from Ben Franklin, Covello would tour the neighborhood, talking with its diverse members, advocating solidarity, "for the necessity of all people sticking together in the fight for a better life" (p.

223). Often his most tempestuous encounters were with Italian Americans:

> One group of younger Italian workmen argued against the Puerto Ricans coming into the neighborhood and working for less wages. "They're not like us. *We're Americans*. We eat meat at least three times a week. What do they eat? Beans. So they work for beans. That's why we have trouble here." I asked them, "What do you think your parents ate when they came to America? You don't want to remember. I was there. *Pasta e fasul,*" I said. "Beans and macaroni—and don't forget it. Don't forget that other people used to say the same things about your mothers and fathers that you now say about the Puerto Ricans." (p. 223)

Despite the poverty and desperation that often characterized life in East Harlem, Covello remained convinced that the through the school and education, solutions could be found to the problems of each generation of new Americans.

THE INTERSECTION OF LIVES

The educational journeys of Rodriguez and Covello offer a useful framework for examining important issues in the education of new Americans. There are some striking differences in the importance they place on learning from and within immigrant communities, yet interesting similarities in their struggles to define who they are as Americans.

Home Language and Culture

Rodriguez grew up in a neighborhood where only his family spoke Spanish. Once his parents became convinced by school personnel that they should speak English in the home with the children, Rodriguez' home language environment was fundamentally changed, and his community was the larger *gringo* world; he makes the logical decision to pursue a public identity in that world and leave behind the limitations of a broken English home. Covello's story, largely unfolding in a working-class, multiethnic urban setting, is about the importance of school as a center for the community, where students of many languages and cultures can come together in the process of becoming Americans, and transforming America. In Rodriguez' story, the scenes of which vary from the middle-class neighborhood of his childhood to exclusive parties in Bel Air, school is presented more as the means for individual mobility, a place where someone given the right tools can succeed in mass society and achieve a public identity. Having been himself educated in an immigrant school, Covello realized that English was necessary, but that the school's familiarity with a child's home language and culture would ease the child's learning, and open lines of communication with parents. For this reason there were several bilingual teachers on his staff at Benjamin Franklin.

Educational research since the 1970s has returned to themes raised in Covello's *The Heart Is the Teacher*, suggesting that the home language and cultural practices of nondominant cultural groups are rich in meaning and valuable for the education of their children, and, some insist, for all members of society. Heath (1983) reflects the concerns of many researchers by calling on teachers to recognize that language differences exist between the "ways" words are used at school and at home, and to try to provide scaffolding that will allow students from nondominant groups to build on the language skills they already have, and learn the ways of school. Unfortunately, the educational success stories of immigrant children such as Covello and Rodriguez cannot erase the fact that historically, a disproportionate number of immigrant and minority language students are placed into lower tracks and special education classes (Oakes, 1986). For students, this signifies unequal educational opportunity, and leads inevitably to lower status jobs.

However, it has been suggested by Ogbu (1982, 1991) that some cultural minorities may have an easier time adapting to the dominant culture in school than others. He distinguishes between "voluntary" minorities, such as immigrants who chose to come to the United States, and tend to place more value on and trust in schooling, as a way to make it in the new country; and "involuntary" minorities, such as African Americans, many Mexican Americans and Native Americans, who were forced into the U.S. social system by means of slavery, war, and conquest. Involuntary minorities tend to view their options as already limited by society, and schooling as a waste of time—in effect, they often adopt a "resistance" stance towards school (see also Anyon, 1995). For such involuntary minorities, occasional educational "success" for a few individuals often leads to alienation from both their own cultural group and the dominant culture, relegating them to the no-man's land of the Rodriguez' "scholarship boy."

A question arises, however: Just how "voluntary" are the experiences of many immigrants relocating to the United States? What have been the range of choices that they entertain? Did the Irish of the 1840s, for example, choose to immigrate to America, or did the potato famine and massive starvation choose for them? When facing the alternative of continued lives of grinding poverty, is it surprising that many from the south of Italy, such as Covello's family, chose the uncertainty of the tenements of New York? When faced with the choice between genocidal regimes, the brutality and squalor of refugee camps, and the move to a strange land and culture, is it surprising that refugees such as the Hmong have opted for the latter? The choice of these and many millions of immigrants have been reluctant, at best, and such reluctance must be accounted for in Ogbu's typology.

Portes and Rumbaut (1990) make a useful distinction between four types of recent immigrants to America, and their relationship to schools and education: Labor migrants, by the nature of their migratory labor, their poverty and their often-times undocumented status, have fewer educational opportunities to offer their children; the vast majority of refugees also live in poverty, and although many refugee parents have few of the linguistic or cultural tools valued by the dominant culture, many see education as the means for their children to live a better life; professional and entrepreneurial immigrants, on the other hand, can offer their children access to better educational opportunities because of their own significant educational and/or economic resources. Thus, in many ways, children of labor migrants and refugees, despite any parental wishes for their educational advancement, are more likely to find themselves in urban and rural schools that are poorly equipped to handle their linguistic, cultural and educational needs. Some, like Covello and Rodriguez, achieve success; others, like many youths among involuntary minorities, become alienated from the school as well as the home.

School as a Bridge

What Covello and Rodriguez share is a belief that anyone can succeed through education, yet also a yearning for the lost family ties that often accompany educational success. Rodriguez' story illustrates that minority children can, indeed, be given the "cultural capital" to succeed by schools, yet the success of such "scholarship boys" seems largely material, and rather hollow: Despite his love for them, he can no longer communicate with his parents. The silence of Rodriguez' father at family gatherings is paralleled by the increasing silence between Covello and his father. Although these immigrant parents advocated education for their children, and encouraged them in their studies as best they could, they are largely left by the wayside, silent, as their sons advance in their careers. Covello, at least, realizes that this gulf between immigrant children and their parents must be bridged, somehow, and he makes an effort to involve parents in the school, and engage students in service to the immigrant community.

The quandary teachers who work with nondominant groups face, according to Gee (1990), is how to recognize and honor the "discourse communities" of students while at the same time giving them the tools to operate in the dominant discourse community, what Delpit (1987) refers to as "the rules of power." Gee advocates that teachers teach students to "make do" in the dominant discourse, learning the literacy tools that will allow them to participate effectively in the larger society without requiring them to "reject" their own community. These educational resources are art, in Gibson's (1988) terms, suggesting that immigrants can adapt to the dominant culture without being forced to assimilate; that they need not be forced into dichotomies such as Rodriguez's public and private identities.

Important research on the relations between schools and minority language communities draws on Vygotsky's (1978) cognitive theories, which suggest that the young learn about the world through interaction with more knowledgeable members of the community and culture, and that meaning is socially constructed and mediated through language. Moll and Greenberg (1990) extend Vygotskian theory to argue that *funds of knowledge*—valuable resources for everyday living—are exchanged among the immigrant home and community, and that these "funds" are indispensable resources for schools. Moreover, Moll and Greenberg argue that connecting schools with the homes of minority language students will give students and teachers new learning opportunities:

> We are convinced that teachers can establish, in systematic ways, the necessary social relations outside classrooms that will change and improve what occurs within the classroom walls. These social connections help teachers and students to develop their awareness of how they can use the everyday to understand classroom content and use classroom activities to understand social reality. (pp. 345–346)

In important ways, the research of Moll and others recovers the resources existing in immigrant communities that Covello and other educators of a previous generation had once mined.

How best do we prepare young people with the skills necessary to participate in a dominant culture and language that may be very different from their own? Reading the lives of immigrant children such as Covello and Rodriguez remind us of the importance of learning English as well as important tenets of American culture, if immigrants wish to succeed academically, socially, and economically in the United States. However, their lives also poignantly illustrate that when immigrant children reject their native language or culture, serious family and societal consequences may result. Caught up in the identity crisis of who we are as Americans, educational practitioners and policymakers often overlook the unique contributions that the life stories of the new Americans can provide. A better understanding of how new Americans see themselves, the schools, their communities, and the American society could help to break policymakers of their dependence on the two-dimensional images of immigrants handed down from the past. Moreover, a better understanding of the lives and learning of immigrants could help educators better teach diverse children with a respect for their cultural and linguistic backgrounds while fostering a common identity as Americans.

Lives Within Communities

In interesting ways, these two immigrant stories address themes of individualism and communitarianism running through the American experience. Rodriguez' narrative presents the quintessential American individual who works hard, loses something of his past, but gains freedom and the ability to create his own future. Covello's narrative, on the other hand, is about the importance of community. Historians Tyack and Hansot (1982) portray Covello the educator as a "community organizer": "His ideal was a school that was community-centered, rather than subject-centered or child-centered. And he used the school, its students and staff, as an agency for organizing the people of East Harlem to improve their lives" (p. 208). Rodriguez' autobiography illustrates that individual hard work, initiative and creativity are worthy characteristics to encourage in schools. Nevertheless, if educators seek to forge a community and a society that is more than the sum of its parts, and to challenge reform efforts that continue to ignore the needs of many Americans for social and economic justice, important lessons can be learned from Covello's community-centered education in East Harlem.

The lives of Covello and Rodriguez also illustrate ways in which immigrant children are transformed by their experiences in America, but also how they contribute to American society. Rodriguez, as a writer and critic of education and culture, suggests the importance of all children achieving a public identity as Americans. Covello as a teacher, curriculum innovator, principal and community leader, suggests that by valuing the languages, cultures and ideas of the *pluribus*, educators can find ways to create unity within schools and communities.

The autobiographical writings of Covello and Rodriguez remind us as well that immigrant parents are often marginalized not only by the larger society, but by their own children's public "success." Covello recounts how he eventually lacked the words to communicate with his father. Rodriguez tells of how, when he came home from college, it was a struggle to make conversation with his parents sound anything more than an interview. The voices of mothers and fathers soon are silenced, as the young men make their way in America.

If we believe that meaning is socially constructed, that funds of knowledge exist in immigrant homes and communities, and that parents are the primary educators of children, it is necessary for us to hear again the voices of immigrant parents. What are their learning experiences? What values do they hold, and how do these values influence their children's od ucation? What contributions are they making to America, and the next generation of Americans? When the voices of parents are missing from immigrant autobiographies, a role is created for the narrative inquirer to present such voices, in the beauty of their own words whenever possible, in life history and biographical texts.

I have written the life history of Shou Cha, an adult Hmong refugee in America, in order to bring such a parental voice into a dialogue about the role of education and the meaning of being American. Part Two of this study chronicles Shou's lifetime of learning. In a prelude to his life, Shou describes a violent encounter with America that has shaped his subsequent educational experiences. Chapters 3 through 6 recount Shou Cha's educational journey from Laos to the United States, his adoption of evangelical Christianity, his relationships within his family and across generations, and his efforts to make peace between communities, schools, and family members, and between himself and America.

Reading the life of Rodriguez provides us with a personal lens on the present, a time when programs designed to support members of minority groups, such as bilingual education and affirmative action, are being reconsidered or eliminated entirely. It is a time when many Americans believe that individuals must learn to take care of themselves, and depend no longer on government support for their *difference*. Reading the life of Covello provides a personal lens on America's past, a time and a place where the school worked actively to build a strong *community* out of a variety of ethnic enclaves, a community of individuals who would support each other, and appreciate the differences that made them strong. Writing the life of Shou Cha provides us with the opportunity to consider the past, present and future of a member of our diverse society, to acknowledge once again the role of the community, as well as the individual, in the educational process, and to hear the voices and learn from the lived experiences of some of the newest Americans, the Hmong.

II

A Hmong American Life History

Life History Chronology

Year	
1860s	War and destruction in the southern provinces of China. Choua Pu Tung, Shou Cha's great-great-grandfather, leads a large group of Hmong south into Laos.
1890s	France gains control of the opium monopoly in Southeast Asia.
1917	First leader of the Hmong Chao Fa, "Angel of the Sky" movement leads an insurrection against the French colonial authorities in Southeast Asia.
1954	Defeat at Dien Ben Phu spells the end of French colonial rule in Southeast Asia. Division of Vietnam into north and south.
1960	Royalist, communist and neutralist factions jockey for power in Laos. Vang Pao, general in the Royal Lao Army, offers Hmong support for the American CIA's "secret war" against communism in Southeast Asia. Over the next several years Vang Pao's troops are used to interrupt the flow of troops and supplies along the Ho Chi Minh Trail, which runs through Xieng Khouang Province in Laos.
1961	Shou Cha born in Luang Prabang Province, Laos. American and Russian military involvement in the struggle for power in Laos. Over one hundred thousand Hmong evacuated from their villages in Xieng Khouang Province because of the widening conflict.
1965	Gulf of Tonkin Resolution signals the expansion of American military presence in Vietnam.
1968	Shou Cha is learning to hunt, fish and help with the family farm. In Vietnam the Tet Offensive marks the beginning of the end for American military forces in Southeast Asia. In Laos, Vang Pao's forces come under heavy attack near Long Chieng.
1969	At its peak strength, Hmong "secret army" numbers 40,000. Over 60,000 North Vietnamese operating in Laos.
1970	For the first time, the American public learns of American military involvement in Laos.
1972	Seventy percent of all American air strikes in Southeast Asia aimed at targets in Laos, mostly within Xieng Khouang Province.
1973	The Geneva Peace Accords signal an end to U.S. military involvement in Southeast Asia. An agreement is reached between the warring parties in Laos, specifying the withdrawal of all foreign military forces.

continued on next page

1975	The Lao People's Democratic Republic is proclaimed. The last Americans leave Long Chieng airbase. General Vang Pao is officially relieved of duty, and he and some of his lieutenants are flown to Thailand. Several months later, these first Hmong refugees are resettled in the United States. Members of Vang Pao's army systematically rounded up by the new authorities in Laos and sent to "seminars" in reeducation camps, where many die from malnutrition and forced labor. Fearing reprisals because of their support for the Americans, thousands of Hmong flee to Thailand on foot in the next few years.
1976	Hmong village life is undergoing political, social and economic reorganization as a result of new government policies. Shou Cha suggests to his father that the family leave for Thailand, but his father rejects the idea at this time.
1978	Shou Cha gains his father's blessing for his plan to relocate the family to Thailand. Shou crosses the border with a group of villagers, arrives in Nam Yao camp, and takes a course in photography.
1979	Shou Cha returns to Laos with the "resistance" and helps his family and other villagers make the journey to Thailand. They join thousands of other Hmong, together with hundreds of thousands of Vietnamese, Cambodians, and Lao, who are entering refugee camps along the Thai border.
1980	Shou Cha meets his wife, Mai, at Sop Tuang refugee camp. He begins studying English and the Bible with the missionaries, and teaching Hmong language lessons at the missionary school. Shou is unable/unwilling to attend the spirit ceremony following his father's death, and a religious rift separates him from some members of his family. Mai has a miscarriage.
1982	Shou Cha and Mai's eldest son, Sammy, is born. Shou begins preaching in Phanat Nikhom camp, a refugee processing center near Bangkok. Some months later, Shou, Mai and other members of their family arrive in Chicago. Shou begins working the first of a series of low-paying jobs and continues to participate with the evangelical church.
1983	Mai Jia is born in Chicago. Shou has a dream that leads to his decision to join the ministry and attend school in Milwaukee.
1985	Mai, alone in her living room, gives birth to Paj Huab. Shou begins the second year of his ministerial training in Milwaukee.
1986	Yisay born.
1987	Joshua born. Shou completes his ministerial program. He continues to teach Sunday school and occasionally preaches.
1990	Rebecca born. Shou takes his family and his ministry to Windigo, Michigan.

continued on next page

1992	Gong Wendy born. Shou works odd jobs and continues trying to build the ministry.
1994	In November Shou Cha is shot at a convenience store near his home. He receives support from fellow ministers, neighbors, and the directors of Horace Kallen School, who ask him to join them as a bilingual assistant and Hmong community liaison.
1995	Former Hmong soldiers and American military and intelligence officers meet in Colorado to commemorate Hmong support of the U.S. war effort in Southeast Asia, and the Hmong presence in America.
1996	Shou continues his work with the ministry and with Kallen School and begins evening classes towards his high school diploma. On weekends he commutes to preach with two different Hmong congregations across the state.
1997	Summer, the Cha's eight child, is born. The Chas buy a house on Windigo's south side.

Note. This chronology of important events in the life history of Shou Cher is intended as a reference for the reader. A fuller narrative and important themes in Shou Cher's life history are explored in the following chapters.

3

A River in the Mountains

One day, the Hmong and their neighbors had a dispute over ownership of land. The King ordered both parties to depart at nightfall and to return before sunrise. He decreed that each would be the owner of the land they had traveled over during the night. The party that did not return on time would have to remain at the place where the rising sun caught them traveling.

At daybreak, the Hmong found themselves on a high mountain ...

—Livo and Cha (1991, p. 57)

The history of the Hmong people can be traced back at least five thousand years. Over time the Hmong have wandered, or been driven, southward through China, from the fertile river valleys to the harsher environment of the high mountains. Centuries of struggle with the Chinese empire climaxed in the so-called "Miao" Rebellion in Guizhou Province from the 1850s to the 1870s. The rebellion ended with a province destroyed, millions reported dead, and the Hmong people serving as scapegoats for the wider peasant revolt against high taxes and the injustices of the central government. To preserve their lives and their freedom, many Hmong moved southwards, into Vietnam, Laos, Thailand, and Burma.[1] In a brief overview to the Hmong's long history of struggle and relocation, Trueba and Zou (1994, p. 3) ask: "What would make us think that the (Hmong)—after centuries of migration—have retained an ethnic identity, a sense of peoplehood?" Shou Cha's narrative reminds us that stories shared from generation to generation are an important source of cultural identity, especially so within an oral culture such as the Hmong.

How far back does an individual's life history go? What incidents should be included, and that should be left out? One of the ways I have

---

[1] For a very good analysis of the rebellion in Guizhou, and the role of the Hmong people therein, see Jenks (1994).

come to understand the education of Shou Cha is by examining his reflections on the history of the Hmong people, as told to him in his childhood; the many skills he learned as a child in a remote mountain village; his knowledge of people, learned through interactions with family members, villagers, soldiers, guerrillas, and missionaries; and the intense thirst for knowledge and understanding of the world that led him to books, photography, language classes, and ministry.

This chapter's title, "A River in the Mountains," is doubly significant: On the one hand, it represents the historical-geographical context of Shou Cha's story, which begins in oral traditions concerning the driving of the Hmong people out of the fertile valley of the Yellow River in China, and into the mountains; and more recently, the story of thousands of Hmong who fled the mountains of Laos and made the dangerous crossing of the Mekong River to refugee camps in Thailand. On the other hand, the mountains are symbolic for the solid foundation of Shou's knowledge in the history and culture of his people, while the river, fed by countless springs and streams, represents the variety of sources that have contributed to his lifetime of learning.

THE SETTING

The Chas live in a brown, aging two-story rental on the northwest side of Windigo. As I park in the street, Mai Cha pulls up and maneuvers around me into the driveway. Two or three children have come out on the porch to greet her, and another two children follow her out of the car. I introduce myself, and we shake hands. She is an attractive woman, not quite 5 feet tall, with dark hair, brown eyes and a bright smile. She asks me to please come inside. The outer vestibule is filled with several pairs of women's shoes on a rack, coats of various sizes hanging, boots, and other odds and ends. When I enter the inner door Shou Cha gets up from a nearby table and greets me, saying, "Are you Don?" He is a handsome man in his mid-thirties, with dark hair, bright eyes, and a lively, expressive face. I find myself in the presence of someone with a special vitality and warmth. He invites me to sit down on a used sofa in a large living room that is lined with oversized furniture featuring a view of the street and a raised shelf for the big screen TV. Shou sits down next to me. Several children are moving on the stairs to our right, and in and out of the room.

A little later I go upstairs to use the bathroom. There is peeling, blue paint on the walls of the upper hallway, and animated voices coming from behind the closed door to the children's room. The place looks unfinished, as if someone were in the middle of repairs. In the bathroom a few errant cockroaches run along the ceramic surface of the tub.

Mai reenters the house without my ever noticing that she had left. With her are two of the older children as well as Jerry Lee, whom I am surprised to see in the Cha home. A few months earlier I had interviewed him and other members of his family before they moved to the north. Evidently, Jerry was going to follow through with his plan to remain behind in Windigo to finish high school. Shou introduces me to the children, and tells Sammy, his eldest son, that I'll be coming around and can help him with his homework. Sammy and Jerry carry what looks to be a 50 pound sack of rice into the kitchen. Soon I smell rice cooking through the door.

Mai brings out a tray with coffee, cups, sugar, and cream for Shou, herself, and me. Later Shou and I repair to the small table near the entrance to record some of the family history.

THE ANCESTOR

When I asked Shou Cha if he had heard stories about the Hmong and how they came out of China, he said:

> My great-great-grandfather was a marshal from China. He was a representative of the governor in Laos. He fought the war back in China and escaped with a group of people to Laos. And he was famous. My father always told us, and relatives always told us that our great-great-grandfather was a great one! His name was Choua Pe Tong.

> My great-great-grandfather would sometimes call on the Thunder Angel. Here in the United States you just call it thunder and lightning. You have the thunder. But American people don't believe that there is an Angel or Supernatural Power up there with the thunder. But to the Hmong people, they believe that the thunder is not just scientific. It's not. There is something supernatural in it. So my great-great grandfather could call the Thunder Angel to help him, if necessary. And he did. He would call, and the Thunder Angel would appear right away, no matter how sunny it was. Also, rain would appear right away to fight the war. That's what happened to my great-great grandfather. I didn't see it, but that's what they say!

For the Hmong of Laos, the earth, water and sky were filled with living spirits who could be called on for aid, or who could punish the transgressor and the foolish. The thunder angel was one such powerful spirit. Called on for aid in war, this spirit would also punish those Hmong who broke certain taboos. Shou tells me, for example, that if an adult Hmong were to drink breast milk, he would be struck dead by a bolt of lightning.

Shou proudly recalls stories of Choua Pe Tong:

I remember my father told me that when Choua Pe Tong settled in Laos, his house was quite long. Compared to America here, his house could be as long as a block. So, imagine how big his family was! So many people supported him. He was kind of like a chief leader or chief soldier at that time. My father, my uncles and other relatives always told me that he was a soldier-leader, a marshal. I can imagine how tough he was! And when he came to Laos, he received a position as a representative of the governor. Because he had the right, he had the authority to punish someone who disobeyed his decisions, or discipline someone, for a whole region, for part of Luang Prabang Province.

Although he recalls with clarity facts about an illustrious ancestor long dead, Shou has little to say about his grandparents, whom he never knew. He says:

My father was isolated from his family when his wife died and he had to move from my grandparents' area back to the north of Laos, to northern Luang Prabang Province, where there were more people, so he could look for another wife. And he found my mother to be his wife. So I have never seen my grandparents.

VIEW FROM THE MOUNTAIN

The Hmong had wandered southward into the mountains of Laos, yet they had formed a strong relationship with the land. The land yielded up its bounty to the farmer and the hunter. Shou grew up in a mountain village in the province of Luang Prabang, in northwest Laos in the early 1960s. He describes his family's livelihood in this way:

We had a big farm, but not as big as in the United States. For our people, back at that time, we didn't have just one kind of farm, we had a corn farm, we also had a rice farm, we also had a poppy farm, and a sugar cane farm, too. They also raised livestock, pigs, chickens, goats, horses. And some cows. Some raised ducks, too. Some of us sold livestock of different kinds, but mostly it was just for themselves.

The mention of the poppy farm piques my interest. Opium was grown by the Hmong for medicinal use and for trade. The Hmong had learned the difficult cultivation of the opium poppy in China, and had found an ideal climate for the poppy in the mountains of northern Laos. From the late 19th to the mid-20th century, the French had a monopoly on the opium traded in Southeast Asia, and they were instrumental in the expansion of opium smoking dens throughout the region (Chan, 1994).

I ask Shou to tell me more about the poppies. Were they grown for medicinal purposes? He replied:

Opium is a medicine, if you know how to use it. I should say the number one medicine in the world. But if you don't know how to use it, it kills your life. It does not mean that you die right away, but it means that your life is going to be miserable. But it's a number one medication. For example, if you cut your finger, somehow by accident, and you put the milk from the poppy on there, it heals, too. Anything you got, you have illness, sickness, no matter what, you use the opium poppy and it helps, it heals, and that's it. But after you are healed, you have to stop using it. You do not want to get addicted.

In analyzing the role of opium in his own family, Shou recognizes a very powerful medicine as well as the danger of addiction: His father, who used opium to heal members of the family, became addicted to opium smoking as he treated a painful, lingering illness of his own.

Shou recalls a tremendous amount of learning taking place in his youth as he grew up in the mountain village of his home:

I learned well. I learned how to harvest, I learned how to treat the farms, from a very young age, I learned how to farm, make a farm—take totally jungle area and turn it into farm, I learned how to do that. I believe even today I could still do it in the old system."

We look at pictures of traditional Hmong farm implements in a book that I had brought.[2] I learned that Shou's father was a blacksmith, and he could make all of the metal implements—sickles, axes, chisels, brooms, crossbows. Shou tells me that he is familiar with the use and the making of most of these implements:

I have used almost all of them. My cut here is because I used a crossbow." Shou shows me a scar on his left wrist. "Because I was holding the piece of wood and I tried to fix the hole and the knife was so sharp and it accidentally cut me. And I remember that my father beat me for doing that, spanked me, and then he said, "You should be careful!" And then he helped me to stop the bleeding. I was 12 years old, and at that time, by that age, we knew how to use a crossbow.

With the crossbow we hunted for anything flying, or anything related to mice, squirrels, or birds. We even hunted for monkeys. But you had to put a wood poison on the arrow tip to kill the monkey. When you shot at the monkey, the monkey would not run far. It would just fall down.

---

[2]The book was Roop and Roop (1990).

We would hunt larger game with traps and guns. There were not that many animals in the forest. There were deer, and even tigers. But we didn't hunt tigers much. There were not too many, and in that area they were so dangerous. Fortunately we did not have many tigers.

When I asked Shou how he learned how to hunt, he replied: "We would go with someone once, and then you learned by yourself. And then you helped someone else to learn, and help one another."

Though Shou himself did not travel more than a few days walking from his village, wandering merchants would come to the mountains a few times each year, providing young people like Shou with a glimpse of the towns and cities of the lowlands. Shou says:

> I lived on top of the mountain, no town, no city. On the mountain top, every year we had businessmen who would come by and they would trade for anything. They traded clothes, soap, anything that we needed. They used the horses to carry those items through our villages. And because we were on a mountain range, and it was so far walking, about three hours, or even half a day, to reach another village and a lot more people, almost every year the businessmen would come by at that time, and they would sell and we'd buy. So they had a market there. The businessmen would go by themselves to the lowlands, to the city, to get those things to sell.

> Personally, I didn't travel a lot. My father demanded that I not travel a lot. But I traveled too, not very far. When I was a teenager, I was a boy who was a leader. I liked to go ahead, go ahead. When I was younger I would go with someone, but as I got older I led someone. Each year I would travel 3 to 5 times. The destination would be a few days, walking.

Shou reveals a certain nostalgia for the beautiful jungle that surrounded the village of his youth:

> *There was country-side music where I lived.*
> *Back at that time,*
> *in that area,*
> *you would have loved the jungle!*
> *When you were in the village it was kind of hot,*
> *because*
> *there weren't many trees.*
> *But when you are going between the villages,*
> *there were a lot of trees and*
> *under the trees there was lots of shade.*
> *It was kind of cool,*
> *and there were a lot of insects,*
> *so there was a lot of music!!*
> *Bird music and insect music of all kinds!*

Flowers bloomed where I grew up.
On top of the mountain where I lived
in the deep jungle, and elsewhere
there are very beautiful flowers on the trunks of
trees.
Almost the whole year around there are flowers
on any mountainside,
red or white,
purple or yellow.
I bet you that
if you went there you would like it."

In his youth Shou learned a great deal about the world of his ancestors, the world of his village, and the world of nature. His strong connection to the past of the Hmong people, crystallized in his stories of his heroic great-great-grandfather, would serve him well in the future, when once again he and thousands of other Hmong were to embark on a series of long journeys. Shou also shows an incredible resourcefulness in his ability to understand and utilize disparate learning systems, tools, and beliefs. As a youth he learned the things necessary for his cultural environment naturally, by observing others and then doing it himself. In this way he became a proficient farmer and hunter. He was fortunate to have a skilled craftsman for a father, and this is illustrated in the variety of different tools he could make and use. Shou also reveals a great deal of knowledge about the healing power of opium, "the greatest medicine in the world." As an adult he has embraced the world of Western science and medicine, but he still retains respect for the power of traditional practices and traditional beliefs in the spirit world.

THE POET

Shou Cha has practiced traditional Hmong music and song since childhood. Just as they learned to farm, hunt, and practice medicine, Hmong children learned traditional music, including funeral music, New Year's music, and personal music. Also, Shou learned a variety of song that occurs without musical accompaniment, which is called *kwstxiaj*.

Shou says that, typically with such song, what is going on in your personal life is compared to the life of nature. He provided me with this example in English:

There is a bird singing on the mountainside
on the mountainside
And my girlfriend
If I cannot marry with you

CHAPTER 3

I will never die.
There is a bird singing in the meadow
My girlfriend
If I cannot marry you
I might die
I will never go.

Shou says that the meaning of this song is that, although the body of the boyfriend may die, his spirit will not rest, but will stay with her. Traditional songs would include four series of pairs such as the stanzas just discussed.

Shou Cha also helped me better understand the song of Lee Txai that appears later in this chapter:

Unhappy and yet not broken-hearted,
I come to this foreign land,
Without young brothers, without old brothers,
like a crazed dog wandering from here to there.

Broken-hearted and yet not unhappy,
I come to this foreign land,
Without young brothers, without old brothers,
and the others eat, while I watch like a dog waiting
for scraps.

Shou identified Lee Txai as a leader of the Chao Fa movement within the Ban Vinai camp. His song varies from traditional Hmong song in much the same way as the religion of the Chao Fa varies from traditional Hmong religion. Nevertheless, within it Lee Txai had wedded old and new elements of a changing Hmong culture to create a song that expressed the mixture of stoicism and despair with which many refugees addressed camp life.

As we work together with his life history, occasionally rendering his words to poetry in the text, Shou tells me that "I do not belong to this Earth," as a lament, bears most similarity to a traditional Hmong song. Nevertheless, such oral poetry in English, like Shou's life itself, has been fully transformed from the traditional. It has become something new, and has a beauty of its own.

THE WORLD OF BOOKS

Beyond the traditional learning of his village life, Shou Cha also understood the importance of more formal educational endeavors. Although he only attended school 1 day, he learned to read and write while working on his family's farm. He was fully literate in Laotian and Hmong when he reached the Thai refugee camps, and this served him well in his continuing education and employment.

Shou describes his one day in a village school in Laos.

> I stayed with my sister my first day I went to school. Everyone else was working. I was so young that I couldn't work with the others. The farm was quite far, too. I do not know why, but I happen to remember this event for my whole life.

> Back in Laos the teachers were too authoritarian. They had the right to punish anyone they wanted. So I was scared of the teacher very much. The teacher was Hmong, from another part of Laos. He did not do anything to me because he knew that my sister just brought me to the school because we did not have someone to take care of me at home." Shou speaks with great feeling as he remembers, "I was so scared and so ashamed of myself, I did not do anything. I thought I was a hardship for my sister. That is the only day of school that I remember. After that I did not go to school anymore. Just for that 1 day. I was probably 7 years old.

However, Shou is quick to point out that his education continued outside of this one day of formal education. He learned to read and write during his breaks from working on the farm. He acknowledges the support of his older sister in this learning, and recognizes also that she was an intelligent woman who was prevented from advancing in a career because of established gender roles within Hmong culture:

> Only one day of school in Laos in a school building. But I also went to school in a different system, a totally different system. I learned, though, but not the way you do in a school building. Well, the same sister I told you about earlier, she graduated one grade after another, and she went to Long Chieng base to serve as a military nurse; because she graduated from school very quickly and she was a good student. But, unfortunately, she was a girl, and no one supported her much, and she could not go so far as a man or a boy could.

> As time passed, we moved to a place where there was no school. So she came back to stay with us for about 3 years. In that 3 years I and my brother attended school from her—not in a school facility, but she taught us when we were farming. When me and my brother were ploughing, burning the woods, or any time like that, from morning to noon we would do that. Then at noontime the girls and my mother and my sisters prepared food and brought it to us. And I and my brother had to study, and we would study half an hour or an hour, and then we would go back to work. Then after that, in the evening, we would come back from our work on the farm, then we would also have the time again to study—about 1 hour. We did that for the whole year, and then we completed the alphabet book of Lao. So we knew how to

read, and we started to write. And we memorized the stories, not like in the school system, but we had to read them many times, many times! So we did. And we wrote. And that is when I lived on the top of the mountain, and you did not have books or school supplies, nothing at all. So when we burned the wood and the charcoal became soft, we used it as chalk. And we used that to write on any boards or on flat stones. So we did that. And we also tried to buy papers. So we did that for a couple of years, and then we escaped from that village, and we came to another province they call Sayaboury and we came closer to a town or city, where we could find a better system of study. So we continued! No one taught us that we should continue. We just had to continue to read or write or find any book—so we did. And luckily we just continued to learn.

One of the more fascinating aspects of Shou's discussion of his learning to read and write outside of the school is the educational role played by his sister. The traditional Hmong family was a patriarchy, and women's roles were well defined. Traditionally, women would marry young and be heavily engaged in childrearing and agriculture. They neither served as authority figures nor participated in formal education. Walker-Moffat (1995) states that even when schools were available to most Hmong children living in refugee camps, girls typically dropped out after a few years. Considering this traditional role, it is fascinating that Shou Cha's older sister not only completed her schooling in the village, but pursued a nursing career in Long Chieng. Equally impressive is Shou's acknowledgment that his sister was held back from promotion because of her gender: "Unfortunately, she was a girl, and no one supported her much, and she could not go as far as a man or a boy could." Perhaps Shou recognizes the debt he owes to this sister who taught him and his brother how to read in the fields of their home.

THE WORLD FALLS APART

In 1959 the CIA, concerned about the growing communist insurgencies in Southeast Asia, began seeking the support of the Hmong of Laos.[3] The Hmong under the leadership of General Vang Pao agreed to provide military support and to help build air bases for the Americans near their villages. By the early 1960s the Americans and the Russians were heavily arming the opposing factions within Laos, and war engulfed the Hmong people in the north. As is usual in war, the first casualty was the truth:

---

[3]There is evidence that the Americans became involved in opium trafficking in Southeast Asia, and that Long Chieng base served as a collection site for heroin processing. Alfred Mc-Coy documents Vang Pao's involvement in the trade, including his establishment of a heroin lab at Long Chieng, and the use of American helicopters to bring harvested opium into the base from outlying villages. See McCoy (1991).

Most Americans were not told of U.S. involvement in Laos until 1970. What the Hmong were told was that the American's would come to their aid should the war go badly.[4] Shou Cha was not yet born when the Hmong under the leadership of Vang Pao agreed to fight with the Americans against communists in Southeast Asia. A decade and more of the "secret war" in Laos left thousands of Hmong dead and dozens of villages destroyed, especially in Xieng Khouang Province on the border with Vietnam. Shou Cha relates that although his village in Luang Prabang was further removed from the conflict, the effects of the war could be felt there:

> The war was not in our area. The war was in the northeast; there weren't very many scary things where we were. But the war included everything, too. I say that because all the people in our part of the country had to enlist to go to the war. And if you didn't enlist, no matter. The village leader would catch you for the war. Age 15 and up. I know that my uncle went to the war because they caught him. The village leader had the right, because he had been told to do that. I think they obeyed the government so much that they just had to join. Others, because they were caught, and they had to participate. But you know, you were on a side. Like me, I was on the side that was friends with America, and then you had to fight your enemies. So we did. That was the scary thing. We didn't hear the sound of fighting coming across the mountains or from another village. No, we didn't hear that. But we heard that the war was this and that, and that you had to go to the war. And that was a very scary thing, too. But we had war, too. The real war was in Long Chieng or Xieng Khouang, but where we lived, in Luang Prabang province, sometimes, we did not realize it, we heard that the war was just about 3 days' walking away from you. That's a scary thing.
>
> I remember one time we had to escape and hide ourselves in the jungle or in the cave for about 2 weeks. And that was because, just like I said, the war was around our region. So we had to escape, we had to stay away, so we did. And we were lucky because at that time it was just after the New Year, when we did not do anything, we just had to relax and after about 30 more days we would go and begin another new farm. So we stayed about 2 weeks out in the jungle. We could not come to the village because the war was close by. Scary things. For people who go to school, if the war comes to your country, you have to wait to learn, too. And then we all had to be careful and report to the village guards, so that they would know and they would protect us. War is not so good, but we had to protect the country.
>
> My oldest brother got killed. Not by the enemy's shooting, but by participating in the war. My oldest brother got killed by a land mine. In the evening they went out to protect their base, and they went to lay mines. My brother was one of the ones who did that. He was very talkative. When you (lay mines), you just go out and do it, and you have to remember where you

---

[4]For a more complete history of the relationship between the Americans and the Hmong in Laos, see Hamilton-Merritt (1993).

put it. Now in the morning, you will have to go back and pick it up. So at night, when they put it there, each person just goes alone and does it, so he remembers well. But in the morning, they went together, and take that one, and then that one, and then that one. And they were good friends and they talked a lot. Then my brother forgot where his mine was, so he got killed accidentally.

Shou lends me a videotape in which, he says, the American government acknowledges its friendship of the Hmong. The video documents a gathering of former soldiers of the Hmong "secret army," U.S. military and CIA personnel, and a few government dignitaries in Boulder, Colorado, on July 4, 1995. At this event, marking the 20th anniversary of the arrival of the first Hmong refugees in America, General Harry Aderholt, who supervised U.S. military action in Laos during the war, addressed these words to the aging Hmong soldiers gathered together in their combat fatigues:

> I want you to know that what my government did to your people is inexcusable. Through all these years the CIA and the State Department pressured you to increase your activities in northern Laos. Your response was always positive, irregardless of the terrible suffering you endured. I saw you sacrifice your young men, your homeland, and your freedom. What did we do for you, our staunch, loyal ally? We withdrew without ever looking back. (quoted in Thao & Lee, 1995)

When the last American troops left Saigon, Vientiane and Phnom Pen, they left behind allies such as the Hmong. Their villages in Xieng Khouang Province were largely destroyed. Their homeland in northern Laos was occupied by thousands of North Vietnamese and Pathet Lao troops. The Americans, for whom they had tied up traffic on the Ho Chi Minh trail, for whom they had built and protected air bases, for whom they had fought and died, were going home. The Hmong had no home to go back to, just a long walk through the jungle to the uncertainty of Thailand and the future.

THE NEW VILLAGE ORDER

See a tiger, you will die; see an official, you will be poor.
—Hmong proverb

With the proclamation of the Lao People's Democratic Republic in 1975 many changes came to the Hmong villages. Old village leaders were replaced with new. Small private farms were consolidated and collectivized. Traditional gender, family and communal relationships were challenged. Free public education was extended to the remotest mountain villages.

"Seminars" were arranged for those who were unable or unwilling to adapt to the new changes, and many never returned from their stays in the reeducation camps (Hamilton-Merritt, 1993). When I asked Shou Cha how life changed after the communist took over Laos in 1975, he replied:

Totally changed. Totally changed. Something that I remember is that power changed in the village. Before 1975 the village leader where I lived had the power to decide what to do, or to judge, or to solve any problem that occurred within the community. After 1975 the communists operated so differently. You, as the village leader, were not in power. That's what they changed. The power belonged to all the people. You don't own the power. If you said you owned the power, then you had to "study." And "study" meant disappear forever. It meant never come back. You would have to go to a "seminar," and you would never see that person again.

So everything changed. Our economy changed. Back at that time we had to cooperate, working on things together, and the economy was decided on by the government! The whole village, we had to work in big fields. No matter that you worked here a part, there a part. But one big field. You did not own a particular field for yourself. That's what they did. And almost all of the mountain people—like the Hmong, the Khmu, and some other tribes like the Yao, they did not like it very much. But they had to do it. If they didn't do it, they had to go to a "seminar," which means they would never be back! (he laughs) And that happened very often.

The fields belonged to the whole village, and that was because of the economic system of communism. Some of this was good, too. Back before 1975, small villages or top-of-the-mountain villages did not have the education system. After 1975, they established a school system, schools for each 30 to 50 families. And we had night school, we didn't have the day school. Every night you had to go to school, and in the daytime you had to go to work.

In these schools we studied the basics—writing, literacy. If you didn't go to school, or you disobeyed the rules, then the teacher had the right to report to the village leader, and he would report to the higher political leader. So if you disobeyed, you would have to face the "seminar," too. Back at that time you could not leave your hair long like this," Shou gestures to his own hair, which comes a bit below his ears, laughing. "They would say, 'You cut your hair, or you go to seminar!'

I say, "You say the village owned everything. Who decided who got what?"

It was not successful. The first five years they forced people to collectivize but it did not work. So people got hungry, and starved a lot. But they put things together, and they changed the leader system. They liked you to work all together, and they divided together, but it was not working. So they changed the system a little bit. And it was this: I have a field, and you have to come and help me, cooperatively, working until mine is finished. Then we will go all together to work with your field. And while farming, you could dance, and have music. And someone danced, someone worked, and someone cooked. And they did that. It was fun, but some wouldn't do what they were supposed to do—they were dancing or they were singing, they weren't working!

They tried that for awhile and it did not work. A lot of people in the country tried that. And then they changed their system again. At that time, whatever you got from your field, you gave a percentage to the government. If you had ten, you had to give one or two to the government. It was not working. Now they changed their system again. I believe that now in Laos they work their fields, they can sell, they have the economic right to do that, but if they sell livestock, then you have to give a percentage to the government.

I ask, "What was it that made you leave the country?"

We didn't like the government system. Because if you made a big mistake you'd go to a seminar and never come back. The one thing was this: If you had ever worked with the government before the communists came, and someone released that information to the new government, then you would have to disappear. Now, village leaders, and soldiers, those kind of people were considered the most dangerous.

Another thing we did not like is that you had to share your family. What that means is that, for example, if my wife wants to share her body with another man who works with the government, as a soldier or something like that, she had the right to do that. I don't have the right to stop her. OK? According to Hmong people, no, that's not what we should do. I as a husband have the right to stop my wife from doing such things. If I don't have the right to stop it, I am not the man for her. So that happened to many people. So, we didn't like the idea. Even if my wife likes to share her body with someone else, no, I don't like it. That is the scary thing. If I don't like it, and if I stop it, then I have to go to the seminar.

I question Shou whether the Hmong women were forced into sexual relations with soldiers and government officials. His answer reveals a depth of understanding about the traditionally low status of women in Hmong society:

When a group of soldiers came to a village, they helped the ladies carry the water from the river, they helped the ladies grinding rice, they helped the ladies go somewhere to do this or that, and they showed *so much respect*. They would even call them "mother" or something like that to honor them. By doing that, any lady would care for them, or fall in love with them. Yes, that happened. And because her husband was the kind of person just to treat her commonly, they didn't have to be so good or so bad, then the other one treats her *so extra nice!* Then she somehow is convinced.

I ask, "Were the communists actively trying to change the relationships between men and women?"
Shou replies,

> Yes. If I myself had been convinced to follow that policy, I would do that, too. I would share my wife, and I would just go and share the other's wife. That happened to some people. It did not happen to my village—yet. But it happened to some people somewhere else, already.

> For Hmong people, the family relationship is very, very strict. And I think that is the best way that we can live, and don't ever try to destroy it. That is what I think. You as a husband should trust your wife, love your wife, and the wife should just submit to the husband, and that is what you should do. If I am the husband, I have the right to discipline my children and my wife the way that I think is good. If I discipline them wrongly then the village leader had the right to tell me what to do, or my wife had the right to go to her own family, and then she had the right to tell them, and they had the right to put a restriction on me and the discipline between me and my wife. That is what we keep, and that helps! But to say that you want to go anywhere and you want to say goodbye, no.

Evidently, the new order in Laos proved chaotic for Hmong village life. One can imagine the consternation of a patriarchal society at the threat presented by the Laotian government's encouragement of "wife-sharing" policies. Interestingly, Shou Cha shows the flexibility to appreciate concepts from apparently disparate ideologies and beliefs. Although he was not interested in participating in the "wife-sharing" practices encouraged by the new Laotian authorities, he understands how such practices could be attractive to some, particularly females whose spouses showed little respect for them. Moreover, Shou acknowledges that the communist government in Laos brought schools to all the villages, and not just for ideological study. The new government sent those who disobeyed to "seminars" from which they would never return. On the other hand, during the war, Hmong village leaders sent 15-year-olds to a war from which many would never return. Clearly, the new communist government in Laos was challenging the traditional economic, political, and family order, but it was also challenging the imagination of young people like Shou. Unlike his parents, he is literate, and through reading he gains a window onto the outside world. He, too, is a representative of a new order.

THE RIVER

In 1973 the Paris Peace Accords signaled the end of American military involvement in Southeast Asia. In Laos a peace agreement was signed between the warring factions. Two years later, the Pathet Lao communists
pressured the Laotian king to send Vang Pao out of the country. As the
Vietnam War came to an end, the North Vietnamese Army and Pathet
Lao closed in on Hmong strongholds in the north of Laos. Vang Pao and
several of his supporters were airlifted out of the airbase at Long Chieng,
but thousands of Hmong men, women and children were left behind to
fend for themselves, no longer with American support. Many died in a
war of attrition carried out by the new Lao People's Democratic Republic
and their Vietnamese allies (Hamilton-Merritt, 1993). Moreover, much of
the high mountain agricultural system had been destroyed in the war,
and the Hmong faced an economically bleak future (Cooper, 1986).

In 1975 and the following years a vast exodus occurred as Vang Pao's
soldiers and their families, Hmong clan leaders, and all those who were
either unwilling or unable to live under communist rule left Laos for
Thailand. The road was often treacherous, and encounters with communist troops could prove disastrous. Moua Yang, another community liaison at Kallen, walked 20 days through the jungle with his family to the
Mekong River, only to find it heavily guarded by government troops. They
spent 3 months wandering without food until they were able to find a safe
place to swim the river and reach Thailand. The crossing of the Mekong is
the theme of countless Hmong *pandau*, or story cloths, which depict vivid
scenes of this part of Hmong history. Shou Cha relates that he and his
family had the good fortune to cross the border in the north, away from
the watchful eyes of the communist regime in Vientiane:

> My friend in the Thai refugee camp said that if you made a *pandau*, and that
> *pandau* created something like the story of the people who came from Laos
> to Thailand, and were killed by the communist soldiers, and also killed by
> the Thai soldiers, when the camp patrol saw that picture, they would grab
> it! Because that goes against the authority.

> *There was a group of Hmong who were leaving Laos.*
> *They tried to cross the Mekong River*
> *somewhere near Vientiane.*
> *And the communist soldiers said*
> *'Go ahead!*
> *If you don't want to stay,*
> *Cross!*

Go across!'
And of course they wanted to cross it.
And so they came across.
And in the middle of the river
the soldiers shot.
And the Mekong River turned red with blood,
everyone was dying,
and it was terrible.

For me, thank God, I'm lucky, but I did not cross the Mekong River. And we came in a different direction, not by Vientiane. There were 3 hundred people in our group. We went through the jungle, of course. We walked for 10 days and 10 nights. On the 6th day it began to rain very hard and I got sick. Three days later we reached a road, and then we came to Thailand. I was very sick when we crossed the border. And someone who came from Thailand to assist us, he carried my bag, so I could go through and we came to Thailand. I just came myself first, then I could go back and bring my family. So that's what happened to me.

Like I said before, I was the kind of man who said, I want to go, so I did. But I came with about 3 hundred people, almost a whole Hmong village. I and my cousins or nephews, we went together, and we took about eight families with us. Before I left the first time my older brother got married—because he had so many girlfriends! So he had to marry, and he did. So I had the right to go anywhere, and of course my father trusted me. So I left Laos, and my father still took care of the family, as he should.

On my first trip to Thailand, I did some labor. I was obligated to carry someone's items, clothes. I carried for them and they paid me for that. So when I came to Thailand, I took a course. At that point it was photography. So I used all my money to learn that course!" Shou laughs at the memory. "I learned how to manage, I learned how to take photographs, I learned how to do the negatives, everything. I paid the whole amount for that, and I graduated from that program. So when I went to Laos, I knew what to do, I knew what to take pictures of, but I was not a journalist. I did not do that. I took what I liked. So I have something to remember.

Shou's wife Mai has been listening to our conversation, and she leaves the room for a moment. When she returns, she brings two photos to the table. In one of the photos, a much younger Shou stands in the midst of a poppy field with another young man with shoulder-length hair. Each has a large white squash in one hand, and a rifle in the other. In the second photo, Shou kneels in the foreground with the rifle aimed. Standing on his right is his older brother, whose hair is shoulder-length. On his left is another man, and their appears to be a woman behind him, in the background. Large trees of the tropical forest appear in both photos.

I ask Shou why he and the other man are carrying rifles.

You could not go to Laos and carry weapons if you did not go with some kind of political organization. So we went from Thailand to Laos as a revolutionary group. We went under the refugee camp's leader, who was appointed by the Thai government. And if you tell them that you go to Laos to fight communists, and if you ask for weapons, then they would say, yes, you can. So these rifles were brought from Thailand.

I ask, "Did you have to use the guns at all? Did you do any fighting when you were going back and forth?"
Shou laughs.

No, we used them for hunting! That helps. Because if a soldier challenges you, then you have to shoot him. But mostly we had to hide ourselves. Because the only thing you want is not to fight anyone. You know that you don't have the power to fight the whole country. You just have to protect yourself and bring your family to Thailand. So that is what we did. But back at that time, officially, you didn't have the right to bring people to Thailand. But you had to bring them, because you know that you loved your family so much.

I notice that Shou's nephew has long hair in the photograph. When I mention this, Shou says:

"I do not know if you know the Chao Fa?[5] That hairstyle was part of that. He copied the style." Shou points to the other photo. "This is my brother, who has the same style. Mine, back at that time, I cut short. So almost every time, any village, I had the potential to go inside the village because my hairstyle was kind of short. So I could go in."

"So that allowed you to travel easier," I suggest. "And no one would look at you and say, oh, he's a member of the Chao Fa."
Shou says, "That's right. Or from the forest. They usually call them Forest People. Because when you came from Thailand you stayed in the jungle almost all of the time! So if I had short hair I could walk through the village."
I asked Shou if his father had made the second journey with him to Thailand. He said:

No, he did not make it. If he had come earlier when it was easier to come, then he would have made it. He came in May, and back in Laos, a tropical land, May was the bad time, when it rained a lot. In jungle country it was so rainy that you could not walk in the forest. We just had to walk through the

---

[5]Chao Fa, or "Angel of the Sky," is a religious and political movement inside Laos which gained a number of Hmong adherents after the departure of Vang Pao in 1975. This movement is further discussed in the next chapter.

jungle, nights and days and nights and days. And he was quite old, and not very healthy, so he could not walk. So that is why he said, "you go, and then you come back." And I did. I went there. But unfortunately, he did not wait for me. He died before I came back.

THE REFUGEE CAMPS

Unhappy and yet not broken-hearted,
I come to this foreign land,
Without young brothers, without old brothers,
like a crazed dog wandering from here to there.

Broken-hearted and yet not unhappy,
I come to this foreign land,
Without young brothers, without old brothers,
and the others eat, while I watch like a dog waiting for scraps.
                        —Song of Lee Txai, Ban Vinai refugee camp,
                           1980 (in Vang and Lewis, 1990, p. 157)

By the late 1970s the eastern Thai border was home to 21 refugee camps set up to receive hundreds of thousands of people fleeing Vietnam, Cambodia and Laos. These camps were supported by the United Nations High Commissioner for Refugees (UNHCR) and staffed by volunteers, among whom were many missionaries. However, the Thai government was influential in determining official and unofficial refugee camp policies. Camps were opened and closed by Thai authorities, and refugees were shifted about. In general, the Thais favored repatriation of refugees, even though many feared for their lives if they were returned to their homelands. "These periodic shifts from camp to camp effectively terrorized the refugees, because they could never be certain when they would be uprooted again or, worse yet, sent across the border" (Long, 1993, p. 49; see also the Lawyers Committee for Human Rights, 1989).

Tens of thousands of Hmong were living in camps in Thailand by 1980, principally in Chiang Kham, Ban Nam Yao and the large camp at Ban Vinai. Ban Vinai, the largest Hmong settlement in the world at that time, contained over 40,000 people in an area of less than one square mile (Long, 1993). The reeducation of refugees destined for America began in these camps in Thailand. Tollefson (1989) suggests that refugees were presented with an unrealistic portrait of life in the United States, while at the same time they were made to feel the unworthiness of their own cultures:

The counterfeit universe presented to refugees in the educational program at the processing centers is planned and purposeful. The unrealistic vision of life in the United States, the myths of American success ideology, the denigration of Southeast Asian cultures, and the effort to change refugees' behavior, attitudes, and values result from systematic decisions by policymakers throughout the educational bureaucracy. (p. 87)

Camp life was squalid, crowded and dangerous for refugees who feared reprisals from Lao communists, Thai communists, and Thai government soldiers. Despite the difficulties of the camps, however, many Hmong refugees did not want to "board the bus" for America (Ranard, 1989). The lessons of American success they learned in the reeducation programs were more than counterbalanced when they received letters from relatives in America, and read their tales of isolation, poverty and fear in strange cities.

Shou Cha, interestingly, seems to have some fond memories from his time in the refugee camps. There he found his new religion, evangelical Christianity. There he learned English, and began his career as a teacher in formal settings. There he met and married his wife, Mai. When he first arrived in Thailand, Shou stayed in Nam Yao camp. He describes how, 8 months later, he went back for his family, and he brought them to Sop Tuang camp, which was closer to the Laotian border.

Nam Yao is further from Laos that Sop Tuang. You walk from Sop Tuang to the border with Laos, just about one half day. But if you walk from Nam Yao to the Lao-Thai border, it takes about two days. So, it is more difficult. Also, there is a Thai base very close to the border, too. And they were very strict, because they got attacked from Laos, or the Thai communists, so they were very alert about that. So it was quite good for you to go from Sop Tuang to Laos. I stayed in Sop Tuang or Mae Jarim about two years.

I ask Shou if he had learned his English in the camps, and if he had good teachers. With a self-deprecating laugh he says:

Oh, what can I say about that? I don't know if they were good or not! I attended Oxford English classes, and I learned Oxford One and Two. And then I got 'A's' for that. And also I participated every day in basic English from the missionary program, about one half year, and I worked with the mission for children. And I learned something from them, and they taught me. So, as fast as I learned English I worked with them, and by learning, by working together.

Actually, I was a teacher with the mission. I was a teacher, no matter how little I knew. I guess they trusted me enough to be a teacher, so I did. My brother and I were teachers. When I was a teacher, I taught whatever I knew. And I learned from the Bible, and I taught it, and I learned and taught. We learned together. I was also a teacher in the other program, but not an English teacher; I was a Hmong teacher! A Hmong literacy teacher. I taught the Hmong children how to write Hmong. I was a teacher of religion in the camp; I was a teacher of Hmong literacy in the camp, too.

I did not decide to come to the United States because I remembered that my family was still in Laos. So I had to go back to get my family. My brother had the same idea. So we went back. After that I was the one who was going to come to the United States. Until I got married. After I got my wife, we became Christians, and helped the missionaries in the camp.

How Shou Met Mai

Psychologically the refugee camp could be a hard place for a mountain people who were used to roaming freely. Fenced in and often with little to keep them occupied, many Hmong became despondent. Ironically, Shou Cha was to meet his wife while searching for a cousin who had taken his own life.

One of my cousins had two girlfriends, and they were sisters. Then one of them got a short knife, with which she intended to kill her sister. If he married the younger sister, the older sister was gonna kill her. But he did not love the older sister as much. So his father just said some joking words to scare him. So he happened to borrow his mother's money to buy some soap to wash his clothes. That is what happened. And I was there. I did not think that it was so serious, but he, by the words that his father spoke to him, he went off and killed himself with poison. And I and everyone who knew him went to help look for that boy who killed himself. I was walking with a friend somewhere in the center of the camp and I met my wife walking by. I met her, but I did not think about getting married with her or anything. But I also was a Christian already, so I prayed, and prayed and prayed and then I believe that I met her in a certain way, and that God gave her to me. So it is part of this and part of that.

Mai shows me two more photographs, taken the day of her wedding to Shou in Sop Tuang. Although they were converts to Christianity, Mai and Shou performed a traditional Hmong wedding ritual: In one of the photographs they are leaving food offerings along a trail on the outskirts of the camp; in the foreground an elderly shaman offers a prayer.

The Miscarriage

His conversion to Christianity does not prevent Shou from retaining some beliefs in the power of the spirits of land, sea and air that filled the traditional Hmong world. When his wife had a miscarriage, Shou found an explanation in the realm of the spirits, rather than in the hard life of the camps. He says:

> Our first pregnancy was a miscarriage, because we believe a supernatural spirit attacked and destroyed her pregnancy. That is another story. I and my wife believe that was from a phenomenon. Hmong believe this, and also Lao and Thai people. We believe that any valley that has water has certain supernatural phenomena there. And that refers to what we call "Ja" which means, "dragon." Those are super spirits. The Ja, that phenomenon in that small stream causes a problem. That happens to any pregnant women who crosses a small stream. There is the potential. Some ladies who are pregnant don't dare to cross any stream. Even if there is a valley where rain water comes through, that can cause a miscarriage. So I think that happened to my wife.
>
> Back at that time, that day, I and my wife went to the small stream, which was in a very steep place. The camp where we lived was on the top of a mountain, so that stream was slippery. So we went there, and I and my wife had clothes to wash. It was lovely. The stream was not very big, just a bit bigger than your shower. So we washed the clothes, and when we came back from that place, I went back to the building where I worked, which was the office of the missionary school. So I stayed there for half the day, until about dark. Then one of my little sisters came up and told me that my wife had a big stomach ache. But I still stayed at the office. It was not very considerate of me. I do not know why I did that, but probably I was learning something, or staying with the missionary, I don't remember. But I did not stay long. Then I went home. And she knelt beside our bed, all bloody. Then I came and saw that. Then we knelt down and prayed. And she told me that at that moment, the pain stopped. Right there. It became better and better. And in a couple of days we went to the hospital for treatment, too, but she told me that at that moment the pain stopped. So that miscarriage was affected by a phenomenon."

Resettlement

Though some Hmong, especially those involved in the resistance, spent years inside the refugee camps near the Laotian border, Shou and his family were there a relatively short time. His learning of English, his conversion to Christianity and work with the missionaries probably increased both his willingness to leave Southeast Asia, as well as his chances to be sponsored by a religious group as a refugee to the United States.[6] Shou describes how this journey to America developed:

---

[6]This conversion experience and issues related to Shou's religious beliefs are discussed more fully in the next chapter.

When I came to Nam Yao, unfortunately, my step-brothers and sisters who lived there already left. They were in France. The oldest one is still in the camp, in Nam Yao. At that time I came, and I slept in Ban Nam Yao. My youngest half-sister got in contact with me. She had gone with her family to Chicago already. She had an American friend and he was a deacon in the church, too. So they asked him to sponsor us, and they said yes.

When we left the camp, I was so bus sick. So we were just about two hours out of the camp and I got sick. And when we arrived to the capital town of Chavam Nan Province, I had thrown up already. And I asked God, oh, no Lord, if I go like this I cannot go for another twenty hours, because we had to ride that to Bangkok, which takes a long time. I asked God, and at that time we arrived in Bangkok and I did not throw up. I was OK. We lived there and even though I was not a minister, I was not even an elder, I preached, I taught, everything! Oh, thanks to God, I do not know why he put me in that position! Shou laughs as he recalls those days. I was not a teacher but I just did like a teacher. So we lived there and my wife got pregnant in the camp.

I ask Shou if it was a long process in leaving the camp and coming to the United States. He replies: "Years. For example, you register this year, 1996, and in 1997 you can get an interview. Unless they are rushed through and they just come for you."

Shou and his family eventually reached Phanat Nikhom, where refugees accepted for resettlement were processed before the trip to another host country:

It's a long story. But when we came to Phanat Nikhom camp, nearer to Bangkok, my wife also had her second pregnancy and that is our first son. So we lived there almost 1 year, and she got the baby. Then on the flight to the United States, I was scared about how I could manage to come because I was so airsick. So I asked God again if I could manage to go to the United States without getting airsick, and, thank God, I did not get sick. But when we arrived in Chicago, everything was so bright! So exciting. Imagine baseball at night! I understood English enough, and our sponsor talked to me and I could understand.

Shou Cha had left the mountains, crossed the river, and made the long journey to the United States. He had experienced life in a small village and life in crowded refugee camps, and now he was in Chicago, a glittering metropolis of steel and concrete. For the moment, the excitement of the bright lights and baseball at night are enough to carry him through. Soon, the grim task of supporting a family on minimum wage jobs, and the occasional violence of the city streets would shatter any illusions he holds about this land of promise, but tonight, he holds onto the dream.

SOURCES OF LEARNING

Like a river in the mountains, Shou Cha's lifetime of learning has been fed by multiple sources. As a youth, growing up "on top of the mountain," he was immersed in ancestral histories and cultural practices that grounded him not in a location—the history of the Hmong, clearly, is a history of movement—but in the traditions of a people. He learned to hunt, fish, and farm and to create and utilize the tools necessary for livelihood in the mountains. He also learned the importance of his relationships to family, clan, village—and the Americans. For Shou's early life was also influenced by the many changes that alliance with the Americans brought to the Hmong of northern Laos. His village was largely untouched by the war that ravaged neighboring Xieng Khouang Province, but the conflict and its aftermath would influence his life and learning in many ways. His greatest teacher would be his sister, who was educated at schools sponsored by Vang Pao's military command. He would see many uncles and brothers go off as recruits to the war, and some would never come back. After the departure of the Americans and leaders such as Vang Pao, Shou, like thousands of other Hmong, would forsake the land of his birth, and help lead his family on the dangerous trip to Thailand.

Throughout these many changes Shou's narrative is filled with examples of his resourcefulness in taking opportunities to learn and prepare for a future life outside of Southeast Asia. He was able to complete several English language courses, as well as work as a teacher of Hmong language at the missionary schools in the camps. He spent a sizable amount of money on a photography course, and was thus able to photograph some of the events taking place within Communist-controlled Laos. Moreover, Shou reveals a high degree of political astuteness when he attempted to get his family out of Laos: He was willing to join a "revolutionary group" in order to bring his family to safety, although he had no plans for making revolution; he obtained a gun, ostensibly for fighting communists, which he hoped only to use for hunting. As he says, "You know that you don't have the power to fight the whole country. You just have to protect yourself, and bring your family to safety."

Shou's life in Laos and in the Thai camps mirrors the Hmong people's long history of movement, struggle and adaptation. This history is tragic in many ways, yet it reveals the Hmong's power to survive and adapt to new surroundings. In Trueba and Zou's (1994) words: "The long struggle against class oppression, national oppression and adverse natural situations strengthened the resolve of the (Hmong) people and allowed them to bear hardships and persist in the face of struggle" (p. 77).

Shou Cha is a Hmong refugee who arrived in America, literate in at least three languages, with diverse skills relevant to traditional and modern societies. Perhaps most importantly from the standpoint of learning, however, is Shou's ability and willingness to accept new ideas without discarding what he considers to be important traditional beliefs. This is evidenced both in his earlier story about the Thunder Angel and in the story of his wife's miscarriage and the *ja*, or water spirits. At a time when he was embracing Christianity, Shou did not discard older knowledge he had learned about the world. This ability to cross paradigmatic borders between seemingly disparate belief systems allows Shou Cha to make his way in a postmodern world of many meanings, receiving new ideas into the flowing stream of his thought.

Like Lifton's (1993) protean man, Shou has learned to adapt to widely changing circumstances and worldviews. Like a river, his learning is shaped by the contours of the physical, mental and spiritual landscapes that he passes through; yet, Shou's identity as a learner has its roots in the mountains, in the foundations provided by Hmong culture and traditions, and, more recently, by Christianity. Fundamentalist Christianity would provide Shou a gateway to literacy in English, teaching opportunities, and refugee sponsorship; it would also require him to renegotiate his relationship with important family members and traditions. Acceptance of "the Word" would open the door to America and the future, yet it would close other doors to the past.

4

The Word

Once upon a time there had been books. A tribal legend described how long ago the Miao lived on the north side of the Yellow River, but the conquering Chinese came and drove them from their lands and homes. Coming to the river and possessing no boats they debated what should be done with the books, and in the end they strapped them to their shoulders and swam across, but the waters ran so swiftly and the river was so wide, that the books were washed away and fishes swallowed them.

This was the story. When the British and Foreign Bible Society sent the first Gospels and these were distributed the legend grew—the once upon a time books had been found in the white man's country, and they told the incomparable story that Jesus loved the Miao.
                    —from *Stone Gateway and the Flowery Miao* (Hudspeth, 1937)

It is a wintry afternoon in Windigo. The light snow that fell earlier in the day has melted, but the wind has been turned up a few notches. The weather contrasts sharply with the previous evening, when I stood in my shirtsleeves on Shou Cha's front porch and asked him if I could be a guest at Salvation Church, where he teaches Sunday school. Now I am sitting in my car in the church parking lot, feeling uneasy, unwilling to leave the chill and solitude of my car for the expected warmth of the sanctuary.

A large Hmong family arrives in a van, and seven children jump out. The mother and father look very young. Through the glass front door of the church I can see a young child playing on the stairs. Another car, a blue station wagon, pulls up and several kids jump out, yelling and running. A father's stern voice in Hmong is heard. Although many, like the Cha family, probably live in rental housing and have fairly low incomes, I notice that the Hmong who are parked around me have some very nice cars.

Salvation Church looks about 10 years old, with brick and aluminum siding. Inside, in the sanctuary, there are ordered pews, with seating for approximately 200 people. A small Hmong gentleman in a gray suit is talking to the congregation. There are various families, many children, several babies, and a handful of adults; about 50 people all together. Kids play in the aisles and pews. One child with a red and white T-shirt that says, "Keep on Tickin,'" juggles with two coins in the center aisle. Rebecca, one of Shou's younger daughters, comes up the aisle at one point, sees me, smiles sweetly and waves. Mai also waves to me from her pew when she sees me come in.

At the entrance I am greeted by a man in this 40s, who has a pronounced limp—a wound from the war in Laos? He smiles, introduces himself, shakes my hand, then he leads me down the stairs to the room where Shou Cha is giving the Sunday school lesson.

The Lesson

Around the walls of the room are several framed posters with close-ups of individuals from many lands and a consistent message: "Taking the Gospel to the Unreached." The message is printed in English, French, Spanish, Vietnamese, and Hmong. The room has tables arranged in a horseshoe shape. Shou sits in the center, facing out. The young people, six boys and six girls, face inward around the table, girls on one end and boys on the other. I take a seat at the end of the boy's section, next to Shou's son, Sammy. The age range in this Sunday school class seems to go from about 10 to 17—Jerry Lee appears to be the oldest child present. Shou asks the children to "Welcome Mr. Hones." They say "Welcome" dutifully.

When I enter, the class is engaged in singing Hmong songs from a hymnal. Interestingly, the last song they do is only three lines, and goes to the tune of "row, row, row your boat." Next, they do Hmong language lessons. Shou leads them through Hmong letters and their sounds, and the corresponding letters in the English alphabet. The kids have a handout for this, which Sammy shares with me. The lesson is being conducted in Hmong, and Shou calls on everyone—including me—to have us tell him the appropriate sound. I notice that when he asks a Hmong child for an answer, other children whisper the answer to their comrade.

Next, Shou has the children read silently a passage from Leviticus concerning different animal sacrifices to make for fellowship, sin or guilt. The children are instructed to read or pray silently for 15 minutes. Afterwards, Shou writes several key vocabulary on the board:

fellowship
offering
priest

> sin
> blood
> lamb
> unclean

Shou then asks the children to tell him what these words mean. When he comes to "sin," he asks:

"Can we offer our sin to God?"

The oldest girl says, "I think so."

"Why?"

"Well, isn't that like how we get to heaven?"

"Yes—We offer everything—our bodies, our minds, even our sins—all to God."

When Shou gives an example of what used to be considered "unclean"—such as a woman who is menstruating—some of the older girls roll their eyes. I notice that the kids have a little bit of fun during the session, whispering, making occasional wisecracks. They don't seem to be in awe of Shou, and although his voice can be very serious, there is a twinkle in his eye.

Conversion and Literacy

The posters on the wall speak of reaching the unreached, and as related in the last chapter, Shou Cha was "reached" by Christian missionaries in a refugee camp in Thailand. His conversion experience was to change his relationship to his family and to the larger Hmong community. Conversion to evangelical Christianity would facilitate Shou's learning of English, and church sponsorship would ease his transition from refugee camp to America. Conversion would open doors for Shou to begin his career as a pastor and as a teacher, with the church Sunday school as his educational setting. Conversion would also represent a break with his past, with the spirits of his ancestors and with his father, who would die without having embraced Christianity.

The Sunday school lesson at Salvation Church provides an example of the often intimate connection between religion, language, and culture. The extension of the "Word of God" has often been facilitated by the extension of literacy. Before the rise of national school systems, the church was a primary site for literacy education, especially where Protestantism held sway (Graff, 1987). In the specific case of the Hmong, Protestant missionaries in the 20th century have gained many converts through the popularity of their Hmong language bibles (Tapp, 1989a). Salvation Church provides one of the few opportunities for Hmong youth in Windigo to practice literacy in what, for many, is their first language.

WORDS LOST AND FOUND

Although their traditional beliefs are animistic, in their long migrations through China and into Southeast Asia, the Hmong have become acquainted with Taoist, Buddhist, and Christian beliefs. Christian missionaries have been active among the Hmong of China for over 100 years. Tapp (1989a) has argued that the Hmong and other ethnic minorities have embraced Christianity with some frequency in that it offers them a way to distinguish their culture from those of the dominant societies within which they live; moreover, conversions are often driven by the desire for literacy, and the improved social, economic, and political benefits that literacy entails. Missionary schools have also offered the Hmong in their isolated villages, and later, in refugee camps, an opportunity for formal education. Hmong stories tell how once they had a written language and that it was lost during the wars with the Chinese. Missionaries often used such stories to make inroads into Hmong society, especially when they could present the Hmong with bibles translated into their own language. When the British missionary, Samuel Pollard, set up his church in a Hmong area of South China, thousands would come down from the mountains to hear him preach, but always they would ask for the "books"—the bibles that he had brought for them (Tapp, 1989a).

The Christian and Missionary Alliance converted Shou Cha.[1] The Alliance, like many American foreign missionary efforts, arose and grew at a time when the United States began rivaling the empires of Europe by gaining control of far-flung territories in Asia, the Pacific, and Latin America. Behind the soldiers that were sent to quell resistance in places like the Philippines and Haiti were armies of missionaries come to save the souls of the "heathen."

According to Niklaus, Sawin and Stoesz (1986), since its beginning in 1887, certain principles have guided the work of the Alliance, including a focus on aggressive evangelization rather than education, especially in "the 'regions beyond,' the *unoccupied* portions of the heathen world" (p. 84). However, by the 1970s, the Alliance was experimenting with an "indigenous policy" that set overseas churches free of mission control. As

---

[1]Information about the Christian and Missionary Alliance philosophy and program has been obtained from the following: Cowles and Foster (1993); Bailey (1987); *Manual of the Christian and Missionary Alliance* (1995); Niklaus, Sawin, and Stoesz (1986); *Alliance Distinctives and Government* (workbook) and *Compendium of Pastoral Theology: The Life of Christ* (workbook).

many of the Alliance's members in the United States are from ethnic minorities, an office of specialized ministries was established, "based on the recognized need of people to worship God in a way natural to their cultural and linguistic heritage" (p. 241). A passage that Shou has highlighted in his Alliance prayer book reads, "prayer is cross-cultural and multicultural in practice and in results" (Cowles & Foster, 1993).

To a greater or lesser extent the missionaries also encouraged the Hmong to abandon their traditional beliefs. The Hmong studied by Tapp (1989a) had a rather pragmatic (and humorous) way of distinguishing between the various Christian creeds that the missionaries represented:

> Most Hmong would broadly classify Christians into the categories of Catholic, Protestant and Seventh Day Adventist, according to the leniency towards their traditional customs. With the Catholics one could smoke, drink, and perform most of the ancestral and funeral customs. With the Protestants one could at least smoke, but with the Seventh Day Adventists one could neither smoke, drink, nor even eat pork, and there was consequently some confusion between the Seventh Day Adventist Mission and the Islamic faith. (p. 87)

Conversion to Christianity brought changes to Hmong clan and family relationships, as traditionalists became divided from practitioners of the "new religion." (Tapp, 1989b; Trueba, Jacobs & Kirton, 1990). In addition, some Hmong reacted to missionary incursions in Southeast Asia by embracing messianic movements such as the Chao Fa ("Angel of the Sky"), which combines elements of traditional and Christian beliefs with a powerful political message of Hmong autonomy. Although he is now a devout Christian, traditional Hmong beliefs and Chao Fa messianism have left their imprint on Shou Cha's life.

Traditional Hmong Religion

> A long time ago
> The God Saub spoke from the sky
> He threw down the sacred bamboo wood ...
> Whoever lifts it up
> Will lead the life of a shaman
> and will have power to heal
> —Paja Thao, Hmong shaman
> (Conquergood, 1989, p. 3)

I ask Shou Cha to describe the traditional Hmong religion practiced by his family when he was growing up. Shou tells me that he himself had been apprenticed to a Hmong spiritual healer as a youth, and he reveals a depth of knowledge about traditional shamanic practices that I was surprised to find in a Protestant minister:

> The Hmong religion? You need a shaman, you need a spirit worshiper, and you also need to respect the great-grandparents who have passed away; and you also respect the supernatural in your environment. So that is what you should respect. That means you need to know how to treat your dead relatives, you need to treat them as you should culturally. That is one thing. And the other thing is you need to establish a place in your house, an altar, to worship spirits. You should learn how to do that, too. Sometimes the shaman's spirits get attracted to you. They just come to you and you become sick. Then, if a special person got sick, then finally he would shake and shake and shake, and some other shaman would try to find out what was wrong. Now, sometimes they would find out that you were appointed to become a shaman, too. And you would follow the master shaman who came to help you during the spirit trance.

> My second oldest step-brother who is still in Thailand, was a good, expert shaman. He was invited to go quite a distance, like four days walking. He was so widely popular. That is how he became one. He knows a lot of things. He knows beyond what I know. He still practices.

> Another thing is you treat the supernatural powers around you—a rocky mountain, a river, a fountain, a valley—we believe that there are spirits there. You need to treat them well. You need to honor them, you need to feed them. Perhaps that is close to the traditions of American Indians!

> Take for example the New Year. You know, in the old religion, every year you had to kill a chicken to wash away whatever is impure. So you killed the chicken and went over everyone, and round and round, and you had to use certain magic words to believe that it was washed, and you would not have terrible things or suffering or anything bad for the new year. That's the old way.

> We do not do that. But we treat the New Year as a very, very important feast, too. We praise God for the new year, and bless the old year, and celebrate the new year, God let us live through another year, and if we want to ask forgiveness we can. And if we want to ask for blessings for the new year, we can do that. And we can just enjoy the New Year, we wear the same clothes, we can enjoy together.

I ask Shou about his relationship with the wider Hmong community outside of his church, and specifically with the Lao Family Community, a Hmong mutual assistance organization. He says: "I am involved in the church, and because of that, outsider people who do not want to join the church cannot use me a lot. They used me several times, and I'm willing to help, and I did, but they do not use me very much. I am a man who can be useful. I am here to serve everyone."

Evidently Shou wants to be useful, and to serve his community. Yet I am curious by his use of the term "outsiders" and I ask him to whom he is referring. He responds:

> I am referring to those who don't come to church yet. I don't have very much interaction with the Lao Family, but I am willing to. They ask me sometimes. I do not go there very often because I am quite busy with my own job. The Lao Family director is my friend. We often meet for personal reasons. Almost every time we meet we talk about organization, and we say that we should help one another. Talking about a secular organization and a religious organization, not everything can go together. Serving communities, yes, we can do that, but not everything together. Some things we do apart. We do whatever we need to do. If they lack knowledge or I lack knowledge then we help one another by meeting.

I ask, "Are there divisions within the U.S. Hmong community regarding religious belief?"

Shou replies,

> Yes and no. For example, here in Windigo, we have a practicing shaman. And people respect that. It is what we used to do. Our church and theirs are quite different, but we don't fight, we don't argue. If they want to argue, as a Christian, we do not argue, that's all. But we know that they have to change to receive the salvation of God, so we teach them sometimes. Some might argue, but personally, as a minister, I and my coworkers do not. Some of the Christians who are so strong in faith, they could fight for some things. In some cities (Christians and traditionalists) are not getting along very well, and in some they are.

As Shou recognizes, in some cities in the United States the Christian and traditionalist Hmong are not getting along very well. For traditionalists, encouragement to leave their religious practices for Christianity comes not only from within the Hmong community but from many of their encounters with the dominant culture in the United States. Conquergood (1989) argues that the discouragement of Hmong shamanic practices reflects a larger history of subjugation of traditional cultures. The Hmong, who largely maintained their traditional religion when living in Laos, experienced increasing conversion to Christianity when they arrived at the refugee camps, the gateway to the new life in the United States.

The New Faith

The Christian and Missionary Alliance Church, which operated the school for children at Sop Tuang camp, was one of the many fundamentalist missions that were very active in the refugee camps along the Thai border. These fundamentalists were far less likely to appreciate, or tolerate, traditional Hmong beliefs than their Catholic counterparts. As relief workers the missionaries often controlled access to the means of current and future refugee survival, and a semblance of Christian faith was required of refugees who wished to make it out of the camps. Often the Hmong were forced to say grace before receiving the food distributions, and to say prayers during the English classes necessary for future resettlement. Moreover, church sponsorship was necessary for those who wished to relocate to the United States. Perhaps as a consequence of this latter policy, it is estimated that 50% of the Hmong in the United States practice some form of Christianity, whereas in Australia, where no church sponsorship is required, few Hmong have converted (Lee, 1986; Tapp, 1989b).

I ask Shou how long he has been involved in the Christian church, and he response supports Tapp's (1989) contention that the Hmong had economic, social and political motivations in converting to Christianity:

> Back in Laos I learned a little bit about Christianity. When I was in the camp, I truly became a Christian. Back in Laos, I was not a Christian, but somehow I was so attracted to Christianity. So when it was translated into Lao, and I listened to it, and I loved it so much, but I was opposed to Christianity. Because we always stuck to our (Hmong) religion. So that is the main point. But when I came to the camp, I did not realize if I should stick to the religion or not. But the first thing that hooked me to the Christian program was that I liked to learn English a lot. The other thing was that my whole life I had a vision to have a friendship with the whole world. Everyone in the world I'd love to be friends with. So, in the camp, they established a facility for food for children. Near our place it was kind of sloppy, so near us they established a facility for a kitchen. So I was standing just on the ground near that area, and watching the people, and they did not talk Thai, or Lao, or Hmong, but they talked in English. And I wondered if I could learn something from them. So, I just kind of hooked up with them somehow, and then they asked me to work, and then I worked with them. So that is why I learned English.

In effect, the missionaries in Sop Tuang camp provided Shou with economic support in the present as well as the language—and religion—which would ease his transition to the United States.

Although he admits to belief in Ja, the water spirits, and is respectful of the shaman's altar, Shou Cha feels it necessary to tell me that his Christian religion and traditional Hmong religion are totally incompatible. He says:

> The religion of the Hmong people and Christianity are totally different. Because the Hmong did not know the True God. So they worshipped the god

that they thought was the God. The Hmong religion is totally different. Personally, I believe that anyone who becomes a Christian should totally change, transfer from the old to the new. Everything totally changed. Traditionally, well many of the traditions we don't have to change, even culturally some of them do not have to change. But we have to totally change the religion. Like I said, we had to have an altar for worshipping idols—No! No. Not now. Don't do that anymore. In the Hmong religion, you have to kill a dog, and the dog will be a protector against the bad spirits. And you have to make a fence at your door, and you have to use the blood of the dog to mark the doorpost. We don't do that anymore.

Now, talking about the shaman. If someone becomes a Christian, shamans are totally destroyed by the name of Jesus Christ. But nobody's gonna dare to touch the shaman's altar. Because the shaman has a big altar, too. And there is a big place for the spirits. For the shaman do not have just one spirit, they have probably twelve groups. And the groups work differently. They will join together to oppose a shaman, but they work totally differently. So, when a person becomes a Christian, with the support of the missionaries or a minister, he totally destroys those things by the name of Jesus Christ.

Shou's is a flexible fundamentalism, adapted to his continuing belief in the power of traditional spirits. Although he seems to feel compelled to oppose the "old" religion, he acknowledges the lasting power of the shaman. Paradoxically, Shou rejects the sacrificial offerings called for by Hmong tradition, yet the Christianity he has adopted is steeped in traditions of such sacrifice. In many ways Shou seems to illustrate that the crises of belief within the Hmong community between traditionalists and the followers of the "new" religion may be in part process of transformation: Elements of the old are being mixed with the new to create a Christian religion with a distinctive Hmong flavor.

Chao Fa and Hmong Messianism

This message is to let you know that the Pahawh for the Hmong and for the Khmu' is only being made available for a time now. The group that accepts the Pahawh will be blessed from now on, but if either group does not accept it, that people will remain downtrodden and poor, the servant to other nations for the next nine generations. (in Vang, Yang, and Smalley, 1990, p. 34)

In spite of his Christian fundamentalist beliefs, Shou Cha reveals tolerance, and even admiration, for the Chao Fa, or "Angel of the Sky" movement, which is in many ways a response to Christianity, and a synthesis of elements of new and old religion. The Chao Fa dates back at least to 1917, when the first Chao Fa leader fought against the French colonial regime.

Tapp (1989b) views the messianic movement of the Chao Fa as a "complex reaction to serious cultural disruption" (Tapp, 1989b, p. 88) There was an important connection between such Hmong messianism and literacy: In the 1960s, Shong Lue Yang, a nonliterate farmer, with divine guidance created a Pahawh, or alphabet, for the Hmong and for the Khmu' peoples (Vang, Yang, & Smalley, 1990). After Shong Lue's death in 1971, the Chao Fa promoted the need for a Hmong alphabet and a Hmong king, they rejected Vang Pao's efforts to assimilate the Hmong into the Laotian nation, and they wore their hair long for protection in battle. Their beliefs were inspired in part by Hmong mythology:

> Chao Fa priests espoused the invincibility of those who worshipped properly. True believers could defeat the enemy with magic given by the supernatural intervention of Sin Sai, the great mythological defender, against bad giants such as the Vietnamese and the Lao communist forces. As the communist net of terror and death tightened, Hmong, realizing they were doomed, turned in desperation to the Chao Fa priests. (Hamilton-Merritt, 1998, p. 384)

Shou describes the beliefs of the Chao Fa in this way:

> Chao Fa, they worship the God. They refer to God the Creator. But Chao Fa, those are Laotian words, which mean "The Angel of the Sky." These people created something very different from Hmong culture, too. They worship the Four Angels in the corners of the Heavenly Realm. They also worship the Most High God, but they just call him the God Who Controls Heaven and the Four Angels control the four corners of the Heavenly Realm. But Spiritually and Politically, too. When you are Chao Fa you have to have identity with the political idea and the war. And this goes with war, because it's very powerful, too. For Hmong people, referring to the four heavenly corners is a call to fight. For example, if you have a person who is very sick, and you call those Four Angels, that means that you will fight the bad demons who are persecuting that person. The Chao Fa call on them to fight, to attack in the war.

Shou tells me of the popularity of the Hmong alphabet which is being spread by the Chao Fa movement:

> We have six or seven different Hmong alphabets in the whole world. In the United States of America, in France, Canada, part of China, French Guiana, Australia, those countries where Hmong people live, we use the Roman alphabet. Within those countries there is another totally different Hmong alphabet, too. Why I mention this is that we have the character, we have the will to study. If we pursue that, and have an official alphabet, that

is part of the power in education, too. We have never introduced our alphabet to school, but we have been learning in a totally different way, too.

Shou speaks admiringly of the commitment of the Chao Fa, the "people of the forest." He also passes on news out of Laos: A high-ranking Hmong general in the Laotian army has defected with his troops, and had made contact with the Chao Fa resistance.

Back in Laos today, there are the people in the forest, the Chao Fa, who fight. The only things they need are weapons and food—and people who help from outside. I think they would be very strong, able to take over the whole country. In 1976 and 1977, the Lao government almost divided up the country because of them. That is what I heard.

I heard that the Lao government is kind of scared right now, too. Because the Chao Fa, they never give up. They are still in the jungle, and the Lao government just leaves them alone. And now one of the Lao government's generals has joined the revolution with his troops. That general was Hmong. Now, the whole region under his control and his soldiers joined together and attacked the Lao people. And likely, they already have contacts with the Chao Fa.

Now I am thinking about the way the Hmong people play politics—it is *so strict*, too. *They keep the spirit for a long time.* They keep it for a long time. How much they suffer, I do not know. But they keep it.

Chao Fa is a messianic religion which includes the dissemination of a Hmong alphabet and politics of Hmong autonomy, and Shou can see this is a powerful combination. Moreover, the Chao Fa movement appears to be both a reaction to and reflection of Christianity: They proclaim the return of the Hmong King in much the same way as the missionaries who have visited their villages proclaim the return of Christ the King. They disseminate an alphabet given by God to the Hmong people, much as the missionaries would disseminate bibles. Shou Cha even believes there is evidence that the Chao Fa alphabet was written by a Protestant missionary!

American history contains its own examples of millennial movements, influenced by elements of Christianity and indigenous religions, that sought to bring hope to peoples whose lives were often filled with loss and despair: In this respect the Ghost Dance religion of the Western Plains in the 1880s can be seen as an indigenous reaction to and reflection of Mormon teachings among the Paiute (Barney, 1986).[2]

---

[2]For an excellent dramatic portrayal of the psychology of messianic movements among the dispossessed, see Vargas Llosa (1981).

The mixture of traditional and modern religious beliefs has been equally powerful in the long history of the Hmong people's struggle against oppression. Cheung (1995) reports that when the first Christian missionaries came to Southwest China in the late 19th century, the story they told of Jesus Christ was connected in the minds of many of the Hua Miao (Hmong) with the return of the "Miao King," and an end to their subjugation by the Han Chinese majority. The millennial beliefs of the Hua Miao shifted between the anticipation of change in this world to the expectation of rewards in the next, as Cheung explains:

> The Hua Miao conception of the power order in ethnic interaction changed from their being a people who had lost their kingdom and were waiting for their Miao King, to their being a people who had been redeemed through conversion to Christianity and who had gained access to the heavenly kingdom in eternity, access that the dominant heathen groups were denied. (p. 240)

The sad truth is that Christianity not only separated the Hmong of China and Southeast Asia from dominant cultural groups, it separated them from each other as well. Many converts to Christianity would learn that the "heathens" denied access to the heavenly kingdom were sometimes members of their own families.

THE SACRIFICE

> Go ye into all the world, and preach the gospel to every creature. He that believeth and is baptized shall be saved; but he that believeth not shall be damned.
>
> —Mark 16:15–16

When I was a teenager, two of my elder brothers became involved in a fundamentalist Christian sect that was popular on college campuses in those days. I remember that it was a very traumatic time for the family, but especially for my mother, for whom Roman Catholicism has always been a refuge when there was trouble at home, the helping hands of a godmother, a kindly priest passing out oranges to poor children at Christmas. The new beliefs of my brothers challenged the church that had been the foundation for my mother's life. At one point, away at college, I decided to write a letter to one of my brother elder brothers. In it I upbraided him for hurting our mother, for belonging to a religious *cult,* for being a follower of an *unscrupulous, deceitful* leader. I put into that letter all the angst and superlatives of a 19-year-old who was afraid that his family was falling apart. My brother never responded, and it was several months before we would be able to talk to each other again. My mother, the one I thought I was trying to protect—she it was who told me how deeply I had hurt him.

I wanted to find out more about Shou Cha's Christian faith, and he has provided me with several books from his home library. One of these contains some of the sermons of A. B. Simpson, the founder of the Christian and Missionary Alliance (Bailey, 1987). One passage that has been highlighted concerns sanctification, the separation of the believers from sin and from other sinners, "We put off, not only that which is sinful, but that which is natural and human, so that it may die on the cross of Jesus and rise into a supernatural and divine life" (p. 53). Simpson also wrote that "men deserve to be lost forever if they refuse to accept the Savior who is offered to them" (p. 119). The conversion experience has divided many Hmong communities and families as some accept the new religion while others resist it. When I ask Shou if his conversion caused any difficulties within the family, he told me the following story:

> When I first became a Christian, I, my wife and my other sisters suffered a lot, too. We even went and cried because of those sufferings. We felt the opposition, but we always were feeling better because the Christians believe in the three Gods, God the Father, God the Son and God the Holy Spirit, and the Holy Spirit always counseled us *a lot*. We were accused, we were punished, we were called traitors. But we just had to tolerate it. But we did not personally attack. Even though they felt bad about us, even if they opposed us, we didn't oppose them at all. We just treated them *nicely*. For example, you are my brother, and you are the old religion and I am Christian. You don't like the way I live and you oppose me and you discipline me; well, I might not be pleased with that, but the next day I will come back and will act the same, normal. That's the only thing that they do not understand. But my brother knows that I am a Christian. And one of my cousins, who is a village leader, he opposed me very strongly. But I treated him just as a respected brother, so he did not oppose me a lot.

> Did I tell you about when my father died? I don't know if Americans have this practice, but when someone dies, for a certain period of time you bring back the spirit, and make the last visit. And that's it. That was the last ceremony for my father, and that took place on Christmas Day. And I was a Christian, and so was my wife. So we did not want to participate in the ceremony. The only way we could help, and we tried our best, was to prepare the wood for the fire, to cook. So we did. And then we went and we participated in the Christmas events. So, halfway through the day my wife came and said that my family was not happy with what I did. We were new Christians, so I asked advice from the church elders there.

> "What should I do?" They said:

> "Don't worry, you stay here."

"Don't worry."

So we did. And, in the middle of the day, we came home, and I saw my uncle sleeping on our bed for some reason. He cursed us:

"You did not visit your father's spirit at the receiving ceremony. Because of that you will not have any children!"

It was about 6 months later that my wife had the miscarriage, but that was caused by the phenomenon. Because of that curse, I went back to my friends who were Christians. They said:

"Don't worry. Because God's power is even more powerful than their curse. If you did something against God, then that curse would come true. But you didn't do anything against God."

"God is your father."

"So don't worry."

So I did not worry, but when (the miscarriage) happened, I prayed to God to not let that happen any more. Now we have kids, thanks to God!

I ask, "Were you able to say goodbye to your father in your own way?"
He replies, "No. To the Christian theology, we don't have anything to do with that at all. Because we believe that, according to Romans, 1:19–20, anyone who has not received Jesus Christ yet, his spirit will go directly to Hell.
I am astounded by this statement. Here was a son who seems to have loved his father, and who yearned for the respect of his father; yet, there is no room in Shou's adopted religion for the souls of those who died "unreached." I ask: "But someone like your father, who probably did not have much familiarity with Christianity ... "
Shou remains firm in his response.

He knew about it. He had been taught. My sister who was a nurse with General Vang Pao, she was a Christian when she came back (from Long Chieng). She got sick, and she prayed, and after some days she got well. So she encouraged our whole family to become Christians, but my father denied her. Of course, he did not know or understand everything, that's why he denied. But he heard about Jesus Christ. But I don't know how she proclaimed the Gospel at that time. I think that she just said that we should become Christians. We should drop or get rid of the way we traditionally worshipped. And my father denied her. That's all I remember.

I find myself insisting on the father's innocence: "Maybe it was difficult for him to take the Gospel from a woman, and his daughter. That might have made it more complicated, too."
Shou responds,

She, herself, was not a very strong Christian. But she denied our shaman when she was sick. Now she is in France. She asked me to preach for her one time!" Laughing, he continues. "All my brothers and sisters in the United States are Christians. And my mother is a very strong Christian, but back at that time, at my father's spirit ceremony, she was not." Shou seems to feel that, although the messenger, his sister, may have been inadequate, his father should not have rejected the message that so many other members of the family were to embrace.

Reflecting further on his actions at the time of his father's spirit ceremony, Shou says:

I do not know. My father, physically, was a righteous man. He did not do anything wrong. He practiced righteous things. But still he worshipped certain spirits which are not God.

But I do not know why! Perhaps I did not show respect by not attending the spirit ceremony … I was just trusting God so much that I did not do anything! But because I am her son, my mother did not say anything bad. But she was not very happy. She said, "You should not do this. And when you do this, your uncle is very upset."

> *That night,*
> *because of that curse,*
> *it hurt me, my wife, and my sister,*
> *it hurt us a lot.*
> *I remember that night*
> *it hurt us a lot.*
> *My sister was not able*
> *to deny the ceremony herself,*
> *so she participated.*
> *She was with them.*
> *But when I came back from the Christmas events,*
> *we went to*
> *a place on the outskirts of the camp where*
> *there were no people,*
> *below the school buildings,*
> *and we prayed.*
>
> *We said,*
> *"God, we do not want to hurt anyone.*
> *But now we are hurt, and*
> *we do not know what to do …"*
> *And when we prayed, we were crying.*
> *I, my wife, and my sister said,*
> *"We do not want that curse, but*
> *we have no choice,*

because of You
we do this."
After we prayed, we came back.

Running throughout this story of his father's death is the theme of sacrifice: Shou was willing to sacrifice his father, the love of some members of his family, and his hopes for children of his own because of his love of God. God asked Abraham to sacrifice Isaac, his son, his future; Shou Cha is asked to sacrifice both father and son, past and future on Earth in return for the heavenly kingdom. Harding (1992) has documented this theme of sacrifice in the stories of another trained evangelical minister: Reverend Cantrell tells her the story of how he killed his son in a farming accident. Like the story of God's sacrifice of his son Jesus to save mankind, Cantrell, according to Harding's interpretation, has sacrificed his own son to save *her*, the interviewer, *the unreached*.

Unlike Reverend Cantrell's tale, Shou's story of multiple sacrifices does not seem intended to *save* me. Is this sacrificial tale one that he wishes his children to remember? Does it serve to help him renew his own efforts in the ministry? Perhaps Shou's sacrifices made in the refugee camp help to recreate for himself an identity as a sojourner, not of this Earth, whose Father and home is in heaven.

Are there other dimensions to this story, beyond its religious and spiritual significance for Shou Cher? I would suggest that, like many of his stories, it reflects the importance of family: In this case, the need for belonging in a family, on the part of Shou, and the sense of betrayal expressed by his uncle. In such cases, who is more hurtful? The ones who, through their convictions, refuse to go along with established family religious practices? Or the ones who, like Shou's uncle, or myself, presume to place ourselves in the position of judgment, in our quest to defend a father, or a mother, from further hurt? For researchers, this story of Shou Cher's sacrifice highlights as well the interpretive dilemma faced when one has a visceral reaction to the expressed beliefs of an informant.

THE AMERICAN DREAM

Chicago, Shou Cha's first home in the United States, has never been an easy city for the poor. Sinclair (1906) chronicled the squalor and desperation of the city's working and living conditions at the beginning of the 20th century in *The Jungle* and Kotlowitz (1991) has personalized the struggle of the forgotten poor of the city's public housing at the century's close in *There Are No Children Here*. In between, at the height of the Depression, my father went to Chicago to look for work. I have always liked his stories from that period. When he went to see the local ward boss to ask for a job as an election worker, he was asked, "How many people in your family live here? How many votes do you represent?" My father didn't get the job, his future wife and 11 children not being part of the electoral picture yet. He lost a girlfriend once when he was asked by a man in the street, "Buddy, can you give me some money for a meal?" My father responded, "Didn't I give you some money yesterday?" The man replied, "Yes, but I'm hungry again." My father gave the man 50 cents, only to be upbraided by the girlfriend for being too easy. When he had worked for sometime at Montgomery Ward in the mailroom, my father asked at the personnel office, "How do I get ahead in this business?" He was told to take night courses in accounting. So he studied accounting at night school until he went away to the war. As an accountant schooled in the world he would work for over 40 years and raise his family, this man with the soul of a Irish bard.

Shou Cha would also make an important career decision in Chicago, influenced not by a supervisor but by a dream. He arrived in Chicago sponsored by a minister who was a friend of his sister. There he lived in poverty, trying to support a growing family by working full-time at two or three low-paying jobs. He also continued his involvement with the church, and was soon preaching again. Living in Chicago, struggling to support his family, he had a dream that influenced his decision to go to school and become a minister. Shou vividly retells this dream, which he had more than 10 years ago, and uses a blackboard to draw me a picture of the setting of the dream, a high mountain trail between the past life of his village in Laos and the "bright time" of the future:

> By that time, in Chicago, I was so, so poor! Really! And the state of Illinois does not support a low-income family, no matter how low you are. And my wife had her second pregnancy, so I could not support us. And I was so discouraged. And I worked, and I cried, and I did not know how I could live. But then I even got laid off. Then at the time I got laid off, I read the Bible for about 3 months. I read the whole New Testament. So at that time I had a dream that was a change in my life, I do not know why.

In the dream

> > *I was on a trail*
> > *part way*
> > *between the village of my past and*
> > *the bright time of my future.*
> > *On the way I passed certain*
> > *travelers—*
> > *Livestock owners,*

people on horseback,
people in cars,
many travelers—
but I was the fastest one on that trail.
I was running.
As I passed the people they fell
away from the trail.
At first through grassland,
Then through dark jungle.

The dream was that
I should suffer a certain time.
The dark time,
or suffering time,
included tigers,
dark night,
scary sounds,
attacking animals,
you could not see the way you were
traveling,
mud,
so dark,
even darker than night, and
a long way to go.
On a journey.
A big tall jungle forest, such as in
Laos.

After passing that deep forest,
the bright time will come.
After I suffered I could go on
living a bright life,
to serve the Lord,
to call people to come
to the second Ark of Noah.
An ark of the sky
You know what I mean?
Back in Noah's time,
it was an Ark for the Flood.
But now it's not the Ark but the
Second Ark,
which escapes the Fire.

Fire will flood the Earth.
Then I will go and call my relatives,
my friends
to come and get on the Ark,

so they can go and
escape this land.
When I go to the bright time in my
life
I will see them,
I will call them.

To my wife I said
"Get ready while I am gone.
I will see you on the ark when it
comes."
"I miss you."
"I miss you, too."

With that dream, I woke up. And that put me on to going to religion school. I went up to Milwaukee and attended the program. And that is why I am a minister now. I did not go just because I wanted to go. Because I believe that in dreams, someone, from somewhere, the Great One, the God, put me in that position. That is why I went. That dream leads me here. That's a major change. Because of that dream, I went to the ministerial program.

In the dream Shou is leaving the village of his past and literally running into the future. Other travelers are moving along the same path, but none are so eager to reach the destination as Shou. Moreover, he is leaving behind this world with its pleasures and problems, and embracing its apocalyptic conclusion, and renewal. The "beautiful jungle" of Shou's youth, described in the last chapter, has been replaced by the dark, dangerous jungle that haunts his dreams in America. Perhaps for Shou, life in Chicago was an abnegation of the American dream of prosperity, and he replaces it with the dream of the Apocalypse, the destruction of this world followed by the "bright time" to come in the future.

To what extent does this recounted dream parallel Shou's reorganization of his life story to reflect his mission? His workbooks for the ministerial program contain several selections devoted to the theme of the Second Coming. In one response to a workbook question, Shou has written:

Christ ('s) second coming will appear in the sky
premillenium to gathering all believers to the air no
matter someone object (to) it or not but it should
happen as many signs fulfilled today.

The Theological Program

Following his dream, in a veritable leap of faith, Shou left his employment in Chicago for the uncertainty of the ministry program in Milwaukee:

After 3 years in Chicago, I was one of the elders who preached a lot in the church. So one of our church elders recommended that I go to a Bible school. He brought a proposal to a college, and they accepted me. But I felt that my English would not be good enough to participate in college. So I asked God about two things: I either would got laid off, and go to school; or whatever God wants me to do. And I asked God a couple of times, and I got laid off. Getting laid off was kind of sad, but I did not feel sad, because I had a purpose, to go to the ministry.

But then I did not go directly to where I thought I should. Like I said, I thought I could not participate in a college class in a Bible College, because my English was even lower than now, in reading, in speaking and in writing. But I was so lucky back at that time. There was a Theological Education by Extension program, and when I was in Milwaukee, that program had been opened. Other Christians already participated. So I went there, and I was lucky enough that they were willing to open another center or another class. So I participated, and I did it, and I finished that.

That program was developed by the headquarters of the Christian and Missionary Alliance, but before that it had been established in some Latin American countries. They adapted it to the United States. I was supposed to take three years, but the teacher who taught us was kind of busy, so we took about 4 years to finish. They had three levels. I finished my first level, which was the basic course. But I did not complete the advanced level until I came to Windigo.

We went for a 2-hour meeting each week. We had to do the homework. Each week we finished a unit, and in the meantime, you worked accordingly. So you worked, you studied, and you had meetings. The work was assigned by the teacher, which they called the center leader, but assigned according to the church. At that time I really did so many things. I was one of the church leaders, an elder, yes. My first year I was a Sunday school leader, and the second year, the Sunday school superintendent, which was part of the education, too! Another year I was the church elder for a whole church, and that church was quite big, with a lot of members, about 300. The church was growing, and everything had to be learned, adapted changed. For 3 years I did that, and in my 4th year I was another church leader in a different church. I joined the first church and then we established another church, and I was one of the ones transferred to the new church, and I participated in that new church. My first year there was as co-minister, even though I was not a minister. They did not give me such a license, but I helped the preacher, who went with me to the new church. We took turns preaching! And I was one of the Sunday school teachers for the youth, too. I taught the youth. In my 2nd or 3rd year, I do not remember well, I was again a church elder for that small church. That whole 5 years I attended school. I went to ESL class, part-time. I worked a little bit, but just part-time jobs. I went to the two schools—ESL and the theological school. Then, in the middle of that year, I moved to Windigo.

Even before I became a Christian I worked for the church, for children who the missionaries called together and taught. So I taught. That was back in the camp. I was one of the ones that helped them. After a year (the missionary) put me in a school building. I taught what he taught me. Songs, some Bible, and I served food, for a couple years. And I was paid for that, too. So when I moved to another camp, to Phanatnikhom camp, the missionary told me, 'Shou, you will be a leader for your family.' And I said, 'what does that mean?'

When I came to Phanatnikhom camp, there was a church with no leader, no preacher at all. And I practiced preaching, because we did not have a pastor (laughs). And I just did it, and we had about 10 families joining together. I just had to study, and I preached. So I did.

When I came to Chicago, for a half year I did not preach, because they did not know that I had that gift. So they did not ask me. But somehow, after that much time, I started to show off, or whatever, and I started to preach, and we did that several times more. We would take turns for about 2 years. After that we moved to Milwaukee, and I also stopped preaching for 6 months or a year. And then I started to do that job again, but not every Sunday. When we were attending the theological class, I preached quite a lot. Almost every month, I preached. And when we joined the new church I preached about that much too. And then we got a new pastor who did not allow me to preach, but I was a Sunday school teacher. And I was also assigned to preach in a different church. In Windigo, I do similar things to those.

Interestingly, when I ask Shou what had brought him to Windigo, he says:

This church in Windigo was established in 1989. Before the church was even established, I and my friends came to Windigo to see if we could plan a church. So we came here the first time and we thought that it would be a good idea to start a church. It was not thoroughly researched. If it was, then we probably would not have started a church, I do not know. But the second time I came, and the third time I moved in! And when I moved to Windigo I also participated in school, too.

I recall Shou's reflection about his thoughts prior to the shooting incident in 1994, when he and his wife were seriously considering giving up the ministry. After receiving so much support from fellow pastors while in the hospital, Shou decided to continue with the ministry. However, it seems clear that at some level, he considers it a mistake to have ever attempted to bring the Gospel to the "unreached" in Windigo.

Shou continues: "I moved here in 1990. One of my friends, who moved here, too, originally started the church. In his first 2 months he did the door-to-door ministry. He did that, and so when I came, whatever families he had already established, I just worked with them. Right now we have

11 families." Shou laughs as he says, "I tell you, almost everywhere I go, I just follow someone, watering the seeds!"

In the summer Shou picks up extra preaching in nearby cities. Shou says,

> Because there is no school in the summer, I don't have enough income. Within that, I knew in my mind that it was good to practice the Word I knew already coming from the Lord. In Windigo the church I am working with does not have a pastor, and I volunteer doing any kind of work, and they also voluntarily are helping me, so we are helping one another. I also have a very small fellowship group in Bay City. I visit them late in the evening every Sunday. One night as we came out of the door, one of the ladies said, 'We are very happy that you are here. You seem so friendly to us.' So that was very encouraging to us. Our purpose in Bay City is to finish reading Galatians over the summer. I teach them, but I also request that they read the book themselves. So they do it. One week I asked, 'Did you read it?' and one of the gentlemen said, 'I finished the whole book.'

Beginning in the refugee camps and continuing through his ministerial work in Windigo and neighboring communities, Shou has gained valuable preparation and experience in the word of literacy and the word of religion. He has taught Hmong literacy and Sunday school classes for youths, and engaged groups of Hmong adults in the reading of extended passages of one of the classics of world literature, the Bible. Religious work for Shou has been intimately connected with the extension of literacy as well as with a moral education that draws from biblical and Hmong traditions. As a religious educator, he exemplifies the ongoing transformation of Hmong American culture and the Christian church.

CHANGE AND CONTINUITY

> There are only fish that follow the river.
> There are no rivers that follow the fish.
> —Hmong proverb

I relate to Shou the comments of a Hmong shaman in Chicago (Conquergood, 1989), concerning the traditional religion, and how he sees fewer and fewer people are practicing the old ways. I ask Shou if that is something he sees as well in the wider Hmong community. He responds:

> One thing is that this society changes. Another thing is country that you live in, the environment, and another is the medical science. Everything af-

fects our old religion. For example, the environment where you live. In the United States, such a house as this is totally different from where we lived in Laos or Thailand. You can't put an altar for your worship. And of course, back where we lived, you should not stay above your altar of worship. But in the United States, you know, you sleep upstairs and put your altar downstairs. That is not appropriate. Another thing is that in this society people go to school a lot, and they have to learn. And education effects them, and they do not have much time to practice their religion. And that takes a lot of time, too. So they don't do that a lot. There is also an interest in new things. So the new things have come and the old things have passed away. So that's what effects the shaman's practice, too. The very big thing is that in this country, we practice medical science. Helping, healing of sickness. That also effects the shaman. This country is, what should I say, 50% Christian. And the others do not practice religion. Many of them are still very active Christians. Even those who don't go to church very often, still put their hopes in God. So everything is very positive for Christianity.

Perhaps Shou seems to be overly optimistic about the chances for Christianity in a nation where other belief systems, including those of the public school, those of science, and those manufactured on Madison Avenue, compete for the allegiance of young and old alike. I interject: "Haven't you also given some reasons why young people might turn away from church altogether? What is your thought about the future—young people, such as those in your family?"

For the future, we either change into something, or something changes us. If we don't really practice what we should, then I think my children or grandchildren will forget about Christianity. One key that I think is this: As society changes, we also should change. We cannot help it. Whatever appears today, you have to figure out some way to change and go along. For example, if I were a shaman, I would not stick to my shaman practice my whole life. It would not work. My children would not go with me. After I let it die, the religion dies. That's a problem with religion today. I do not know about my children's future, but we should change along with society.

I ask, "Can you maintain some link to Hmong tradition through the church?"

Because the society changes, I guess most of the Hmong culture will be changed, too. And I believe it will change, unless we keep the combination (between Christianity and Hmong) so strong. If we don't keep the combination real strong, then it will change. No matter whether Hmong people like it or not, it has already changed. Totally changed. So even if we keep a Hmong church, I preach in my own language, we sing our songs, and when we come home we keep our culture, we keep our way of life, we do that. But I know we are changing. And Hmong always change. Hmong keep one thing forever, but the other things change.

I ask, "What's the one thing you keep forever?"

Shou Cha responds, "The relationship. The relationship and the respect. Things like that you keep forever. If you lose it, then, that's it, your gone."

As will be seen in the next few chapters, relationship and respect are values that Shou Cha mentions often when he discusses what it means to be Hmong in America. In this he is not alone: The importance of family, clan and community relationships and respect, especially for elders, within the Hmong community has been addressed at length by others (Chan, 1994; Donnelly, 1994; Unger, 1995). Paradoxically, Shou Cha, as an evangelist, is seeking to bring the transformative power of Christianity to the Hmong community in Windigo, and this new religion continues to transform traditional family relationships. As an agent of change, can he hope to remain grounded in Hmong culture? Burridge (1991), in his study of the missionary experience across time and across cultures, suggests that converts such as Shou Cha can only find a home in the metaculture of Christianity: "Caught between waiting on the spirit and the desire to persuade, or, maybe, coerce, neither missionary nor serious Christian can have any permanent sociocultural identity. He or she is grounded not in culture or society but in the metaculture" (p. 228).

Shou Cha's life in "the Word" presents the complexities of a man whose fundamentalist beliefs do not deter him from adapting to new situations and making use of new ideas. Lifton (1993) argues that the fundamentalist self arises, like proteanism, at times of great change. Whereas proteanists exhibit almost chameleon-like ability to change their colors and beliefs to match new surroundings, fundamentalists try to get through the shifting tides of life by strict adherence to certain traditions, and separation from those who do not believe. Yet, as Lifton points out, proteanism and fundamentalism seem to work together in complex ways: "Although an antagonistic negation of proteanism, fundamentalism tends to be intertwined with proteanism; they may even require one another" (p. 160).

Certainly, Shou's adherence to fundamentalist beliefs led to his painful separation from family at the time of his father's death. However, in many important ways, religion has served Shou Cha just as he has served religion. Christian beliefs ease the transition of the Chas to life in the United States, especially in smaller cities such as Windigo where church-going remains an important community event. Through his training in "the Word" in the theological program Shou gained valuable experience that he would use later as a paid minister to several Hmong churches in the Windigo area. Moreover, with his first encounter with missionaries in Thailand, Shou began his career as a teacher, and, through succeeding experiences with church Sunday schools, he developed an educational philosophy and methods that would serve him well as a bilingual assistant at Horace Kallen School. With his strong beliefs in the power of traditions as well as the power of change, Shou Cha follows in the footsteps of many American educators who envisioned schooling as a process of conversion.

AMERICAN EDUCATION
AS A PROCESS OF CONVERSION

The strong connection between literacy and religion in Shou Cha's life is paralleled in the history of American education. The Second Great Awakening in American Protestantism in the 19th century influenced the rise of the Common School movement, many of the whose leaders were evangelical preachers (Fraser, 1985). Through the schools these Protestant ministers sought to bring the Word to those persons who they deemed were sitting in darkness, whether they be Native Americans, immigrant Catholics, or others who had yet to embrace evangelical Protestantism (Glenn, 1988; Jorgenson, 1987). More generally, schools in the United States could be seen as tools for *converting* the young of many different cultural backgrounds into an *American* system of beliefs and values. Often these new beliefs and values conflict with those of their parents, forcing students to make the kinds of uncomfortable decisions that continue to influence their relations to their family and to society.

Historians Tyack and Hansot (1982) suggest that many of the advocates of common schooling in the mid-19th century

> were convinced that America was literally God's country, the land He had chosen to bring about the redemption of mankind. The version of millenialism they most commonly shared was not that of an apocalyptic Second Coming, but rather the gradual creation of the Kingdom of God on earth and the triumph of Christian principles in government and society. This process of redemption was not passive or deterministic, however; the common school crusaders regarded themselves as God's chosen agents. (p. 3)

One of the ways these agents brought fundamentalist Protestant morality into the schools was through *McGuffey's Readers*, a series of fabulously successful textbooks. With early encouragement from evangelical schoolmen such as Lyman Beecher, McGuffey's sold between an estimated 122 million copies between 1836 and 1920. According to Fraser (1985), these texts "reflected American white, middle-class, Protestant morality as it was circa 1836, but they also became one of the major makers of American morality in the decades ahead" (p. 189).

Although they were not ministers themselves, Common School leaders such as Henry Barnard and Horace Mann could not help making parallels between schooling and the religious experience. Barnard compared the schoolhouse to a temple, "consecrated in prayer to the physical, intellectual, and moral culture of every child in the community" (quoted in Rushdoony, 1963, p. 56). Moreover, the creation of normal schools for the training of teachers was seen as part of the overall missionizing effort. In a lecture on special preparation of teachers in 1838, Mann said:

> Normal schools had to come to prepare a way for themselves, and to show, by practical demonstration, what they were able to accomplish. Like Christianity itself, had they waited till the world at large called for them, or was ready to receive them, they would never have come. (quoted in Rushdoony, 1963, p. 41)

John Swett (1911), superintendent of schools in California, made it clear that the mission of common schools need not stop at the borders of the United States, but should be taken triumphantly abroad by expanding American power. He penned these words of missionary zeal:

> Earth is rousing from her slumbers
> on the shore of every sea;
> toiling millions without number
> marshaling for Liberty.
> Raise the shout of exultation
> let the banner be unfurled.
> Education
> for each nation,
> Common schools for all the world. (p. 180)

Interestingly, even Progressive Era educators who saw no place for traditional Christianity in the schools proclaimed a messianic role for education. G. Stanley Hall (1911) wrote that "the vocation of teaching should furnish many true saints for the calendar of this new religion, and would if the schoolroom were indeed a worship of the Holy Ghost" (p. 668). John Dewey (1897) recognized the important role of teachers in bringing about his "Great Community," saying, "the teacher always is the prophet of the true God and the usherer in of the true kingdom of God" (p. 15). Harold Rugg (1941) argued that public education must be given "a driving purpose, so clear and magnetic that thousands of teachers and millions of parents and youth will be energized by it" (p. 277).

What the narrative of Shou Cha teaches us is that conversion can exact a heavy price on the converted, especially in the bonds to family, community, culture and history. Yet Shou's narrative also illustrates that conversion can often be accompanied by greater access to literacy and the ways of dominant culture. At the same time, converts such as Shou Cha have the ability to weave seemingly disparate worldviews and practices into new traditions and a new system of belief.

Intertwined in Shou's life with the word of religion is the word of literacy. Like the Hmong villagers in China a century ago who came by the thousands to receive Bibles translated into Hmong, Shou's interest in literacy has been facilitated by his work with the church. Through the church, he has learned to read and write in English, and through the church he can promote Hmong literacy among children of his community who have grown up in America. In China, in Southeast Asia, and now in the United States, literacy has been a vehicle for the Hmong to challenge their status as an outcast group within a larger society. Schools have much to learn about the *words* of religion and literacy in the everyday life of minority groups. In *Ways with Words*, Heath (1983) has argued that teachers must find ways to connect curriculum and practice in the schools with the literacy practices and needs of the community. Similarly, Moll and Greenberg (1990) argue that substantial literacy learning occurs through extended family, neighborhood, and other social networks and that schools should acknowledge and benefit from such *funds of knowledge*.

For minority individuals and groups, the words of religion and literacy can become tools for inculcating the ideology of the dominant culture and an acceptance of the status quo (Graff, 1987). Conversely, the words of religion and literacy can enable people to see their world in a different light, and to realize that, as they are transformed, so can they transform reality (Freire, 1968). Both of these processes of acceptance and transformation are present in Shou Cha's narrative. Through the *word*, he and other Hmong people in the United States, Southeast Asia, and elsewhere attempt to transform the economic and social realities they face in lands of exile.

Through the *word*, Shou hopes to prepare his children for success in the dominant American culture; through the *word*, he tries to pass on certain Hmong values, traditions, and language to the next generation of Hmong Americans.

The Cha family. Front row, left to right: Yisay, Joshua,
Gong Wendy, Rebecca. Back row, left to right: Sammy, Mai Jia,
Mai, Summer, Paj Hua, Shou.

Coauthor Shou Cha with other pastors.

Leonilla and Donald Hones with their children on their 50th Anniversary, 1993. Front row, left to right: Kay Ellen, Sarah, Agnes, Leonilla, Don Sr., Karen, Mary. Back row, left to right: Gerard, Tim, Luke, Don Jr., Greg.

Ariana, Kathleen, Don, and Orion Hones.

5

Generations

One of the strongest imperatives of our [American] culture is that we must leave home. Unlike many peasant societies where it is common to live with parents until their death and where one worships parents and ancestors all one's life, for us leaving home is the normal expectation and childhood is in many ways a preparation for it.

—Robert Bellah (1987, p. 370)

It is snowing again in early March. One Saturday evening I find Shou and Mai home with the five youngest Chas, and we make impromptu plans to go sledding at the golf course near my house. The kids are excited: They have never been on a real sled before, and I have brought three of them, gleaned from yard sales over the summer. The five of them take turns with the three sleds, often riding double. Shou goes down once or twice with the youngest girl. I notice that at least two of the girls are not wearing mittens. The following Saturday brings another snowfall of a few inches, and I meet the Chas again on the hill. This time, the little girls are wearing mittens and hats. This time, as well, we are joined by Mai Jiu, Sammy, Jerry, and some other members of the church "youth group." When we find the golf course gate locked, the older boys go over the 10-foot fence in one movement, with the practiced ease of adolescence. Shou and I take it more slowly, carefully looking for footholds. Meanwhile, the younger children enter the golf course by crawling through a low place nearby. The older boys attempt to ride one of the sleds like a skiboard, standing up. They draw apart, congregating near the steeper, more dangerous part of the hill, stretched or squatting in the snow, talking and watching the younger children ride in pairs down the hill.

The full moon rides out from behind the clouds, and Orion the Hunter appears high in the south. Rebecca, the second youngest girl, smiles when I tell her that those stars have the same name as my son. Shou looks up, and points to the three stars of Orion's belt.

"In Laos," he says, "we call that the Water Carrier. See, on either side is a pail of water on a pole, and in the middle is a man with the pole on his shoulder."

Mai has been preparing dinner, and the smell of steamed rice greets me when I enter the Cha house later that evening. Sammy lets me in, and Jerry says hello from the living room. The rest of the children are sitting or standing in various places around the room, eating egg rolls from the ends of forks, and watching television.

At the round table by the kitchen places have been set for Shou, Mai, Jerry, Sammy, and myself. Shou gives a prayer in Hmong before we begin eating. There is steamed rice, shrimp with mushrooms, spicy parsley ("a little bit hot," according to Shou, and he wasn't kidding), and mounds of egg rolls.

The Cha family appears to be a happy one, yet my interviews in the home reveal that there are some potential conflicts within the family, especially as their children reach their teenage years. Interestingly, both children and parents place great importance on fostering family relationships, but their viewpoints are quite different: The older children took these issues seriously enough to prepare and present a sermon about them at the family's church.

CHILDREN ARE JEWELS

I recall the service that the youth group at Salvation Church had organized. Jerry Lee gave the sermon, from Ephesians, 6:1–4:

> Children, obey your parents in the Lord, for this is right. "Honor your father and mother," (this is the first commandment with a promise) "that it may be well with you and that you may live long on the Earth." Fathers, do not provoke your children to anger, but bring them up in the discipline and instruction of the Lord.

The focus of Jerry's sermon was about the importance of communication between parents and children. He went on in true preacher style, for a good half hour or more. Fortunately, Shou was interpreting some of his main points for me from Hmong to English; yet I wanted the opportunity to talk more with the older Cha children and Jerry about their relationship with parents and elders. It was the first time they had ever organized the church service, and everyone in the youth group contributed suggestions to the sermon Jerry delivered.

Jerry, Sammy, Mai Jia, and I sit on the floor, cross-legged, in the boys' room, with the tape recorder between us. The room is faded light blue, with two beds. There is a large boombox on a chair, and a chess game is set up on a small table. The overhead light is burnt out, so the room, like most rooms in the Cha home, is quite dark. The interview is a bit awkward—after all, I am asking them about some of the issues that arise between them and their parents, a touchy subject to speak about with a relative stranger. Mai Jia says nothing, occasionally nodding or shaking her head in response to my queries. As in most of my encounters with him, Sammy speaks little. It is Jerry, eldest, and not one of Shou's children, who does most of the talking.

One point of contention between Hmong children and their parents is on hairstyle. Jerry says: "Just because we have a different hairstyle doesn't mean that we have done something wrong."

Sammy concurs: "My dad wants me to change my hairstyle. He doesn't like it split (parted in the middle)." Sammy doesn't know why, although Jerry's sermon suggested that some parents identity such hairstyles with gangs.

Jerry continues: "People look at these little things like hairstyle and turn them into big things, like gang membership."

It is interesting to contrast this hairstyle issue with the hairstyles observed in from Shou's teenage photographs in Laos—especially with all the young men with the Chao Fa hairstyles at that time. Shou is probably right in guessing that a person's hair choice speaks of some kind of affiliation. In the old days, Hmong men wore their hair long. Especially in the days of Shou's grandfathers, when men wore their hair in ponytails. On the other hand, Timm (1994) notes that Hmong parents often fail to distinguish between groups of teenage friends and "gangs."

According to Jerry, this issue of teen relationships is further complicated when Hmong American youths form friendships with members of the opposite sex:

I think over there in Laos our parents were different. When they were young, usually if he was a guy, and they were a guy, it was OK. But if he had like a girl, then people would start saying stuff, gossip, rumor. Usually over there when a guy has a friend who is a girl, usually it's a girlfriend. Very rarely do they have a friend who is a girl. I'm not sure, they are shy, maybe. They don't talk to girls much. So usually when they have a girl, it's a girlfriend. Here it is different.

When I ask if they have friends who are both boys and girls they nod in the affirmative. I continue: "If you invite a girl over to the house, how would they handle that?"

Jerry replies:

I think they would ask questions. They will ask, who are your parents? If her parents are nice and respectful, then usually it is OK. If they know the parents, no problem. If they don't know the parents, then they will ask more questions, where are they from, etc. Also, about having friends who aren't Hmong. Our parents would ask lots of questions.

Sammy adds: "Sometimes, I've had other friends over. Sometimes my friends come over, and they say, 'Why are they here? Why don't you go outside, or go somewhere else?'"

Educational issues were prominent in the youth group's sermon. Jerry elaborates why:

> Our parents keep on telling us to do better. They really want us to do better. Some of them never went to school, and some have gone to school. They really want us to take advantage of our education, because they want us to do better. I think the more they keep on telling us "you should do this, you should do that," we try to do it. We try to do better. But if they encourage us, that is real good. When they let us know that it is OK to make mistakes. Often they want us to do no mistakes, do the best it could ever be, even if it is so hard, just do it, and we will try to do better, and we try harder and harder. Once in awhile we need more encouragement. But not always, not always. For me, when I keep on hearing it always, always, then I'll just start dropping out. Parents should learn more, too, so they will see that education can be tough. Actually, it will help them to succeed more, too, in jobs.

Jerry's comments allude to the high, and sometimes unrealistic, educational goals that Hmong parents hold for their children. Trueba, Jacobs and Kirton (1990) report: "Most parents did not have a concrete idea of what their children did or learned in American classrooms and invested the schools with a magical power to teach children" (p. 71).

Walker-Moffat (1995) has a somewhat different perspective on the role of refugee parents in the education of their children. In her view, they are ready to create a learning environment for the children at home, but the lack of communication between most schools and parents inhibits their efforts:

> Regardless of their educational background, parents will want to participate in the education of their children. This is especially true in many Southeast Asian homes, in which education is a family affair ... Yet today the reality is that there is little dialogue between Southeast Asian parents and their children's teachers. (p. 158)

Although Shou Cha works as a bilingual aide in an elementary school, like many Hmong adults he has little formal education. This makes it all the more difficult to have a realistic understanding of the academic challenges facing Hmong youth in schools.

Nevertheless, Jerry feels that the parents in his church learned a great deal from the youth sermon: "The parents liked the sermon. They realized a lot of things. They might change their minds about some things."

Jerry finishes with a beautiful metaphor:

> *Children are God's jewels.*
> *When a child is missing,*
> *you should try to find him,*
> *as you would a jewel.*
> *If your child is dirty,*
> *you should wash him,*
> *like a jewel.*
> *If a child is broken,*
> *you must fix him,*
> *like a jewel.*

FAMILY IN TRANSITION

In the field of psychology the image of the family has changed dramatically over the last 40 years, with the cohesive, Eriksonian family of the 1950s giving way to the chaotic family of the 1990s. Problems within the family are felt all the more acutely in an age where other forms of communal support have deteriorated, and the family has effectively become the "locus of emotional and spiritual repair" in a world turned upside down. Walkover (1992) argues that the "family might make up for the collapse of communal traditions and harsh indignities of a capitalist economy" (p. 182).

Handlin (1951) was the first American historian to explore the effects of immigration on the lives of immigrant families and communities. He argues that for many of the European immigrants of the past century, family life had not been isolated in their native country, but an integral part of the community. Moreover, for peasant farmers, the work of the family had been shared, whereas in America, for economic reasons, the family forces had to be divided, dependent as they were on the combined income of individuals. This caused disruption in the extended family, as "the larger unit was now a source of weakness rather than of strength ... Steadily, the relatives dropped away; the husband, wife, and children were left alone" (p. 229). In addition, Handlin writes that the sharp contrast between the worldviews of their home and of school was not lost on immigrant youth, and, "as the children of the immigrants grew up, they felt increasingly the compulsion to choose between the one way and the other" (p. 248). For these youth, "there was a yearning for identity, to be a being" (p. 255).

It is important to remember that cross-culturally, families vary greatly in their relationships and their practice and there are no universals (Coontz, 1988). The Hmong arrived to this country with strong extended family and clan networks mostly intact. Nevertheless, like earlier immigrant groups studied by Handlin and others, the Hmong have faced increased levels of familial strife in the United States. Berrol (1995) suggests that "the potential for intergenerational conflict is present in every family, but exacerbated when parents are foreign-born and children are not" (p. 91). In a study of Hmong families in Wisconsin, Timm (1994) writes:

> The primary ideological conflict between Hmong culture and American culture is a focus on the family as compared with an emphasis on individual freedom ... The tug between these two value orientations is at the heart of the Hmong dilemma in the United States and is causing problems within families, across generations, and in the Hmong community. (p. 37)

Shou and Mai seem to understand clearly that the problems they experience with their own children are widespread in the Hmong community, and that finding a way to improve the relationship between family members is of paramount importance.

MOTHER AND FATHER

The wife is the loom, the husband hangs the thread.
                                                         —Hmong proverb

Like many Hmong, Shou and Mai were quite young when they began having children: He was 20 and she was 13 when Sammy, the eldest, was born. Now they have seven children, whose very names reflect the transformation of the Chas and Hmong American culture: Sammy, born in a Thai refugee camp; Mai Jia "cool breeze girl;" she was the first child born in the United States, in Chicago. Paj Huab "flower cloud;" she was born at home in Milwaukee. Jesse, Joshua, and Rebecca, named for famous biblical characters, were also born in Milwaukee; they are the three children who attend Kallen school. Gong Wendy "whispering pine;" the second name, "Wendy" was chosen by the other children, in honor of the Peter Pan character; Gong Wendy was born in Windigo.

Mai talks about the difficulties of having many children:

> When you have one or two, it is easier. Three is still easy. But four, five, six—that is more difficult. When the older ones know how to change diapers and take the little ones to use the bathroom, then it is easier. But when they

are still young it is still difficult. If Shou is not home, and it is just me, I have to do everything.

When Shou was working 20 hours a day in Chicago it was hard for Mai at home: "At that time I didn't know how to drive. I didn't know how to take the bus because I didn't speak English.

Shou would be gone all day and all night. When I needed some milk or some diapers it was difficult." Shou and Mai are happy that their children have mostly come in pairs—a boy, two girls, two boys, and two girls. It is nice for the children, and also a "blessing from God." Interestingly, Sammy, the eldest, has no one with whom to be paired, although this past year he has been able to share a room and much of his time with Jerry Lee.

One important memory that Shou and Mai have of their children is of the birth of Paj Huab, the third child, at home in Milwaukee.

Shou recalls:

I remember one time when we had our third child, Paj Huab, in Milwaukee, Mai had her labor in the house. I was in Chicago. Mai went to the hospital for some treatment, but afterwards came home. But Paj Huab did not come home. She had to be kept in the hospital for some checks, because she was delivered in the house. So Mai was very sad at that time, too. Even crying. And I could not tell why. Because she had a baby, and she was home, and the baby was not home. So that was very hurtful for the mother. For me it was OK, but I can see that it was hurtful for her.

I ask Mai, "Were you alone when Paj Huab was born?"
Mai replies:

Yeah. His brother and my sister-in-law were there, but at that time, it was very early, about three in the morning, so I did not wake them up. But I felt different, so I just sat down on the sofa about 2 or 3 hours. I couldn't get up. I felt the baby coming out, so I caught her. At that time my brother-in-law and his wife came and helped. It was the first time for them.

It is fascinating that, in the midst of labor, Mai chose not to disturb her brother and sister-in-law. Moreover, she shows consideration for the fact that "it was the first time for them" to help a woman after her delivery. In doing so she showed an interesting combination of respect for others and individual resourcefulness. With such qualities, it is no wonder that Mai has been able to keep strong extended family relationships and maintain a household of active children while Shou is often away at work. Still, for the past year, Mai has been working full-time herself putting computer cable together at a factory that is a 40 minute drive away. Without the support of her brother's family and other help, raising seven young children while both parents work would be extremely difficult.

When I asked them about their roles as parents, Shou replied:

> As a father I do certain things different from Mai. I don't help her a lot. Sometimes I do some cleaning, but she does the most. And she knows everything. My role is to discipline the children for whatever reason. I discipline more than her. She does that, too. But in our tradition, the children do not respect the mother as much as the father.

Shou pauses to shout across the room at one of his daughters: "Hey, Rebecca! You need to quiet down please."

Shou continues:

> Discipline is necessary. God gives authority. I do more discipline, and she does more caring. If I discipline very strongly and the children cry, they can run to their mom. And their mom will say, OK, I am here to help you. But you have to listen to your father—he is right. But Mai also disciplines very much. She carries the children more than I do in certain ways.

> Sometimes they fight, and we have to judge. We call them together and say, well, who is at fault? If they won't say, I say, Honestly. You know that God is with us here right now. If you don't tell me the truth, God is going to punish you, don't you know that? Tell me the truth! So they say, Well, actually this is what happened. And sometimes Sammy says, Yes. I did this. So, because he tells me so honestly, I reduce my punishment. I say, since you told me so honestly, I will give you one spank instead of five. How's that? Is it fair? He says, Yes. It is fair. To the other one I will say, this is part of your fault, too, because you returned fighting. If you are in the right, you do not have to return fighting. You just have to let us know. If you fight back, then I have to punish you, too. Remember two important things: One is that you are at fault. The other is, next time, make peace. Because if next time you do not make peace, I am going to come back to you and deal with this. I will punish more than this. Then they offer their butts for the spanking. I will not spank anywhere. I will not spank arms, hands, or face, or head or legs, or anywhere else. I know spanking hurts, and I know sometimes it can destroy their body, too. So the only good place to spank is on their butts. I explain this to them.

Despite this stress on discipline, Hmong adults whom I have met in the Cha home seem to exhibit many nonaggressive characteristics when interacting with children. Within the Cha family, children are given responsibility for themselves and for each other, such as taking care of each other at school; children share and cooperate willingly, as I observed during our sledding adventures in the winter; and there is a great deal of body contact between parents and children. On one visit to the Cha home, for example, I found Shou and two other adult Hmong males collectively caring for 25 small children. One man, perhaps a former "revolutionary" like Shou, was giving a bottle to a baby. Thus, I have observed Hmong males as well as females serve as nonaggressive, nurturing models for their children.

When I ask about the different characteristics or personalities of the children, Mai and Shou tend to focus on qualities of helpfulness, respectfulness and educational success:

Mai begins: "Paj Huab does everything that I want her to do. She does everything slowly, but she listens to me when I say, do this or do that. She does everything. She makes me happy." I recall that Paj Huab seemed to take a lot of responsibility for the other children when they were sledding and later, when they stopped for hot chocolate and cookies at my house.

> The other ones, like Mai Jia and Yisai and Joshua, when I have many things I want them to do, they just do one thing. Sometimes they say, "Mom, I'm not your slave!" Mai laughs. "I will say, 'Mai Jia, put your shoes outside there.' She says, 'No.' I say, 'Put Joshua's shoes outside.' She says, 'No. That's not my shoes.'"

Shou and Mai take their children's school work very seriously. Shou says:

I went to Paj Huab's teacher conference yesterday. She got all As, which is good. So, she does most of the things at home, and she also does a good job at school. She works slowly, though. Slow but good. She also reads the most books. She concentrates on reading so much.

At her school there is a "nuts about books" contest, and Paj Huab has the most nuts on her T-shirt. Shou thinks the other children need to read more.

He continues:

> I think my children follow some of my family's characteristics. Paj Huab is kind of slow, like me. The difference is that she does a quality job. Mai Jia is totally different. She could care less. I mean, she does not care how beautiful she writes. She just goes through it very fast. I do not have that characteristic. She can do her homework, and she does not need help. However, neither one of them asks me for help with their homework. They know how to do it. Sammy I helped with a lot of homework when he was in elementary school. Right now I say, no I cannot help you. Your work is really too difficult for me. Besides, I am too busy. So he does it himself, but he also has a different personality. He does not do much.

> We have a rule, that if you do certain things, you will receive certain rewards. So, if they get all As from school, we will give them a certain prize. If they get As and Bs, then we give them a certain lesser prize. If they get a C,

then they receive a lesser prize. So they know the rule, and if they listen to everything at home, the directives, and say, OK, we'll do it, and they follow it, who ever follows most will get a special treat. We let them go to certain places. For example, they like to watch TV on weekends. So I say, OK, if you are the one who listens the most and does the most, you get the choice to go and choose any videocassette that you want. So they do, and that helps, too. But Sammy does not care. Because he knows that he does not want to do everything that we ask him to do. He does not care. But when Paj Huab goes to the video store, he says, Hey, Paj Huab. Choose this one. Then I say, No. She has the right to choose it or not. But sometimes she just shows compassion and chooses the one that her brother asks for!

Mai mentions that Sammy no longer wants to accompany the rest of the family on most outings:

Right now Sammy is bigger, and he does not follow us very much. If we go to the store, or go anywhere, he does not want to go. When Jerry is not here, he doesn't want to do things with us. He looks so different. Yesterday we were talking. I said some things that were not good to him. And he got angry, and said: 'The parents do not understand the children, and the children don't understand the parents either.' Right now Sammy is difficult.

Shou adds:

To be a parent at any period of time is difficult. When there is a baby, it is difficult, because they can easily get sick. And when they are older it is difficult. The Hmong people used to say that, as a parent, you are parenting them from the time they are babies until you are gone.

It is evident that Mai and Shou care deeply for their children and want what is best for them. Like many Hmong refugee parents, neither of them has much formal education, yet they encourage their children to do well in school, and find ways to celebrate their accomplishments. They also are concerned that the children maintain traditional values of respect toward their elders, and cooperate fully in household work and other activities. In these ways Shou and Mai are not very different from many other parents across America, or indeed across the world. However, they face a greater challenge as refugees: For they seek to maintain familial relationships that have been transcended in both time and space by the overwhelming changefulness of life in postmodern America.

RELATIONSHIPS ACROSS GENERATIONS

When I was growing up my heroes and heroines were my older brothers and sisters. My eldest brother was the Cowboy, the one who had gone out west to the mountains, and who would return for Christmas in Michigan, tanned, trim, and full of stories. Two of my older sisters were adventurers across the sea, sending me postcards from France or Italy, writing about how they supported themselves cleaning houses or working with small theater companies, writing more about their adventures in the hills of Ireland or the islands of Greece. When I turned 18 years of age my parents were going to give me a suitcase, and I was going to be an adventurer, too: This was my dream, a dream of free wandering with the all the world before me. My brothers and sisters became heroes and heroines as they *broke loose* from the family.

According to Coontz (1988) all families are based on complex relationships involving a system of rights and obligations:

> (The family) provides people with an explanation of their rights and obligations that helps link personal identity to social role. At the same time, the family constitutes an arena where people can affect their rights and obligations. It is also ... a place where people resist assignment to their social roles or attempt to renegotiate those roles. (p. 2)

Family relationships play a large role in Shou Cha's narrative. The Hmong are traditionally a patriarchal people, who honor obligations to fathers, elder brothers and leaders, where the collective good tends to override the rights of the individual family members (Dunnigan, 1986).

I am not a refugee, but I am a parent, and as the 9th of 11 children, I have a lot of respect for parents who can manage the complexities and personalities of a large household. Father to father, I ask Shou, "How do you keep a good relationship within the family?"

Shou says:

> One thing that we do is that when we eat, we eat together. The other part of the relationship is to help your brothers and sisters. If he forgets to put his shoes outside, you do it, because you help him. If you help him, he will appreciate it, and I also will appreciate what you do. During the winter season we do not do certain things together. But in the warm weather we go outside and we play together.

> I remember last year we went to the park. And they had not experienced what the park looked like. So we went there, and we walked in the woods, and they complained to me and my wife, "There is nothing interesting here. We are bored." So we were just walking on the trail, and after that we walked into the woods. And then, in the meantime, it was about to rain. And our baby was very small. And then there was the sound of thunder and the flash of lightning, and they were very scared. And they came together and stayed close to us, and we walked under the rain and we came back to the

car. The part of it that was very good is that it showed us we should keep the relationship.

One year I was in charge of the whole ministry in Michigan, and I was to direct all of the ministers' families to do certain things. We were interested in going camping, so we did. And certain ministers from all over the region, about six families, went camping with us in the north. We didn't have a tent. So we made a teepee. We had the sticks bound up at the top, and we had a big, big piece of plastic. So we covered it up, and we slept inside, the whole family. It was so frustrating, but it was so fun. I know it was not so good, but my children helped me to set it up. So we enjoyed sleeping there.

Whereas in the United States Shou tries to foster family relationships through activities such as going to the woods or the beach together, he grew up in a time and place where relationships were fostered through collective work in the fields and forests. Shou's account of how he gained his father's trust for the eventual move to Thailand illustrates some of the dynamics of traditional Hmong parent and sibling relationships:

I came to Thailand without my family. One thing was that my father was quite old. He was not very strong to lead his family. I was grown, and I was strong and he trusted me. He had a couple of sons, but I was the youngest and he trusted me because I had proven myself. Earlier, when we moved to Sayaboury Province, he did not trust me. I was quite young. We did not like the system running the country, so I mentioned that we should go to Thailand. He said, 'No. We cannot do that. And you don't have the knowledge—you are without knowledge to bring us there.' Which was putting me down *a lot*.

I did not mention anything. But about 2 years later, I and my brothers went to a different village, walking about 3 days. We wanted to move from our village to the next village, because that place would grow things better. So we tried to."

Shou recalls that his older brothers had eyes for the girls of the local village, and little progress was made in clearing the land for the new farm.

So when we came home, I told my father, "No, it's not a good time for us to move this year. I'm gonna tell you—the farm that we created was *so small*, and it's too late to create a new one. One day my brothers came to farm, to create a farm out of the forest, and the other 2 days they went with their girlfriends. I was the only one to stay in the jungle the whole time, and can you do it yourself? No. I can't do that. I needed their help." So my father believed me, and he asked my brothers if it was true, and they said, "Yeah, we don't have a really big farm." So, we did not move. But that year, *he trusted me!* So that year we tried to stay in the old village where we were, and then the next year, I mentioned to move, and he trusted me, so we tried to move to another village. And he also trusted me when I mentioned coming to Thailand. That's why he let me come. You have to do something for your father to trust you!

Shou's elder brothers rise and fall in his estimation to the extent that they can fulfill their obligations to the family. My elder brothers and sisters gained my admiration when they broke free of the family and struck out on their own. And yet, as I think of my own children growing up in a society where individualism and conformity to consumer culture is exalted, and the wisdom of the very old and very young is forgotten, I find more value in Shou's conception of familial duty and responsibility. In such a world, I believe all of us must find some ways to meet the changing needs of the community, the family, and the individual.

DUTY TO THE GROUP

Shou says that it is very hard to get used to the "colder" relationships between people in the large cities of America. He also recalls how, when he first arrived in Chicago and wanted to break up a street fight between two men, his sponsor told him not to get involved. This was a difficult lesson to learn. I ask him: "Many people in the United States think we are missing a sense of community, a sense of responsibility for each other. With your own children, what would you like them to believe when they are out in the community and witness things like the street fight you saw in Chicago?"
Shou says:

That is a very good question. I do not know how they teach in school. And I believe they teach a good way. But when they come home, here, we add something. Since I am a minister and I have learned a lot about family counseling and family changing, too. I actually add something which is good for the family—which my great-grandfather practiced, too!

Respect, relationship: For example, when my children come in, I say, 'You should say, Hi.' That's one thing that we should practice from teenage years on. I can see that many people do not practice this. That is one thing, to keep your reputation where you are, not to lower yourself down. Because when you show respect, people respect you. When you do not respect people, you will lose your reputation, too.

Shou stops to call Mai Jia over, and he says to her, "I need you to wash this cup for your little sister. Something down there is not clean. Thank you, girl."

When they come home here, and they don't clean the house, I say, 'It's part of your job. You should know that. You need to clean that, and I need to see that it's clean.' And so they do it. If they don't do it, I say, 'Do you understand what I said? Then, if you understand, do it, as part of the family. And you know that you live in this house, and we should do these things, that's part of what I want you to keep forever.' And I explain it, and they do it. And we help one another. When we talk about religious stuff, and family, too, we also say that when you do (your work) you receive a blessing from God. Because you are working nicely for your family. And that is what the Bible says, too. I add something to it which goes back to my great-great-grandfather, who practiced this, and so did my family when I was young. We help each other. That is one thing that we keep.

At several points in our continuing conversations Shou has suggested that he wants Sammy, his eldest, to be a leader, an example for the other children to respect. I recall my own experiences with Sammy, sharing his Hmong worksheet at the Sunday school, studying math, and playing chess and checkers. I say: "Sammy had been very helpful to me when I was trying to follow the Hmong language lesson at the church. Also, I have found him to be a hard-working student when I help him out with his math. So there is a side of Sammy that wants to participate, to help, and do well."

Shou agrees, and tells me the following story:

I remember when we were in Milwaukee and Sammy was the first one to go to the elementary school. And I had such high expectations for them: I thought that they knew everything. And I didn't bring them the first day of school. And all of the children went to school by themselves on the first day. And they did not know which class they should go to. And I was not there. Sammy was in second grade, and when Mai Jia went to school, he helped her look for her class. He even went to the office and asked them where Mai Jia's class was. So when they came back home, I said, 'I'm sorry. I should have gone with you to school. I did not realize it would be difficult. I thought that you would know everything. It was so good that you could do it.'

What I think happened is this: Sammy would not do anything if he saw that his father was there. If sometime his father is not there, he knows that he has the responsibility to do it. But he is a little bit too harsh. Sometimes he is even more strict with the other children than I am. Sometimes he might mistreat them, and they say, He beat me! He beat me! And Sammy says, Yeah, I beat them because they did this! I say, yes, but it is too harsh. You should not do that.

I remember when I was about his age or a little bit older. I used to carry my youngest sister who is now in Minnesota. One time we were walking, just me and her and the older ones, but they didn't take care of her. There was a very steep ravine. There was not water in there, but it was about 5 feet across and 15 feet deep. And my youngest sister could not cross it. My older sister and brother did not carry her, they just went ahead by themselves. So I had to wait for her. I even put her on my back, and tried to find a way to carry her over. I remember that event today.

Shou believes that Sammy is like that young boy who carried his sister: He may not go out of his way to look for good deeds to perform, but when they need him, he helps his siblings across the ravines that separate the world of their home from the world of the American school and society.

THE DIALOGUE

I ask Shou and Mai, "Do the children communicate important issues with you?"

Mai responds:

Sometimes they have troubles, but they are afraid to tell their father, because they think maybe he will beat them. So they tell me about it. They explain it to me, and I explain it to Shou. So, if we have time, we call the ones who have trouble together, and talk to them.

I'd like to talk to them about it, but I don't think it would work. So almost always, we don't talk. Mostly the girls talk to their mothers. And then the boy does not go to the father much. He goes to his trusting friends. This is what happens in the Hmong community a lot.

Shou then tells me a story which reflects his own difficulties in communicating with his father when he was Sammy's age:

I did not talk to my father very much at that age. It was the only night that I talked to my father, the one night in the world that I never will erase from my brain, the only night. That night we talked as *special guests*. We talked about *everything*!

I was quite sick. Back at that time we did not have good medication, and my father was an opium man. So we used opium as a medication. I was sick and he and I had to smoke opium together.

> *That special night*
> *I do not know how we began,*
> *but I talked,*
> *he talked,*
> *I talked*
> *he talked.*

We talked about brothers and sisters.
We talked about special accidents we had seen.
I talked about some events I had experienced,
and the kinds of friends I saw.
And I remember we talked about hunting, trapping.
That is the part that is still in my brain: The way I hunt, the
way I trap,
and hunting squirrels.

I talked to him about the time
I went with a very poorly-conditioned gun,
and there was a squirrel running above me
from branch to branch.
And I shot from behind it,
and the bullet went right through it,
and the squirrel was stuck up there!
So I tried every way, but I
could not quite reach it.
It was about,
oh,
as high as this house.
And that place was slippery, too.
So I tried every way, and I took a long time,
about half of the day,
to get the squirrel,
and finally I got it.

I also talked about the time
I went with my uncle to hunt.
We went hunting for about two days,
far away,
walking in the woods about three days.
Then we went to a different rocky mountain, and
somehow,
I missed my family so much
when we were in the jungle
and we were quite high
on the rocky mountain.
I was looking back
to the rocky mountain where we lived,
which was to the north,
by the Mekong River.

When I talked to my father
I said,
"I missed you guys very much at that time.
I had a sense that,

> *if I could be back with my family,*
> *I would."*

"So, I talked a lot about those things!" Shou laughs. *"It was the only night I talked to my father."*

I say to Shou, "It's hard for kids to talk to their fathers."

Shou agrees. "It's hard. I do not know how we can break that wall. Because so many teenagers do not like to talk to their parents. I'd like to break that wall, but right now, I and my son Sammy do not agree about many things. Not everything, but some things we do not agree about."

Perhaps what Shou, Sammy, and all parents and children need is something with the power of an opium cure, but with the more lasting effect of opening channels of communication. Like the stories of Covello and Rodriguez that appear in chapter one, Shou's story of his "only night" of dialogue with his father and of his own inability to communicate with his eldest son illustrate the gulf of silence that often separates parents from children, a gulf that is widened when children spend their lives in the cultural borderlands between home, school, and the street.

Walker-Moffat (1995), who has spent years working with Southeast Asian refugees in the camps of Thailand and in the United States, argues that young people like Sammy may be having more difficulties at school or with their parents because of their changing cultural scripts. To some extent, they are emulating the behavior of other *Americans* whom they meet at school:

> While most Hmong students continue to be models of "correct" behavior, more and more Hmong youngsters are acting like other school children: skipping school, hanging out at shopping malls, and giving priority to being regarded as "cool" by their fellow students. Changes in Hmong children's behavior at school implies that their cultural scripts are changing. They are no longer just Hmong. They are Hmong American (p. 111)

Such changing cultural scripts, and the changing values that accompany them, can cause tension and a breakdown of communication within homes such as the Chas. Such tensions are exacerbated when children wish to conform to the standards of a highly materialistic culture whose values and income are beyond the scope of their refugee parents.

A MATERIAL WORLD

It is late Saturday evening at the Cha house and I sit on one of the used couches in the living room talking to Shou about family. Nearby, Sammy and Jerry sit, watching a movie on the television. The bright, pulsating flashes from the TV are the only light in the room. Although I am in conversation with Shou, my eyes are mostly on the TV screen. In the movie two modern-day gladiators are fighting before a well-dressed crowd in some futuristic Las Vegas. One defeats the other, and then looks to the crowd for a sign. Unanimously, they turn their thumbs down, and with that the victorious wrestler grabs the head of his prostrate opponent, gives it a hard twist, breaks his neck, and leaves him lying dead, to the cheers of the assembled throng. Sammy and Jerry watch on with expressionless faces, while I get ready to go home and help rock the children to sleep, and wish them sweet dreams ...

On a later visit, Shou and Mai inform me that they are limiting the amount of television that the kids watch. When I ask why, Shou response indicates that the sexual content of television programs concerns him more than their violence:

> We settled in the United States, and everywhere in this country there are televisions and commercial things. Some things are not good to watch; they are dirty, bad, or could be adapted to the family and that wouldn't be good. This is one reason why I do not want them to watch. But another thing is that, whatever they watch, even if it is just *Sesame Street*, I will not let them watch on weekdays, because their homework will not be done. Besides, if they just spend their time watching TV, they do not help in the family's work. So there are a couple of reasons. We watch many video movies, but the parts that are not good to watch we do not let them watch. Sometimes we think it is not good for children to watch, but we still let them watch. For example, *Kung Fu. Kung Fu* is nothing that we can adapt to our family. It is just fun to watch, so I let them watch it. Or like *Power Rangers*. I do not like to watch *Power Rangers*, but they are so attracted to it. But they also watch *Baywatch*, which I do not agree with. I do not want you to watch it. I explain it to them, but I do not put a very strict rule about it, so sometimes they watch *Baywatch*.
>
> The most important reason is the homework. With too much TV, they will not get their homework done. And any movie that they copy, or adapt to themselves, I say, No. This is not good for you to do. If you copy it, I will not let you watch anymore. For example, ninja turtles. Ninja turtles have the weapon that is the stick with the rope. The children tried to make that. I said, No. You have to destroy it or put it away. Or if they try to copy *Power Rangers*, I say, No. You will not do it. If you do it, I will not let you watch it anymore.

Besides his disapproval of sexually explicit content found in shows such as *Baywatch*, Shou mentions several times that he does not want his children to "adapt" violent material from television to family situations.

He seems to have a strong belief in the power of television to change the personalities of his children and alter family relationships. This belief is exemplified in a story involving Sammy, a friend from the neighborhood, and a video game:

> Across the street we have a neighbor, and he is very good to me, too. He has a son who is a little bit older than Sammy. They came over and I let them watch TV. And I trusted them a lot. But one thing that happened when his other friend came over, and I was totally mad. They came and played a video game on the TV and spent a whole half day, and the next day, too. So I said: I demand that you stop. These kind of games I want to destroy. I don't want you to play anymore. And I also said, you are his friend, but I tell you: You and Sammy better stop it. I don't like this kind of playing.

> We actually have a video game, because of relative gave it to us. But after that I said, No. It will destroy my family. They were just doing *adookat, adookat, adookat,* all the time, and they fought. So we put it away. No more.

The pressures of living in a materialistic culture are felt strongly in the Cha family. Television has a strong impact on the kids, and so do the expensive clothing styles of other children. Mai suggests that such materialism seems to threaten the Chas' budget as well as their family relationship:

> With the younger children, if I buy any clothes for them, they say they like them. But Sammy, no. Right now he chooses the expensive clothes, so that is difficult for us. If his friend wears the expensive shoes and clothes, he wants to dress like his friend. So I say, my family is not rich. We are poor. So you have to wear the cheaper clothes. Right now he says No.

In her study of the history of the concept of "family," Coontz (1988) says: "The expansion of democratic capitalism may have freed families from older political and social hierarchies, but it has subjected them to other hierarchies of consumerism and envy" (p. 4). Youths from socioeconomically marginalized groups are placed in a particular dilemma when they find themselves in a highly materialistic culture with few material resources of their own. In the Twin Cities, where a sizable Hmong population resides, Ungar (1995) reports that Hmong youth, especially boys, "develop American habits and tastes without the means to pay for them; they become highly Americanized without being socially integrated" (p. 189). Through his clothes, his hairstyle and his choice of games, Sammy is perhaps trying to find his identity as a young American, hoping to find acceptance through a show of outward conformity.

Psychologist Erikson (1959a) writes that identity crises are particularly acute for minority youth. Such crises "come when their parents and teachers, losing trust in themselves and using sudden correctives in order to approach the vague but pervasive Anglo-Saxon ideal, create violent discontinuities" (p. 96). Indeed, Erikson argues that American elementary schools are generally tolerant places, but that minority students in the schools would eventually have to face the reality of their own difference, and their exclusion from the dominant group:

> Children of these ages seem remarkably free of prejudice and apprehension, preoccupied as they still are with growing and learning and with new pleasures of association outside their families. Many individual successes, on the other hand, only expose the ... children of mixed backgrounds and maybe differing endowments to the shock of American adolescence: *the standardization of individuality and the intolerance of "difference."* (p. 143)

Ogbu's (1982) argument that "cultural discontinuities" exist between the home and the school, causing some groups of minority youth to rebel while others excel, provides a more recent interpretation of this dilemma of adaptation. Youth from minority cultural groups are often asked to adapt to a dominant culture that rejects the cultural worth of their group identities, and defines them primarily in material terms.

The Watch

Shou recognizes that social pressures to conform lie behind his son's wish to buy certain brands of clothing:

> That is a very difficult point. I just think that we have to explain and explain and he will just have to understand, and we will have to understand him. I know it is very difficult for him, because he wants it a certain way. I remember he asked to buy a $70 watch. I said, No. Please accept my no, because I myself wouldn't even try to get one. We cannot afford to buy one like that. And suppose we could afford to buy one for you. What about the other ones? It is not fair. As a family we have to do things fairly. So he was kind of mad, but he had to accept it.
>
> According to this society, it is part of parenting that you cannot accept your children's opinion all the time, and you cannot just force them to do what you want all the time. But in Hmong society, you cannot do anything that you want, unless your parents trust you so much that they think you can do a good job. Then you say, father I want to do this. What do you think? If he doesn't trust you, then whatever you do, he will say no. If you want to do something, you have to gain his trust.
>
> When I was still young, about Sammy's age, my older stepbrother, who was about 20 years old, had stopped going to school, and was trying to do something else. And he was not cooperating and doing the farm with the family.

He was old enough, so he asked my father to provide some money to him to make a business. And my father trusted him enough, so he gave him a certain amount of money to start a business. After about 3 months the business was gone. Everything was gone. He could not make a profit. So my father was quite sad. And then after that, my stepbrother asked to buy a watch. Back where I lived a watch was very costly, and there was a very nice but very expensive Japanese watch. My brother asked to have one, and my father said: 'No. I am not going to buy you one. Besides, I don't have much money to buy you one.' So my stepbrother said, 'Why won't you buy me one? I am going to run away!' My father said: 'I don't have money to buy one. Remember, you promised me you would make profits from your business, and you didn't. So I don't have money to buy you a watch. If you marry, yes, I can provide any help to you. But to buy a watch for you, no, I am not going to do it.'

The reason I tell this story is this: In youth, there is mistrust and misunderstanding. Or you are judged wrong. Like Sammy, if I don't trust him one time, or two, three or four times, then I will just tell him, I'm sorry. If you misunderstand him one, two, three times, then the record is there. You cannot trust for him to do other things. And whatever you say, your parent will not believe it.

A watch keeps time, and for Sammy, and Shou's elder brother before him, having a watch meant keeping up with the times. Moreso for Sammy, it may signify an outward show of conformity to a set of dominant American values, and an attempt to belong to a group beyond his family and Hmong community. For Shou, the watch also keeps time, the number of times that misunderstandings have occurred, that trust has been gained or lost. For refugee parents like Shou who are attempting to foster traditional values among children growing up in a materialist culture, it must often seem that time is running out.

PREPARING FOR THE FUTURE

Like all parents, Shou Cha has certain hopes and dreams for his children's future:

Back when I was in Milwaukee, I also participated in schools quite a bit. I was trained as a PPP—something about Parents, Progress, and Participation in school. I got a certificate for that training too. After I got that I also learned about preparing my kids to go to college. I hope that they will go to college. To tell you honestly, I would like them to be involved in religious things. Missionaries, or ministers, or something like that. But I do not know if that will be the choice of God, or if they will take that choice. But I also know that certain things like computer science or medical science are highly paid.

Shou has high hopes for his children's educational future. However, he is concerned that teenage marriage, a traditional practice of the Hmong, could threaten the girls' chances for education. Marriages of girls as young as 12 still occur within the Hmong community in America (Trueba, Jacobs, & Kirton, 1990; Ungar, 1995).

Shou tells me the following story of a young Hmong girl who got married recently in Windigo:

> She was one of the girls who was in elementary school and did not even go to high school yet. Somehow, a boy met her—some time, somewhere, I do not know. And then she just kept on communicating with him, and after all she did not graduate. She stopped at maybe Grade seven.
>
> One thing that is a danger. Most of the Hmong people, the girls, didn't pass high school. They would get married before high school. Mai Jia is getting very close to that age. That is the only thing that I am quite scared of. I'd like her to go to school. I'd prefer that my daughters finish college. But at least high school. Shou laughs as he adds, "Which I haven't made yet!"

In her study of the Hmong in Seattle, Donnelly (1994) finds that amid the flux of economic, political, cultural and social changes facing their communities, Hmong respondents insist that they can remain "Hmong" as long as they maintain certain social relationships and respect within the family. Donnelly writes: "The particular social forms can be identified not by the actual content or goals of actions, but by the lines of respect and authority they embody. These place each person in two hierarchies: gender and age" (1994, p. 184). In some ways the Cha family challenges the traditional Hmong relational hierarchies identified by Donnelly. Clearly, Shou, as father, holds a position of traditional power, and both he and Mai expect a high degree of obedience from their children. The fact that the children, especially Sammy and Mai Jia, are beginning to question parental authority indicates a degree of acculturation to American youth behaviors among the children. More interesting is the fact that Shou, as male head of the family, actively encourages his daughters' academic success. Breaking with a traditional pattern, he seems insistent that the girls get an education first and wait to get married. Just as when he questioned the fairness of a traditional society that denied opportunities to his educated older sister, in encouraging the education of his daughters Shou exhibits fundamental egalitarian principles, although he also assumes to know what is best for them.

Donnelly (1994) has suggested that, as Hmong such as the Chas move in the direction of nuclear families based on married couples, rather than extended families based around the patrilineal clan, individualism inevitably becomes a feature of the household. Such individualism reflects pressures from the dominant society, as Donnelly explains: "Teachers, doctors, social workers, co-workers and employers all expect individual family members to speak up, to decide for themselves, and to look out for their own benefit" (p. 189). Unfortunately, what is often lost in this societal expectation of individualism are the potential communal strengths of households such as the Chas where children and parents are still expected to help and take responsibility for each other.

MAKING PEACE IN THE HMONG FAMILY

The Hmong community in Windigo faces its own conflicts brought on by generational and religious differences, extensive poverty, and the difficulties of refugees who find themselves part of a rapidly changing culture. Through his life experiences, Shou Cha has learned that helping one another is the *glue* that holds the Hmong community together, and mutual support could help build the larger community as well:

> In my culture helping one another keeps us glued together. I need help from someone else, and then they need my help. I help them with speaking and translating, because I have stayed longer in the United States, and I help with what I know. But I also need help regarding time, regarding strength or hands. We help each other a lot.

Often when I visit the Cha home in the evening the house is full of guests: newly arrived refugees who find lodgings for a few weeks, church members who find spiritual guidance, and friends who find the warmth of communal relationships. Seeing so many people gathered under one roof brings back memories of the home of my youth, where my mother always found beds for 10 children, grandfather, and assorted visitors. She remembers her life in various homes during the Depression when there would often be additional relatives staying over with her family of 12, as well as a cot in the kitchen for the *tramp*. In her father's youth, the McClear homestead was a regular stopping-off place for members of the Potawatomie tribe on the road between Southwest Michigan and Detroit. The Hmong and other communally-oriented immigrants often seem to stand out in a nation characterized by individualism. Yet extended family and communal ties have always been a valuable part of the American experience.

Clan relationships, as well as relationships with other Hmong from the church and community, remain very important for the Chas. Shou tells me that if he travels anywhere in the world and meets a Cha family, that family must take him in and support him, and likewise he must do the same for all Chas. He explains:

In a local community we have different kinds of organizations, but we always organize to the clan name. We keep that very, very strict. If you deny your last name, your clan, then you have denied the whole Hmong people. And you should not deny it. We have some ways to adopt, but even if you adopt, you should not deny your clan. I am of the Cha family, and I want to adopt the Yang family. I can do that, yes. I become a Yang family member. But I do not deny the Cha family. Because somehow, a sickness in the spiritual world will effect your life in a spiritual way. Do not deny your family. I think that is a very strict rule that we never write down, but it is written in our brains—Do not deny your clan.

The Cha clan of Michigan has elected Shou to chair a committee dedicated to finding ways to improve the relationship within families and across the larger family of the clan:

"My duty to the Cha family is to be a peacemaker." Shou translates from a paper he has from the last Cha clan meeting:

The position is "community relationship and peace for the Cha families". This is not a paid job, it is a volunteer job. The reason we need this is because the Hmong people who came to the United States have lost the communication between families and friends, the kind of friendship we had back in Laos. Our plan is to have the kind of relationship between the Cha families among us in the state, and my plan is to go on and work deeper within families, with parents and children. The reason I plan to do that is because the communication, relationship and peace in each family is also destroyed, is already damaged. The children have lost trust in their parents and the parents have lost control of their children. If I can, I would like to do two seminars, one for the Cha families, to build a relationship between families. The other seminar will be about the relationship within families.

It is likely that this effort to build relationships and open channels of communication within the Cha clan is influenced by, and influences, Shou's work as a liaison between school and community.

Shou, like other Hmong parents with whom I have talked, seems worried by the specter of Hmong youth gangs.

I have heard that the Asian young people have gotten some bad attitudes here in the United States. I am talking about gangsters, very young people, even 12 to 15. In Detroit, Milwaukee, St. Paul, Fresno—almost everywhere my own people live. Looking back to two decades ago when we lived in Laos and presently here, it is totally different, it is totally upside down. We need to work out something, somehow, some way. I want to find out what the reason is for this. It is not the children's fault. It is not the parents' fault. But we have to work together on it.

Although relatively few Hmong youth appear to be involved in gangs in Windigo (Jerry has told me that there are some Hmong gang members at his high school, although he doesn't claim to know them personally), there has been a good deal of media attention on a few cases, such as the Xou Yang case in California, where a Hmong adolescent was involved in the murder of an elderly German tourist (Sabbag, 1995). For Shou it is an upside-down world when children lose their respect for elders, and their sense of familial and community relationship, finding their sense of belonging in gangs instead. Many Hmong elders fear that their children are not only losing their Hmong values, but losing their humanity as well.

For Shou, however, helping others extends beyond his clan and includes the entire Hmong community. His home is a center for Hmong community activity. Every night he has visitors, many of whom stay late into the evening. He believes "it is very good to have someone who cares for you enough that they visit you." Though much of his work is with members of his own church, Shou says he has been able to develop some strong relationships with non-Christians as well:

> A woman, a member of a family who were not Christian at all, got sick back in March. I was asked to pray for them, so I did. That first night they asked me to commit them to the Lord, because our culture is so religious in a special way. So we went to their house and prayed every night. Even though I worked early in the morning and came back late because I had to go to class, too, I would stay up to midnight to support the lady, and by doing that we were getting so close to one another. And since then we have been helping one another back and forth.

> Helping glues us together. They respect me and I respect them. I help them with whatever I know. It is so sad within our culture and community if you know something and never help someone else. However much I know, however rich or poor I am, in my culture, you give and receive help. People will say, 'Oh, he does not need help. He does not need help.' When you pass away, people will say, 'Oh, he does not need help.' So those turning help away are few.

> I was considering moving out of Windigo after I got shot, but the help glues me to here. I cannot unglue it! I just have to stick to it.

Webster's defines *clan* in this way: "In certain primitive societies, a tribal division, usually exogamous, of matrilineal or patrilineal descent from a common ancestor." Like Webster's, many Americans like to think of tradition-rich groups such as the Hmong as *primitive*. Yet, consider what clan membership means to Shou Cha: When he needs assistance, his clan, which he also calls his *family*, is there to help him. When he travels, his clan will take him in. When he needs work, as he did when he applied to work at Horace Kallen school, his clan nominates him for a job. In return, he works for the clan, and beyond, for all the Hmong community. Acknowledging common ancestors, it is an easy step for the Hmong to refer respectfully to their unrelated kin as *uncle* or *brother*.

Traditional relationships help keep the Hmong glued together, as Shou has suggested. In a wealthy nation where many Americans go hungry and homeless, and many others worry about what will happen to them and their families if they lose their jobs, or their health fails, the Hmong have a community support network that provides economic, social, and psychological support. *Which is the primitive society?*

THE ROLE OF GENERATIVITY

Caught between the different cultural expectations of home and society, immigrant youth find themselves forced to identify with the ways of their parents, the ways of the dominant culture, or neither. The effect of this clash of cultural ways on immigrant children and families has been widely researched (e.g., Berrol, 1995; Handlin, 1951; Takaki, 1993).

Specifically with the Hmong, Moore (1989) finds that teenagers tend to identify themselves in three ways: As American-Hmong, with an emphasis on assimilating to the dominant culture; as Hmong Americans, with an emphasis on holding onto traditions; and as Rebels, who reject both the dominant culture and the traditions of their parents, while embracing the excesses of reckless freedom and consumerism. Although their parents seem to fear that some of their children are becoming Rebels, Sammy, Mai Jia, and the others appear to be trying their best to build a bridge between Hmong and American cultural contexts. This is exemplified by their efforts in the Hmong church youth group to engage parents in a meaningful dialogue about intergenerational issues and education. This suggests that these youth see themselves as Hmong Americans, but with an understanding that Hmong culture in America is not a mere reflection of the Hmong culture in Laos of 20 years ago, but is changing and growing. These youth seem intent on helping to explain these changes to parents who have not acculturated as much to the United States, and who fear loss of traditional values.

Parents face much competition in their role as primary educators of children from mass media, other youths, and the schools. Parents who differ from the dominant society culturally, linguistically or socioeconomically often experience additional difficulties in communicating with children who believe that to become like other *Americans*, they need to distance themselves from the home. When children turn their backs on these parents, they lose touch with a valuable source of learning and wisdom, and their parents may become further isolated from both their children and the dominant culture.

Psychologists have long stressed the importance for children and parents of *generativity*, the process whereby members of the older generation pass on something of value to members of the younger generation. Erikson (1950) states:

> The fashionable insistence on dramatizing the dependence of children on adults often blinds us to the dependence of the older generation on the younger one. Mature man needs to be needed, and maturity needs guidance as well as encouragement from what has been produced and must be taken care of. Generativity, then, is primarily the concern in establishing and guiding the next generation. (p. 266)

Generativity represented the seventh healthy stage in Erikson's life cycle; denied the opportunity to guide the younger generation, mature adults may face stagnation and despair.

An immigrant himself, Erikson was aware of the special importance of generativity for newcomers in a strange land, as the following case study of an elderly immigrant illustrates:

> The old man stands midway between those who are driven by inner conflicts or unmanageable drives and those who have been driven from soil and home. Their common symptoms betray a common state in their egos which has lost active mastery and the nourishing exchange of community life ... Homesick-ness turns into a self-accusation for having abandoned a land one was actually driven from. In other words, the ego's capacity for initiative is inactivated by a conspiracy of historical fate and personal history. (Erikson, 1959b, pp. 88–89)

Erikson insists that adult immigrants, therefore, must continue developing, and continue learning in their adopted home. In this way they can initiate the process of generativity, and provide guidance to children who are torn between the often conflicting worldviews of home, school, and the street. Interestingly, Shou and Mai Cha seem to have been able to guide their children, and other young people of the Hmong community in Windigo, in greater understanding of aspects of both Hmong and American culture through their learning and participation in the church and the school. They have fostered the creation of a Christian youth group that fulfills a social, educational, and religious purpose for their children; they encourage their children to do well in school, and Shou's work with the school system allows him to gain an insiders view of the problems and possibilities his children encounter in their education. Moreover, Shou's commitment to earn a high school diploma serves to highlight the value of education for all the children.

Among the four types of generativity identified by Kotre (1984), cultural generativity, the passing on of relevant cultural beliefs, traditions and values, seems most relevant to the life of new Americans such as the Chas. Shou seems to recognize that many things from his native culture are being transformed or lost over time; yet he still insists on passing on two key values of relationship and respect to the next generation. As we shall see in the next chapter, he seeks through his work with school and community to pass on these values to all children. Moreover, Shou's work as a community liaison illustrates that schools can also play an important part in the process of generativity. By actively working to open channels to parents from diverse cultures, Horace Kallen School supports the process of generativity by legitimizing parents' educational role. In this way, the school both acknowledges and benefits from the education that takes place within homes and between generations.

6

Making Peace

> Blessed are the peacemakers,
> for they shall be called children of God.
> —Matthew, 5:9

Horace Kallen school sits in a residential, working-class neighborhood a few blocks south of the interstate highway that divides Windigo into two unequal parts. Its dark, brick exterior conceals somewhat the sounds and sights of the life within its walls, life that shows out briefly through student drawings peeping out at passerbys through classroom windows. Inside, visitors are greeted by the words "welcome" in the many languages of the school. The walls are lined with self-portraits and autobiographical statements of each of the children. Upstairs, the school library is contains countless volumes of multicultural stories and textbooks, arranged by continent and language. In one corner there is a piano, and several children are participating in a music lesson led by a volunteer music major from the university. Back in the hallway, a hubbub drifts up from the gymnasium/cafeteria downstairs. There, children are gathered for the free or reduced lunches, served and supervised by bilingual aides from over a 12 different countries. The room is lined with the flags of the United Nations.

Outside, on the playground, it is a warm, overcast Friday in early May. Children who have been cooped up indoors for so much of the long winter run and shout happily. In the dirt near the monkey bars, I come across Yisai Cha playing marbles with two Vietnamese girls. They each squat about 5 feet apart, and take turns trying to hit each others' marbles, all the while smiling excitedly. The previous week I had scarcely noticed Yisai, the smallest boy on the soccer field, until it was time to go in for classes. Then, without being asked, he collected the bright orange pylons that we use for goals and carried them into the gym.

Today, Shou Cha joins us on the soccer field. He plays hard, even in his street shoes and dress pants, and shouts encouragement to his 9-year old teammates. The children shout to each other in a variety of languages, but English is foremost. Many of their parents come from nations known to anyone familiar with recent U.S. military history: Vietnam, Laos, Cambodia, Iraq, Bosnia, Haiti. A sliding tackle causes a Vietnamese and a Haitian boy to get into a shoving match, and hot words are exchanged. Shou intervenes, separates the two, and bends down to talk with them at eye level. Because of his soft voice I cannot hear clearly what he is saying to them until the last words: "OK, you two, I want you to make peace and be friends."

Schools such as Horace Kallen must address multiple levels of conflict in the lives of children and communities. City leaders surveyed in 1994 by the National League of Cities ("National League of Cities Survey Cities Youth Problems," 1996) ranked gang activities, school violence, and ethnic conflict among the top 10 worsening conditions facing their citizenry, and during that same year, one out of seven teachers responding to a survey by the National Center for Education Studies reported being attacked or threatened by a student (Nicklin, 1996). Although departments of teacher education are beginning to prepare teachers to manage violence in the classroom, more and more teachers in the field are filing civil lawsuits against violent students, and some teachers unions are calling for "zero tolerance" legislation that will require suspension or expulsion of students who behave violently (Nicklin, 1996; Reske, 1996).

What are the causes of such conflict? Kozol (1991) has effectively documented the *savage inequalities* that deny equal educational opportunity to poor children, who realized all too soon that the schooling they receive will offer them little chance for success in life. Ogbu (1982) has examined the *cultural discontinuities* between the school and minority communities, and how *resistance* to an educational system that would seem to divide them from their peers and their families is a natural reaction for children of *involuntary* minority status.[1] Yet, in spite of an increasing awareness of potential causes for conflict, American schools are still strongly influenced by a larger societal urge to enforce norms of behavior, and, in the words of Foucault (1979), to "discipline and punish."

---

[1]Ogbu makes a distinction between *voluntary* and *involuntary* minorities. In his view, voluntary minorities include groups such as immigrants who have chosen to come to the United States, and who typically view school as a vehicle for social and economic success. Involuntary minorities include Native Americans, Mexican Americans and African Americans—groups who have been forced into American society as a result of wars, slavery, etc. Such groups have traditionally occupied the lowest socioeconomic positions in society, and children from these groups often see no hope of advancement through education; rather, they see schools as another form of cultural domination, to be resisted.

Bat-wielding principals such as Joe Clark are lionized in movies such as *Lean on Me*, uniformed policemen and metal detectors are fixtures in many public schools, and newer, bigger prisons are being built to handle those students who are not sufficiently disciplined by their school experience.

Foucault (1979) documents the rise of a new system to "discipline and punish" offenders in the early 19th century. Primary to this system was the establishment of norms of behavior, and a continuum of enforcement that connected schools, asylums, prisons, and other public institutions:

> A certain significant generality moved between the least irregularity and the greatest crime: it was no longer the offense, the attack on the common interest, it was the departure from the norm, the anomaly; it was this that haunted the school, the asylum or the prison. (p. 299)

Foucault's analysis poses an important question to American educators today: How does one judge normal behavior when norms from different socioeconomic and cultural groups come into conflict? Moreover, when factors such as poverty, abuse, and a metaculture of violence and materialism influence the behavior of children, punishing the child, or attempting to "manage" the violence in isolation, may not be the answer (Lindquist, 1995). Rather than merely maintaining discipline, it is perhaps time for educators to become peace makers in a diverse society, between children and adults with different cultural backgrounds and belief systems. In his foreword to *Pathways to Cultural Awareness*, Trueba (1994) writes:

> Could anyone really question the universal need for healing? The daily stories about hatred, cruelty, war, and conflict dividing nations, regions, states, cities, and neighborhoods reveal clearly the open wounds and hurts of many. We all carry profound emotional injuries that affect another deeper sense of self and the ability to recognize who we are individually and collectively. (p. viii)

Spindler and Spindler (1994) offer *cultural therapy* as an answer for educators who would address the multiple conflicts which divide individuals, families, and ethnic and socioeconomic groups in society. Cultural therapy is a process of healing that involves several steps. First, participants (teachers, students, families, and others) must acknowledge that cultural conflicts exist and make the nature of such conflict explicit. Next, participants must address how this conflict involves their *enduring* and *situated* selves. The enduring self is a sense of continuity with one's past and social identity, whereas the situated self is pragmatic, contextualized, and adaptable to changing conditions of everyday life. The enduring self can become *endangered* when it is "violated too often or too strongly by the requirements of the situated self ... (This) certainly occurs as children and youth of diverse cultural origins confront school cultures that are antagonistic to the premises and behavioral patterns of their own culture" (p. 14).[2] Finally, cultural therapy addresses the requirements for *instrumental competence* in schools, which includes academic skills as well as the social skills suitable for participation in the larger society. For example, teachers would be encouraged to prepare members of minority cultures for the requirements of test-taking, while acknowledging that test-taking is predicated on the ritualized norms of Anglo-oriented schools.

The healing principles of cultural therapy offer a framework for interpreting the work of Horace Kallen school with immigrant children and communities. By making diverse cultures and languages an important part of its focus, the school seeks to acknowledge the enduring selves of its students, valuing the traditions and beliefs of their families, while at the same time preparing them with the instrumental competencies they will need to adapt successfully to life within the dominant culture. Through the use of community liaisons such as Shou Cha and monthly meetings with parents, the school seeks to mediating between different worldviews, cultures, and ideologies, explaining the viewpoints of parents to school personnel, and explaining school policies and societal laws to immigrant groups such as the Hmong. Finally, through his role as "peacemaker" between various cultures at Kallen school Shou Cha has engaged in the process of making peace with America. In many ways his job as community liaison has been the antidote for the lingering psychic wounds and sense of alienation that he felt after being shot in 1994.

A FOCUS SCHOOL FOR LANGUAGE AND CULTURE

Horace Kallen is a focus school within the Windigo school district for the development of a multicultural and multilingual learning community. A school brochure states that "the Horace Kallen School promotes a positive international, interethnic and interracial climate by identifying, sharing and supporting cultural values from our Global Learning Community." A majority of the approximately 300 hundred students at the

---

[2]I consider the work of the Spindlers to be of particular relevance to this discussion of the schooling of members of minority cultures. My use of the *cultural therapy* to frame the interpretations within this chapter, however, should not be seen as a departure to previous frameworks I have utilized to conceptualize identity. Rather, the Spindlers offer a cultural and sociological perspective which I believe complements the psychological perspectives offered by Lifton's *proteanism* (as well as Eriksonian and Vygotskian concepts of identity).

school come from families that have recently immigrated from places such as Laos, Vietnam, Iraq, Mexico, and Haiti. Ninety percent of the students speak a first language other than English, and the school uses bilingual teaching aides extensively, along with specialized English as a Second Language ESL instruction for some students. Families choose to send children to Horace Kallen because the school claims to value diverse languages and cultures, and encourages ongoing dialogue between the school and linguistic minority communities. The school also plays an active role in educating the wider community in Windigo. School staff and children regularly participate in city-wide educational conferences and cultural festivals. Kallen also publishes and disseminates various materials, including a booklet on cultural traditions whose writers included refugee children and parents, teachers, the principal, the mayor of Windigo, and the president of the local university.

The school is guided by Diana Canek, an innovative and politically astute principal who has developed a program designed to meet the needs of largely low-income, nonnative speakers of English and their families. The school, now in its third full year of operation, is a direct descendant of Windigo school district's Center for Bilingual Instruction, which Canek used to lead. When the opportunity arose to create a public school of choice within the district, Canek and some of her colleagues jumped at the chance to create a school where language and culture would provide the thematic focus for an elementary school. The school has had the most "choice" applications of any school in the district, and now has a growing waiting list of families who wish to enroll their children. Hmong children make up one of the largest ethnic groups at Kallen, perhaps because their parents value the access to teachers and administrators through community liaisons and monthly parent meetings.

Diana Canek's views on culture have been strongly influenced by Hall's The Silent Language (1959), but also by her own experiences as a child moving between languages and cultures. She grew up speaking fluent Portuguese and Spanish and was quite comfortable in the cultural environments of Brazil, Chile and Guatemala, where her parents worked as diplomats. Nevertheless, she got her first serious case of culture shock, and the school's role in exacerbating cultural discontinuities, when she returned to rural Michigan at the age of 15 after a decade spent abroad.

At an interview in her cozy, dimly lit office, I ask Diana if Horace Kallen teaches its mostly immigrant students about American culture. Her response illustrates the primacy she gives to a sense of culture that is both inclusive and critical, and, as in the process of cultural therapy, to make explicit the cultural conflicts that exist in society:

The concern was raised by majority and minority groups when we were trying to get this school started. But I still defy anyone to tell me what American culture is, so that everyone could be included in it. The minute we start
defining what American culture is we are already going to exclude someone.
I have been blessed with the opportunity to have been raised somewhere
else, and to have come into this culture and figure out how to fit in. Being
Caucasian, everyone assumed I knew what America was, but my psyche
certainly didn't know. It was a very personal struggle for me to figure out
how to operate in this culture. I really don't want anyone else to have to go
through that. And interfere with learning about community, and values,
and friendship, and sharing, and all of these other elements that Hall says
are perfectly normal interactions irrespective of culture. So being an American to me doesn't mean knowing who George Washington is. That is not
critical. If you really were an American, the essence of an American, being
an American is to know that George Washington was the first president of
the United States, to know that he fought against the British for the inde-
pendence of this country, and to also know that he sent smallpox-ridden
blankets to the Indians of the Ohio valley so that he could seize that terri-
tory because they wouldn't sign a treaty with him. That, to me is to be an
American. It is to be a critical thinker, to not be afraid of the truth about an
individual, to not invest too much illusory confidence in a political leader.

Canek understands well that along with a critical literacy, an ability to
work as an individual on projects, tests, and other matters is one of the instrumental competencies children from other cultures need to learn to
adapt successfully in the United States:

The other thing that is unusual about us is the issue of individualism. I
think that probably characterizes what an American is probably more than
anything else. We encourage individualism, we don't want kids to be involved in group projects, although we understand that that is probably
better for learning, but when it comes down to the test, you know, you have
got to do it by yourself. So this spirit of individualism is something that I
think we need to teach in our school. Because that is the issue of survival in
this country. I think we have this tension between the individual and the
community that I don't think other countries have. And that is the kind of
issue that I think kids in this school should understand: You do have responsibility for yourself; but the cultures that come here have a responsibility to the group. So this tension for kids here, and the negotiation of these
two worlds, is kind of what we are here to do.

By acknowledging a role in this negotiation between the world of the
school and the world of the immigrant home and community, Canek highlights the importance of fostering the growth of individuals who are com-
petent in the skills needed for participation in the dominant culture, who

can yet maintain and develop their relationships to distinct cultural communities:

> We are here to say, there is the good of the whole, you can hang onto that, that is a very important aspect of human survival. But you can also blossom and flourish as an individual. And to me that is the essence of what being an American meant to my grandfathers who immigrated, and to my parents who went in between all the cultures, is that you don't have to sacrifice your cultural community to self-actualize as an individual. This school is that transition between those two social behaviors.

Canek is a well aware of the political nature of her work as principal, situated between the powerful institutions in society and the socially and economically marginalized students who attend Horace Kallen school. In her efforts to legitimize the cultures and languages of diverse families and communities, she also seeks to include members of the dominant culture:

> I don't want to present the diversity issue as a threat, or a challenge, or a divisive perspective. I am not interested in creating backlash. I am interested in creating coalitions, and to interpret for the power structure how important this coalition is for their survival. So symposiums. So booklets. So if someone sees that the president of the university and the mayor are involved in our "community traditions" project, that regular individuals who happen to be White Anglo-Saxon Protestants happen to be involved in these projects, and they are in the power structure, then maybe it is okay to talk about diversity. Maybe it is okay to consider it as reality, as something that we all embrace together. *We all have culture.* White ethnic people have culture. Diversity is not abnormal, it is not something you have to manage or deal with, because we all have culture, and we are all diverse, because we are Homo Sapiens evolving.

Rachel Gwynnod, assistant director at Kallen, describes the role of the school as an *ingathering* of children from diverse cultures and an *outflowing* of cultural and linguistic information to the entire community:

> There was some opposition to the idea of this kind of school, set up on purpose to have this kind of student body. After all, how are they going to learn how to be "Americans" if they are around each other all of the time? Of course the school was never designed to be exclusive of monolingual English or Anglo-Caucasian students. There is the potential for this to be not only unique, but very successful, and for kids to thrive and succeed in this kind of environment, to include aspects of world language. To be a hub for kids from all over the world and all over Windigo. Then to turn around and reach out with all the riches and the gifts that we have into the community, with symposiums, taking performing kids all over the city. At

once we are doing an ingathering of kids with diverse languages and cultures, and an outflowing of energy and information into the community. A reconnecting to the community.

Perhaps for our students, the best way to talk about what it means to be part of this country is by studying what community means. By understanding that there are all kinds of variations of people, and ideas, and perspectives that go into making any community, even the small one in Kansas where I was born! Maybe part of discussing America is discussing from a kid's point of view belonging.

Efforts to create civic-minded children who appreciate and tolerate diversity are not unique, though they may buck some of the current trends in educational reform. Proposals such as America 2000 seem to focus more on preparing young people to fill slots in the corporate world, and less on America's 200 hundred years of commitment to civic education and community. Bellah (see e.g., Bellah, Madison, Sullivan, Swindler, & Tipton, 1991) has been critical of an "economic ideology that turns human beings into relentless market maximizers undermining commitments to family, to church, to neighborhood, to school, and to the larger national and global societies" (p. 94). Bellah's emphasis on preparing citizens for a democracy echoes earlier concerns of Dewey, the great philosopher of American education. A strong advocate for education that was experiential and that connected students, teachers and schools with their society, Dewey (1900) also foreshadowed our continuing problem of an educational system that exacerbates class distinctions, "the division into 'cultured' people and 'workers,' the separation of theory and practice" (p. 27) For Dewey, to foster better learning and to build a more just, democratic society, schools needed to embody service and a sense of community:

When the school introduces and trains each child of society into membership within such a little community, saturating him with the spirit of service, and providing him with the instruments of effective self-direction, we shall have the deepest and best guaranty of a larger society which is worthy, lovely and harmonious. (p. 29)

The staff and students at Kallen school appear to be putting into practice such a vision of community; they offer educators and policymakers an alternative model for educating young people to live and work together for the benefit of all members of society.

CHILDREN OF MANY CULTURES

There are about 20 students present today in Ms. Torres' kindergarten class. They are many shades of brown and have names such as Chavez,

Ortega, Belazaire, Newman, Thao, and Lee. The room is very colorful also. Cut out crepe designs hang from the ceiling. There are lots of pictures on the walls, and two world maps. One is hand made. In the corner is a globe. The alphabet, with pictures of animals for each letter, adorns the front wall above the blackboard. Below the alphabet is a handmade poster created by one of the students in class, depicting activities at a Hmong New Year celebration. Numbers from 1 to 10, this time with pictures of sea animals, march across the back wall. Underneath this is a poster advocating "healthy habits" (these include teeth brushing, eating vegetables, etc.). On one of the side walls is a long picture entitled, "kids around the world." On the wall nearest me is a picture of kids with various skin colors and facial features hanging out together—not unlike the kids in this room. With the picture are the words: "We are alike in many ways. We are all special." Various activities are taking place at six areas in different parts of the room. Children rotate between these activities, which include math, computers, language arts, reading, puzzles and games, and listening.

Mr. Cha comes in from the playground where he has been supervising and playing with the kids. The first thing he does after hanging up his coat is to help Rodrigo in the math group. Shou shows the various numbers to Rodrigo on the back wall, and has him count with him. He has his hand on Rodrigo's shoulder. He then helps out kids at the listening group, then the literacy group, and thus around the room, as needed. When the groups switch, Shou goes back to the math center to help them pick up. All the while he vocally encourages the kids to treat their materials and each other with respect, and to learn. The kids keep calling out, "Mr. Cha, come look at this! Mr. Cha, can you help me?"

Shou has a no-nonsense approach with the children, but he speaks to them very calmly, even softly. He sees a girl named Lisa with her earphones on, but jumping around, and using her book roughly. Mr. Cha sits down, close. He takes off her earphones. She puts her hands over her ears. He says, "Lisa, I know you can hear me. You must listen and learn. So you can grow and be the nice girl you are meant to be."

Ana Torres, the teacher for this classroom, is a second generation Cuban American. She is continually amazed at how well children of many cultures in the classroom accept each other.

> Here there is such a mix in every class that you find. Whether it is their levels of speaking, their academic levels, their hair color—whatever—even though there are the differences, there are so many that it just makes it look like one whole class. I don't think the children look at it as all being different, but just everybody being in here, trying to get to the same goal. I feel like I am very fortunate to have kindergarten, because I get the majority of

my kids at the beginning of the school year. It is amazing the first day of school to see those children come in, and immediately, no matter what their background is those first 4 to 5 years at home, they come in and they *accept each other!* They don't even consider making fun of each other. They might stare with kind of a funny look, as if to say, I don't really think he is speaking in the same language that I speak, and it sounds a little different … The children just come to an understanding that the teacher is speaking in English, some other people are speaking in English. If there is an Arabic girl who wants to talk to a Vietnamese boy, they are all going to have to speak in a common language. It pulls them all together.

Wouldn't it be beautiful if we could send these kids out to educate the rest of the people about how to get along? It starts here. These kids are going to grow up and they are going to accept everybody that they run into for the rest of their lives. And if this could have only started way back when. This should have taken place years ago.

Ana describes Shou Cha, her bilingual assistant, as her "savior":

Those days without him are just long! I don't think he even understands how much I appreciate everything he does. This is my second year working with him. Now that we have spent this much time together I can't imagine teaching without him! I guess after you teach with somebody that long, you get used to each other and kind of click. So he knows on days when I am struggling for words or something, he will fill in. Or if he is having a problem disciplining, I can help him. Yeah, we really do complement each other. The way he works with the children is just beautiful. He really has a special way with him, and I think so many children these days really need a male role model this young. In so many school districts you don't see a male teacher until you get to junior high or high school. They get to thinking that all teachers are women. I think it is great to have him in the classroom for that reason. I get hugs on a daily basis, but he does, too. They see him as important. They don't look at me as the number one teacher. They know that both of us are teachers.

I think a lot of the interaction he has with the children comes from his home, and his background. He really does talk to the children in a gentle manner, even when disciplining. The children look him in the eyes and know it is coming from his heart. Sometimes he will throw out this *deep voice* and from across the room it draws a silence.

Ana continues in a voice like an old bear:

'Now you have to sit down!' It is really special how he interacts with the children.

In our lives outside of school, we both have strong religious backgrounds. I think that is very, very helpful when it comes to a point where you want to just yell and scream. I am guilty of that, sometimes, as a last alternative. I think religion has helped me keep my positive discipline, instead of the negative. The negative is always the easiest to turn to. I think his faith really helps him, also. We don't actually come out and preach or talk about religion in the classroom. It is something which we obviously cannot do in this school, because there are no many different religions. But I think the children feel it. I think it is part of our affection. Even if it is not a physical affection, it is an emotional affection they pick up from Mr. Cha and I, which I hope has a positive effect on the children.

Bellah et al. (1991) has suggested that religious traditions are an important element in American identity, and may provide a pathway from a culture that is highly individualistic and materialistic to one that is more communitarian in spirit. Religion may provide a sense of meaning, too, that many Americans, young and old, need in their lives:

> Religious communities ... help us grapple with the ultimate problem of meaning, of trying to find a way to live that is based on something more than cost-benefit calculations or desire; or whether we have a place in the universe at all and any abiding purpose to pursue there. (p. 218)

Religion gives meaning to the lives of Ana Torres and Shou Cha. They do not teach their religions in school, and have no need to: As Ana suggests, their spirituality moves them to form emotional bonds with children, and to engage others in the search for meaning. If meaning-making is to be a purpose for schools, then it must be recognized that spirituality can not be turned on and off, or left at the classroom door: It is all around us, all the time.

I ask Shou Cha what has been particularly interesting for him in his work as a bilingual aide and community liaison. He responds:

> There is another step, and another dimension. Before I worked at that school, I practiced at my religious school. But something was added to me when I got the school job. Something was added to me and my family and something was subtracted. I say that honestly. Some rules in the school in the United States are not really good enough. It needs to be more strict. I am talking about the discipline of children. And I know the rules in the United States, you don't discipline the way the family disciplines, but there is something that needs to be more strict.

Shou, like many parents, is concerned that his children learn in a disciplined environment at school. Perhaps he fears that too much freedom for children in schools could *subtract* from what they learn at home, contributing to laziness, violent behavior, or open sexuality, issues he raised earlier when discussing television programs and stories about family life.

Thus, Shou's view of schooling is complex: On the one hand, it is offers a site for making peace between the school and children of different ethnic communities. However, in order to make peace, a greater degree of discipline is necessary, and if children cannot discipline themselves, schools must provide the discipline for them. Shou translates this sense of discipline into a concept of responsibility for oneself and the group:

> I have some knowledge from the school, too, which is very good. I learn from the teacher who I work for. I see so many children who do not speak English, and of course they do not know the American culture or the way to live, or to keep things, or to take responsibility. I learn that they take that very seriously, too. I also learn that when the teacher explains to the children, whatever she needs to explain, she really makes it clear and she explains it well, and simple enough to understand. And she makes the children responsible for their things. I believe going to school like that is really helpful. Even though I am only an assistant teacher, and though I have never learned in a secular class, I have finished my introduction to education in the church, which is a little bit related. I also finished my course for children's evangelism, too, so it's kind of related. So I can see that school is very different from what I have learned, but some things are similar. I've learned a lot of things.

I ask Shou about his role in the classroom, and he responds:

> Kallen school is good because so many children do not speak English. They do not have the understanding to participate, or go on. And it is good, because we have help, regarding language, and also we have many people who can help you. And we have many children who are like you, who can encourage you by some ways, somehow, invisibly, so that you can go on. That school is especially good for that. The teacher explains, and she teaches, whatever she has planned to do, and after that, she needs help with twenty-four students. That is a lot of children. She helps one table, and I help another table. So many raise hands, to do this and do that, questions about this and that. And because of lack of language, too, I need to explain to my ethnic group, or even show examples, and that takes a lot of time.

Shou understands the importance of fostering friendships among children of diverse cultural backgrounds:

> The girls from the different countries can get very friendly with one another, but boys, not so much, and boys and girls, no. They do something totally against one another just because their skin color is different. So I called them together, and I said: 'You know, I didn't see what you did. Why I am calling you here together is this: Whatever you did, whatever you judged, whatever you think, you are wrong or you are right, I cannot make

the decision. You can make it yourself. But what I am doing here is this: You make peace. You talk about being friends over here.'

As with cultural therapy, Shou tries to make explicit with children the nature of cultural conflict in their immediate lives in the world at large:

I also go back to the wars in the world. I said, 'This country fights that country, and this other country fights that other country. The only reason is that they do the same thing: Someone says, 'that one I don't like.' Someone else says, 'This is not our people and that is not our people; that is why we fight.' So I show them that when they are against one another that is how they make enemies, and I don't like that. I tell them, 'This is not a school for fighting. We have to make friends.' So they hug, make friends, make peace. Something like this is pretty new for them. Sometimes they fight, but every time I work with them and tell them they have to be friends.

Central to Shou's efforts with these diverse children at Kallen School is that he adopts the role, not of judge, but of peacemaker. Moreover, he goes beyond the playground conflict to educate children about the nature of broader conflicts in the world. His message is clear: Wars and civil strife begin much the same as fist fights between two children at school. Once children decide that they have enemies, they allow themselves to be drawn into a lifelong struggle that can never be won. However, peace, too, can begin in the school, as simple and strong as an embrace, or the phrase, "Let us be friends."

I am reminded of how Jerry Lee's father always told his children not to fight in school. The Hmong, said Mr. Lee, knew what it was like to fight enemies. They fought their enemies in China. They fought their enemies in Laos. They fought their enemies, and they lost so much. There was no need to make new enemies in America. With a history of warfare and devastation fresh in their memories, perhaps Hmong Americans such as Shou Cha are ideal teachers of peace for our children and our society. When I ask Shou what he would pass on to the next generation of Americans, he says:

Just this: That we should make friendship. We are just the same people—black skin, brown skin, white, yellow—it does not make the difference. We are just different colors. But treat each one equally and nice. Don't just look at their skin and treat them badly.

LIAISON BETWEEN SCHOOL AND COMMUNITY

Two girls are running outside on the playground of Horace Kallen school. As they chase each other, the Hmong girl falls down with the other girl on top of her. The next day, the Hmong girl did not come back to school, nor the next. Diana Canek asks Pao Xiong why the girl is not attending class. Mr. Xiong looks troubled, saying, "When the girl fell with the other girl on top of her, she got scared, and her spirit fell down. Her parents have asked a shaman to come from Wisconsin to perform the ceremony to recover her spirit. And her mom would like the teachers to make sure that the kids don't play like that anymore." "Okay," says Ms. Canek, "We'll call it an excused absence."

The staff at Horace Kallen have helped to create an atmosphere of open communication across cultural and linguistic boundaries. Beyond addressing such diversity in the classroom, the school utilizes its bilingual assistants as liaisons to different linguistic and cultural communities. Rachel Gwynned, assistant director at Kallen school, suggests that the role played by the community liaisons is fundamental:

> The community liaison's role is so critical. They are the diplomatic corps, the glue, that has always been such an integral part of this type of program. Not only because of the legal aspect of having kids work with adults who speak their own language. Even if it weren't for that, it wouldn't make sense to run the program without their involvement. I'm not Hmong, and Diana's not Vietnamese or Laotian, and we don't know what we are talking about when it comes to defining critical elements in the families' lives, and their language, and what is meaningful and not meaningful for them. Insofar as having a certified teacher legitimizes what is going on in the classroom, having people that speak all the languages of the kids who study here, legitimizes this effort in the eyes of parents.

Canek is well aware of the special contribution Kallen's community liaisons in this work:

> The community liaisons are absolutely essential, especially for two reasons: The amount of stuff a building is supposed to pass out to parents, information that is either district-wide or city-wide or whatever, is just phenomenal. I can send them home, but it wouldn't mean anything, and they are not going to participate in it, even if it did mean anything, because it's Anglo orientation. So, with the community liaisons, we discuss what goes home: They are the ones who tell *me* what the community is interested in knowing about or participating in. I tell *them* things that we are doing so that they can tell the community to participate in them. Every single translation issue goes through the community liaisons.

The work of the community liaisons, in this sense, mirrors the use of bilingual staff at Covello's (1958) community-centered school in East Harlem:

We were not separate, off somewhere in a world of our own, unapproachable to the man, woman or child who could not speak English. How often have I seen the lightning joy on the face of a dubious immigrant parent when he hears the sound of a familiar tongue! How many barriers crumble before the shared language! (pp. 266–267)

Canek underscores the interpretive role that the liaisons play for the entire community:

The community liaisons are not just the Kallen liaisons—they are the entire Windigo School District liaisons. They will go to reinstatement hearings at the Board. They translate for custody issues with probate court. To be able to explain special education forms to people. They will translate intelligence tests, and explain why we even use those. The community liaison is critical in trying to interpret this culture and its expectations to that culture, and that culture and its expectations to this culture. I believe that it is two-way.

The role of the community liaisons is a political one as well, as Canek explains:

The other thing is they will tell me what the community will accept and won't accept. What are the politics, what are the nuances. Years ago, in the city-wide bilingual program, the Hmong community shared with me some of their concerns through the community liaison. I have seen the effects of one Hmong clan feeling disenfranchised, and moving to Fresno. We are talking about lots of people, who get up and leave, because the clan leader is unhappy.

Socially and economically marginalized groups such as the Hmong are inevitably involved in conflicts in school and society. In Windigo, one clan resolved its conflict with the schools by voting with their feet, and leaving the area. Elsewhere, Hmong communities have organized to promote changes in school policies. In St. Paul, Minnesota, Hmong families have joined the Association of Community Organizations for Reform Now (ACORN) in an effort to force the public schools to address various issues of concern, which include the need to hire more Hmong staff people as teachers, counselors, and interpreters, and the adoption of curricula that value and acknowledge Hmong people and culture (United Hmong Parents/ACORN, 1994). Whereas the Spindlers suggest that cultural conflicts need to be explicitly made clear and addressed for a process of healing to begin, organized groups of immigrants such as the Hmong go further by linking the process of education in the schools with the need for social justice.

Covello and Horton are two educators who have argued that a concern for social justice must be a factor in the process of peace making between the school, the home and society. Tyack and Hansot (1982) write that Covello "believed that the school itself should mobilize neighborhood people to bring about social justice" (p. 210). Like Covello, Myles Horton (1990), founder of Highlander School, has argued that educators need to addressing real conflicts in society, community organizing, and making peace among diverse groups must go hand in hand. Moreover, Horton suggests that schools can help channel decision-making powers and responsibilities to members of the community:

> If we are to have a democratic society, people must find or invent new channels through which decisions can be made. Given genuine decision-making powers, people not only learn rapidly to make socially useful decisions, but they will also assume responsibilities for carrying out decisions based on their collective judgment ... to convince people who have been ignored or excluded in the past that their involvement will have meaning and that their ideas will be respected. (p. 134)

Community liaisons represent new channels of decision-making as practiced at Horace Kallen school. By entrusting bilingual assistants with this liaison role, the school has earned the trust of various immigrant communities, exemplified by the waiting list of families who would like their children to study there.

It has taken time to build such trust, and the process is ongoing. Xiong, the first Hmong bilingual aide to serve the children of Windigo, describes the many cultural and linguistic barriers that often separate the Hmong community from the school, and how he and other community liaisons must mediate between two very different worlds:

> There are many things that the parents and the school see differently. Sometimes the parents don't understand the school, and the school doesn't understand the parents. For example, one day a Hmong kid came late from the bathroom so he missed his lunch. We brought him a lunch, and he was eating in the office. There were no chairs for him, and the table was kind of high for him, so he could not stand up and eat, and he could not sit completely down and eat. And then some people in the office thought that it was Okay if he could put his knees down and eat on his knees. In Hmong culture, most parents would not want their kids kneeling down and eating. When they eat they should sit down, or stand up, or eat walking, but they can't kneel down. Some of the staff at the school were not aware of that. So the kid was eating on his knees. And then his mom came, and happened to be there, and she saw her son kneeling and eating. This upset her, but she did not say anything. And I saw this, and I said to myself, 'Oops!' This is something that we should not do. In our culture, if anyone is eating on their

knees, then we say that person in the future will become a slave. My mom and my dad used to say, 'No, no, you never kneel down!'

Children at Horace Kallen must cross distinct cultural and linguistic boundaries every day, making transitions between the multiple worlds of the self, family, school, peers, and the larger socioeconomic community (Phelan & Davidson, 1994). Xiong feels for these kids, but believes that his own experience as a Hmong teen in American schools taught him lessons that he hopes to pass on to schools, children and their parents:

The reason I want to be in the field of education is that I have been in the process of learning to switch from a different culture and language to this culture and language. I saw how I adjusted to this culture and this language, and decided that maybe I could be the one to help the other kids who are in the same situation. Maybe I can help make it easier for them. When I first came, the school here was very different from what I had in Laos. I had to try very hard to adjust myself or I could not have fit into this culture at all. Academics was hard, because it was not in my language. The other part was social. The students here will act differently, will talk differently, will respect their friends and teachers differently. They had a different idea about how to be a student than me. What worked in my country wouldn't work here.

I was the first one of my generation that my parents put their trust in, so whatever I said, or whatever I decided, my mom or my family would respect that. They said, 'You are the only one that we depend on, and you are the first one to step into school and education in the culture of this country. We rely on you.' They didn't speak any English, and they relied totally on me. That made me try to be as positive as I could be.

For students right now, it is different. The parents think they know a little bit about school, and they want the discipline to be the way they want it. The students see differently, and so sometimes there is a conflict.

A practitioner of traditional Hmong religion, Xiong understands that it is important to be tolerant of diverse religious beliefs within the Hmong community:

I have to be very cautious about myself, and be flexible, and respectful of different opinions. If I happen to deal with a family that is Christian, I would respect the way they believe. I would never say, no, no, what you did is not right. I would say, whatever you did is right. The religious part I don't really want to get into. I try to focus on school issues.

Though they practice different religions, Pao and Shou say they have no trouble working together to serve the Hmong community.

The job of the community liaison is complex. A community liaison is a mediator, a bridge, a peacemaker between two very different cultures and paradigms. He is also a public servant, always on call. The liaisons assist teachers in the classroom, interpret for children, translate documents for the school, and interpret for members of the Hmong community when they have interactions with the school, and provide lunchroom and special activity assistance. Pao Xiong underscores that the community liaison's job does not end when school gets out, but continues on into the evening and on weekends:

> If I just did the job, I wouldn't have to worry about the community, the outside. But I have to be responsible inside the classroom, making sure every student gets what they need; and also, when I go home, I have another community out there where everybody knows each other. They will call me in the middle of the night, they can call me anytime, and they will discuss about an issue in the school, and they will ask all kinds of questions. There are all kinds of ceremonies going on in the community, and we have to help each other together. I have a big responsibility, a 24 hour responsibility. My work in the community is tied to my work here. We build trust. And they also see that when I work at the school, I represent them. When I tell them what I have seen, and what I think is good about the school, they will believe that it will benefit their community, and benefit their family.

For Xiong and Shou, being a community liaison represents the fulfillment of a duty to their Hmong community. For Ms. Canek and Ms. Gwynned, a community liaison represents the possibility of opening channels of communication and legitimacy for American culture and the cultures of the home. For all members of American society, the concept of community liaisons represents the challenge of building bridges between schools, the school board, the courts, social service agencies, and parents and children of different linguistic and cultural groups. The importance of two-way communication between the school and families, facilitated by community liaisons, is critical. Smrekar (1996) suggests that such communication not only builds community trust, but academic success for youth:

> Trusting, cooperative and mutually supportive relations between parents and teachers act as a linchpin to promote rewarding and successful academic experiences for students. Conversely, ambiguity, conflict and distance may undercut the level and nature of social interactions between these groups, producing a pattern of inconsistent and incomplete information exchange. (p. 161)

The community liaisons are thus the interpreters and bearers of information between distinct communities and world views. They help make possible relationships between school and community that are not based on a common language or understanding of the world, but on trust.

Shou Cha indicates that a high level of trust with the community also allows liaisons to warn parents when they are in danger of breaking school policies or the laws of the land:

> Sometimes the parents make a mistake that goes against school policy, or even sometimes against the law of this country. And I see it, or Pao sees it, and then we can deal with the people before it reaches the law. We can say, 'This is the first warning and we do not need to see this anymore. This country has such and such a law, this is against the law, so do not let this happen again.' And we also say, 'Because we are the same kind of people, I have to tell you first, I know we are newly resettled in this country, and there are a lot of things to learn, but there are some things we should be careful of, like child abuse, sometimes children are not properly dressed, or things like that.'

In many ways the community liaison program at Horace Kallen school parallels Walker-Moffat's (1995) suggestions for family-based multicultural education. She specifically argues for the use of paraprofessional counselors from the various cultures represented in a school because "parents and students need access to someone who works in the schools who understands their culture and background and speaks their language" (p. 170). Galindo and Olguin (1996) have further argued that bilingual, minority educators must draw on their cultural resources in order to fully realized their potential and make lasting contributions to the education of children. By building bridges to families through the use of such bicultural teachers, counselors and liaisons, schools recreate the spirit of Covello's community-centered curriculum in East Harlem. Moreover, bicultural paraprofessionals, such as Shou Cha, have an important role to play in the classroom as makers of peace between diverse children and the world of the school.

THE EDUCATION OF A NEW AMERICAN

It is quite late, and the children have all gone upstairs. Though we sit just a few feet apart in his quiet living room, the shadows separate Shou and I, and his strong facial features melt into the darkness. We talk about images of immigrants in America, and what it means to be an American.

Shou says,

> Back in Milwaukee, when I had an ESL teacher, we studied about the Roman world. The Romans had a way of becoming citizens, too. We were talk-

ing about the United States compared to the Roman Empire in Milwaukee. The Roman Empire was very powerful, but they fell. They fell. And our teacher asked, 'What do you think? What do you think about the United States? Will it fall some day too?' When I look at it today, it could fall. It could fall.

I can't help thinking of the anti-immigrant mood that has been growing of late in America, and has influenced immigration reform legislation in Congress, English Only initiatives, and a good deal of racial and ethnic strife. The Hmong, in fact, due to their high levels of poverty and dependence on public welfare as well as their maintenance of strong cultural traditions, have helped influence at least one writer to advocate a moratorium on immigration (Beck, 1994). To Shou I say:

In the United States, a lot of people will say that the trouble is the people who want to maintain their culture or their language. Some people see this as a threat. They say that is going to destroy America. If you want to speak Hmong and keep Hmong traditions with your kids, that is a threat. If people want to keep Mexican traditions who are living here, that is a threat. If people speak other languages than English, some people think that is a threat, and will destroy America.

Thoughtfully, Shou responds:

The way I see it, that could happen. But that is not a very big concern to me. Talking back to when the Hmong people helped the American people fight the war in Laos. Suppose that idea carries on, and the Hmong people, population, which grows in the United States, they keep their strength, they keep their idea, and they keep their principle of leading, and they keep their principle of fellowship. Then suppose America somehow becomes politically unstable, then the Hmong people are among those who could help. Because they just help those whom they trust.

Shou hasn't always trusted America and Americans. After being shot in 1994, he did not feel that he had a home in America, and became more distrustful of those who were not members of his Hmong community. Interestingly, his attitudes about Americans and America have changed substantially since he has been placed in the position of liaison between the Hmong community the school, and the society. Shou has told me that, as he has worked with the diverse teachers, liaisons, and children at Horace Kallen, he has begun to feel a part of a larger community. Perhaps this active engagement in teaching and learning from others has been an antidote for the lingering sense of alienation Shou felt after being shot in 1994. His has been a process of cultural therapy, a coming to grips with the conflicts and traumas of his eventful life, a learning to acknowledge changefulness while respecting that which endures in individuals, in families, and in communities.

Shou speaks:

> *Before this job as community liaison,*
> *Isolation*
> *was always in front of me.*
> *I isolated myself from African-*
> *Americans,*
> *I isolated myself from Mexican-*
> *Americans,*
> *I isolated myself from other*
> *Americans.*
> *And now I can say*
> *that is not right.*
>
> *Many different peoples live in the*
> *same town*
> *black, brown, yellow*
> *if they look a certain way, they have*
> *their own community.*
> *I don't deny it,*
> *it is good to serve your own*
> *community.*
> *Please do your best for them.*
> *But then you should*
> *treat others nicely, too.*
> *black, white, brown, yellow*
> *we are the same people.*
> *We are different in skin only,*
> *but we are all human.*
> *We are the same, created by God,*
> *one creator,*
> *and it is very beautiful.*
> *Different colors, and very beautiful.*

At Kallen school we have many, many cultures, but we focus on the major culture: which is the community, the city you live in, and the country where you live! I know that there are some things you cannot add to this culture—of course not! But something that we learn to adapt ourselves to. It's American culture. But that does not mean "white" culture. America, even though I am not a citizen yet, America is this country, is my country!

Shou's life experiences have taught him that all things must change, and have prepared him to adapt to meet the challenges of new languages, cultures, and economic and social realities. Intrinsically, he realizes that children growing up in America must adapt to the dominant cultural and linguistic norms of the nation. Yet he has also laid claim to the American experience: This is his country, even if he is not a citizen yet. This country must honor the experiences of all of its people, black, brown, yellow, white. American culture, for Shou, is like the *pandau* of the Hmong: In order to tell the story, you must weave together threads of many colors.

In many ways the educational philosophy of the Horace Kallen school follows the tradition of Dewey's "Great Community" and Covello's community-centered curriculum. They are engaged in a process of cultural therapy, of making peace between immigrant children and their parents, who are often operating with different cultural scripts; between different ethnic and immigrant communities, some of whom have long-standing animosities that they bring from their previous homelands; between the worldview of the larger society, represented in the school, and the various worldviews of different communities. Community liaisons such as Cha and Xiong are golden, as Gwynned suggests, for they are the ideal peacemakers in this complex web of multicultural relationships.

Shou Cha has had a remarkable preparation for the role of peacemaker between families, communities, school, and society. The lessons of peace have been learned over the course of his lifetime, from his earliest childhood memories up through his work with Horace Kallen school. As a child, he was made aware of the long history of movement of his people, as ever they searched for a land where they could be free, and live in peace. He experienced the absence of peace when war came to northern Laos, a war in which many, including his older brother, lost their lives, while most lost their homes and livelihoods as well. He learned the skills of a border crosser, speaking four languages fluently, able to move back and forth between the unsafe worlds of Thai military officials, communist-controlled villages, and the jungle refuges of Hmong guerrillas.

Throughout his life, Shou has learned the importance of maintaining relationships between and within families. While he has taken an active role as a peacemaker to families within his Cha clan, his relationships between generations of his own family have provided him with invaluable insights. Shou realizes the importance of dialogue, the kind of dialogue he rarely experienced with his own father, and that he now has trouble establishing with his son. Although he claims to have no clear answers as to how such a dialogue can be established, he is sure that the absence of dialogue, and the trust that it instills, spells trouble for Hmong families and the entire community.

Shou's conversion to Christianity began a new stage of his education as a peacemaker. By adopting this religion as his own, he recognized bonds to millions of other believers in the wide world beyond his immediate Hmong community. Shou became a minister trained to take the *word* to the unreached, and dedicated to serving Christian and non-Christian alike. Yet, in the nature of his work as an evangelical minister, is the *word* of faith a monologue that others must accept, or a dialogue to which all can contribute? Paradoxically, Shou's conversion has meant a break in his relationship with the spirit of his father, who never accepted Christianity. At this fundamental level, Shou must experience a lack of peace, a sense of fatherlessness.

Finally, Shou has learned that America, also, can be a place of peace. He has experienced both the isolation as well as the physical violence that is too much a part of urban life in the United States. Returning from the hospital after being shot 2 years ago, Shou believed that there was "no place of peace on Earth." Yet, in the aftermath of his shooting, he learned that his neighbors and his community cared for him, and would help him. He was hired by Horace Kallen school to be a liaison for the Hmong community. There, surrounded by teachers, paraprofessionals, and students who represented the rich diversity and promise of America, Shou learned perhaps his most important lesson: That all people are created equal, that all people are beautiful, and that no one need live in isolation and fear. This has been the education of a new American. Now it is Shou's turn to help guide the next generation in the ways of peace.

III

Learning From a Life

7

Resourcefulness, Relationship, Respect: Learning From a Life

One's Self I sing, a simple, separate Person;
Yet utter the word Democratic, the word *en masse.*
—Walt Whitman (1968, p. 35)

Through Shou Cha's lifetime of learning, and his relationships with history, family, community, and school, three themes emerge that imply an important set of values, *resourcefulness, relationship,* and *respect,* which I will relate to a new conceptualization of the *self.* Beyond their alliterative appeal, these 3 R's are significant in that these values are rooted in Hmong tradition, but they are present in American communitarian traditions as well. Nevertheless, these values are often obscured by a contemporary American culture that is both individualistic and clannish, where participation in civic and social associations has declined (Bellah et al., 1991; Putnam, 1995). Moreover, for many Americans there is a growing fear, fed by stereotypes presented in the mass media, of *outsiders,* whether they be from across the border or across town. In such a world, in such an era, schools need to renegotiate their role as educational institutions in society.

Gutmann (1987) has argued that the schools must recognize their roles as moral agents and that civic education, "the cultivation of the virtues, knowledge and skills necessary for political participation—has moral primacy over other purposes of public education in a democratic society" (p. 287). Schools, the places where we hope to socialize the next generation into their role as citizens of America and the world, are both influenced by, and influence, the mores of the society. Certainly, schools can, and do, reinforce individualism in some of their practices, by placing high value on individual achievement and little value on community. On the other hand, schools such as Horace Kallen can, and do, influence students to value their resourcefulness as speakers of languages other than English; to value their relationships with their families, their peers, and their communities; and to respect each other, their diverse histories and beliefs, and all living things on the planet.

In this chapter, I argue that 3 R's—resourcefulness, relationship, and respect—not only give us a sense of who Shou Cha is as a new American, but a new conception of what it means to be an American as we approach the 21st century. Furthermore, I suggest some lessons for educators, policymakers, researchers, and all Americans from this life history of Shou Cha.

ELEMENTS OF A NEW IDENTITY

Shou Cha's many roles include those of husband, father to seven children, evangelical minister, Hmong community elder, and bilingual assistant, and school-community liaison. For him there is a sense of continuity between his great-great-grandfather who led many Hmong people out of China in the 19th century, and himself, who led over 100 members of his village to safety in Thailand in 1979. Although he recognizes that the Hmong people will change as society changes, Shou Cha suggests that the Hmong will keep their relationship with family and clan , their sense of respect for elders, their fellowship with other Hmong and such friends as have earned their trust, and the leadership that has brought them safely through genocidal wars to the United States. Language and certain cultural traditions and practices may change, but for Shou Cha, certain qualities of Hmongness are not optional. He says:

> Because the society changes, I guess most of the Hmong culture will be changed, too. No matter whether Hmong people like it or not, it has already changed. Totally changed. Even if we keep a Hmong church, I preach in my own language, we sing our songs, and when we come home we keep our culture, our way of life. I know we are changing. And Hmong always change. (But) Hmong keep one thing forever: The relationship. The relationship and the respect. Things like that you keep forever. If you lose it, then, that's it, you're gone.

The words of Shou Cha seem to indicate that his identity as a Hmong American is always changing and adapting; it is an identity based on a complex series of relationships; and, within these changes and supported by these relational ties, there is a sense of inner continuity. But this sense of continuity, for Shou, does not hinge on the maintenance of a language or the outer trappings of a culture. Rather, it appears to hinge on the maintenance of certain values, that are at once Hmong and American:

resourcefulness, which Shou does not name, but which his life illustrates in many ways; relationship; and respect.

The Resourceful Self

Resourcefulness, the ability to deal effectively with problems and difficulties, comes from the French word *resourdre,* "to arise anew."[1] Shou Cha has needed resourcefulness to overcome a series of adversities in his life, including the loss of his homeland, adaptation to a new culture and language, continuing poverty, and the near loss of his own life. His ability to learn and adapt during these crises has allowed him to "arise anew" and continue. Shou Cha's *resourceful self* is perhaps an adaptation to what psychologist Lifton (1993) calls our *protean* era:

> The protean self emerges from confusion, from the widespread feeling that we are losing our psychological moorings ... But rather than collapse under these threats and pulls, the self turns out to be surprisingly resilient. It makes use of bits and pieces here and there and somehow keeps going ... We find ourselves evolving a self of many possibilities, one that has risks and pitfalls but at the same time holds out considerable promise for the human future. (p. 1)

Much like Lifton's protean individual, Shou Cha's *resourceful self* has adapted, grown and changed with the circumstances. He is a man educated in the world as much as in schools. As a youth he learned from experience, mastering the skills for farming in the mountains and hunting in the jungle. He learned the stories of his ancestors, and such lessons from the past guided him in his entry into a complex social group, during times of war and peace.

Shou Cha's life provides evidence to support a theory of adult learning that encompasses the wide world outside of schools, and outside of the experience of people who have grown up in more technologically developed countries. Cremin (1988) has argued that substantial education can occur through family, neighborhood, church and business, and Ryff (1989) has suggested several criteria for successful aging, including self-acceptance, positive relationships with others, autonomy, purpose in life, and personal growth. Moreover, like the Spindlers' *situated* self, Shou's resourceful self is both adaptable and masterful of the instrumental competencies needed for survival in a dominant culture. Certainly Shou has shown his resourcefulness by taking educational opportunities that arise: He took the time to study photography when he first arrived in

---

[1]This definition of resourcefulness, and the definitions of relationship and respect which follow, are from *Webster's New Universal Unabridged Dictionary,* 2nd edition.

the refugee camps in Thailand, and this skill allowed him to document life in Laos when he returned as a revolutionary. He embraced evangelical Christianity, and as he has served the church, the church has also served him in many ways. Shou's participation with refugee camp missionaries allowed him to learn to teach and preach, to gain a modest income, and to learn English, which would facilitate his acceptance as a refugee in the United States. Furthermore, conversion to Christianity opened the door to a larger world, and to an immediate connection with diverse peoples far beyond the Hmong homeland in Southeast Asia. Shou has taken the opportunity to continue his education, through a ministerial program that better prepared him as a preacher and in English literacy, through adult education and high school completion programs, and through daily conversations with teachers and community liaisons at the school where he works. Finally, Shou shows the resourcefulness of a hard-working Hmong American pursuing career opportunities as they arise. In his ministerial work, it is not uncommon for him to spend the evening of Saturday and all day Sunday commuting between far-flung communities of believers.

Yet, Shou's resourcefulness is not unique within his family or within the Hmong American community. His wife, Mai, needs this quality to keep a large family together while her husband is absent, at work, or on the road to a ministry. Their children also show resourcefulness as they find ways to help each other manage the transition from an immigrant home to the school and back again. Finally, the Hmong community is noteworthy for its complex network of mutual support, despite the limited income of most of the community's members. When a family arrives to Windigo, the community helps find them a house, a car, a school for the children, and a job. This type of mutual aid one often finds in refugee and immigrant groups, and their is a long history of such community support in the United States.

Perhaps the traumatic changes in the life of refugees and immigrants facilitate the development of resourceful self. Riegel (1976) has argued that significant learning occurs through the management of life crises, that development follows change. Certainly this can be seen in the case of Shou Cha. The change from leaving a life of farming in the mountains of Laos to life in a crowded refugee camp challenged Shou to find a new meaning for his existence. This meaning he found in evangelical Christianity. The change from life in Southeast Asia to a new life in America encouraged Shou's to become literate in English. The trauma of being shot and seriously wounded caused Shou to think seriously about the United States as a home, yet in the aftermath of that shooting he realized his connection to a broader group of Americans beyond the Hmong community.

Like Lifton's description of the protean self, Shou Cha has moved toward species consciousness, and a sense of commonality with others.

The Respectful Self

The word *respect*, to notice with special attention, and treat with courtesy, comes from the Latin *respectare,* "to look behind." Respect is of central importance in the establishment and maintenance of Shou Cha's complex relationships with other people and the world. Shou Cha's *respectful self* recalls the Spindlers' *enduring* self, with its connection to the past and its sense of continuity with the future. Shou Cha demonstrates a respect for his cultural and familial heritage, recalling stories about his heroic great- great- grandfather, his experiences with his own father and mother, and the Hmong traditions of Laos and America. Unfortunately, Shou's position in the chain of relationships linking his father to his son is compromised by his inability to respect his father's rejection of Christianity. Nevertheless, Shou demonstrates a respect for seemingly disparate cultural beliefs, and has the ability to incorporate tenets of Hmong tradition such as the Thunder Angel and tenets of modern science into a larger belief system. Respect allows Shou Cha to expand his own understanding of the world, breaking down the dichotomies that some would make between "Eastern" and "Western" thought, or "superstition" and "science."

Shou shows a deep respect for education, both formal and informal, and has been active in the schools as a parent and as an educator. Since his childhood he has learned to respect both the experiential knowledge of the world and the knowledge that can be obtained through books. Both Shou and Mai take seriously their roles as primary educators of their children, assisting their children with homework when they can, and encouraging them to continue their studies even when, as parents, they no longer grasp the advanced subject matter of their children's work. Within the school where he works, Shou encourages all children to respect their teacher, the educational process, and themselves. He encourages his own children and the children at Kallen school to dream, to envision themselves not as the people they are, but as the people they would like to be. Education in the world and in the word of literacy has transformed his own life, and Shou recognizes the potential for it to change the lives of others as well.

Finally, Shou has learned to respect the differences between the various cultural groups that make up his school, his neighborhood, and his country of adoption. Like many refugees living in America's impoverished inner cities, Shou has known the fear of the outsider. When he was shot near his home in Windigo, he could have given up on America and its people, and built a wall between himself and outsiders to the Hmong community. Moreover, as an immigrant parent who arrived to this country with a strong cultural and linguistic heritage, Shou also sees the importance of respecting certain borders between communities so that a continuity in minority cultural traditions can be maintained.

Nevertheless, Shou learned through his experience as a bilingual assistant and community liaison to come to terms with American diversity. He no longer distances himself from African Americans, Mexican Americans, and "Other" Americans, for such are the colleagues with whom he works, and the children with whom he teaches and learns. With these associations has come understanding, and this understanding has enabled Shou to play the role of peacemaker in his school, community and society. His experience working with diverse Americans, coupled with his Christian faith, has enabled Shou to respect the beauty in all people.

Bellah et al. (1991) has suggested that a sense of respect for all people and all life must be fundamental to a renewal of the American people and American society:

> When we care only about what Toqueville called the "little circle of our family and friends" or only about people with skin the same color as ours, we are certainly not acting responsibly to create a good national society. When we care only about our own nation, we do not contribute much to a good world society. When we care only about human beings, we do not treat the natural world with the respect that it deserves. (p. 285)

Through new Americans such as Shou Cha we learn again the complexities of the respectful self when one can acknowledge an allegiance to one's group as well as one's membership in a larger whole.

The Relational Self

Relationship, a connection, comes from the Latin *referre,* "to bring back." Throughout his life history Shou Cha describes himself best when he brings back up his relationships to others. Gilligan (1988) supports such a model of the "relational" self, contrasting it with the "mirrored" self so prevalent in modern psychology: "When others are described as objects for self-reflection or as the means to self-discovery and self-recognition, the language of relationships is drained of motion and, thus, becomes lifeless" (p. 7).

In the relational self, "self is known in the experience of connection and defined not by reflection but by interaction, the responsiveness of human engagement" and "within this framework, the central metaphor of identity formation becomes dialogue rather than mirroring" (pp. 7, 17).

For Gilligan, without relationships, the self ceases to exist. In an important respect, the *relational self* alters the unnatural dichotomy of the Spindlers' *enduring* and *situated* selves: One's dialogues are at once with the past and the future, with the inner self and with others, with the bearers of one's cultural and linguistic traditions and with members of the dominant culture. The value Shou Cha places on *relationship* is clear from his many stories involving history, family, community, and society. Shou relates his sense of the present to stories from the past, of his great-great-grandfather, and the long struggle for freedom of the Hmong people. Significantly, Shou seems to see himself as a player in a larger story, the history of his people, and, since his conversion to Christianity, the biblical story of God's relationship to humankind.

Interestingly, Shou takes a long, generational view of family relationships, using stories of his interactions with his father and brothers to try to shed light on his relationship to his son. Significantly, Shou and Mai worry most about their children when they seem no longer interested in doing things together with the family. Shou takes seriously changes that might threaten the family relationship, as he showed when he discussed the Pathet Lao's attempt to alter husband–wife relationships in Laos. Paradoxically, Shou's new Christian beliefs would also threaten the relationship with his family, and particularly to the spirit of his father. Shou's broken ties to those, like his father, who remained "unreached," represents the dark side of change: Some relationships may be unretrievably lost.

Within the Hmong community, Shou has been an advocate for strengthening relationships within and between families, and has volunteered to organize workshops for members of his Cha clan to encourage dialogue and communication between the older and younger generations. Moreover, Shou has worked to build relationships across clans through his religious community, and between his circle of believers and those who practice traditional Hmong religion. This communitarian spirit is exemplified as much by his participation in mutual aid efforts to his willingness to pray at the bedside of non-Christians who are sick.

Finally, through his efforts as a community liaison and bilingual assistant at an elementary school, Shou encourages the development of relationships across cultures between school children, professionals, and community members. As an exponent of *making peace*, Shou has learned from his relationships with diverse children and staff at Horace Kallen school and brings this knowledge of diversity to bear on his relationships with children. Today he can acknowledge that all people are beautiful, whatever the color of their skin or the language that they speak.

Conceptualizing the resourceful, respectful and relational selves may offer a more wholistic perspective into the narrative lives of immigrants such as Shou Cha. At once there is the recognition of movement and change drawn from Lifton's sense of proteanism, the need for continuity as well as flexibility present in the Spindlers' conception of enduring and situational selves, and an acknowledgment of the overriding importance of relationships as postulated by Gilligan. Moreover, the values of resourcefulness, relationship and respect inherent in this understanding of the self are 3 R's needed for the education of a new generation of Americans who can move beyond individualism to a sense of collective responsibility.

THREE R'S FOR AN AMERICAN COMMUNITY

Lifton (1993) refers to America as the "protean nation," the nation of changefulness, and the nation most in search of itself: "Dislocated from our beginnings, we are the home of traditional flux. Our great cultural themes (are) the ever-beckoning frontier and continuous influx of immigrants" (p. 33).

This search for America and oneself is exemplified in the immigrant stories of Rodriguez and Covello in chapter two. Rodriguez' story illustrates a belief in the individual and his or her ability to overcome family and tradition through education, and enter a broader American dialogue. Covello's story is somewhat different: While in his own life experience we see the potential for individual growth and betterment in America, Covello also makes a strong case for the importance of relationships with family, neighborhood and community. The individual, in Covello's world, makes a difference by engaging with others in community, and education is a communal, not just an individual, process.

The values of resourcefulness, relationship, and respect that arise from Shou Cha's narrative offer another way to frame the discussion of the role of the school between individual, community and society. These values are responses of the *self* to individual, communal and societal needs; facilitated by a school such as Horace Kallen, these 3 R's allow for individual initiative as well as responsibility to the group, respect for community traditions as well as flexibility when faced with powerful technological, economic and social changes. These 3 R's provide a bridge between our understanding of where we have been as Americans, where we are, and where we would go.

Living in a nation in flux, where images of the frontier and immigrant arrival have always been strong, Americans have often defined themselves more through identification of a common enemy than through common values or ideals. As Lifton (1993) suggests, recent history has shown that when we cannot define ourselves through our opposition to a common enemy, we are at a loss to describe who we are:

> Over the previous decades, whatever our deficiencies or decline, whatever wrongs we perpetrated abroad or at home, we could still view ourselves, in contrast with Soviet evil, as steady in our virtue. Denied that contrast, we find it hard to see ourselves as steady in anything. (p. 33)

For Erikson (1959a), the immigrant from Germany, there was a certain clannishness present in Americans who constantly made choices between the principles of a religious and political Puritanism and an ever-shifting set of slogans:

> To leave his choices open, the American, on the whole, lives with two sets of "truths": a set of religious principles or religiously pronounced political principles of a highly puritan quality, and a set of shifting slogans, which indicate what, at a given time, one may get away with on the basis of not more than a hunch, a mood, or a notion. The same child may have been exposed in succession or alternately to sudden decisions expressing the slogans "Let's get the hell out of here," and again, "Let's stay and keep the bastards out"—to mention only two of the most sweeping ones. (Erikson, 1959a, p. 287)

With the end of the Cold War identity-conscious Americans have been left with a choice: to seek out new enemies to rally against, in Panama, in Iraq, across the Mexican border, or across town, and to try and redefine ourselves in opposition to the threats, however remote, that these foes represent; or to develop an identity based on civic interaction, on making peace within our own people, and working for peace in the world.

The values of resourcefulness, relationship, and respect provide a bridge to a new sense of identity for the American community, one that moves beyond individualism and the identification of an enemy to greater sense of community responsibility. The Spindlers (1990) have argued that the *real* enemy to the American cultural dialogue is inequity, fostered by "individualistic, self-oriented success, the successful drive for wealth by individuals uncommitted to the public good" (p. 165). Shou Cha, one participant in the American cultural dialogue, has taught us that resourcefulness can imply the best of individual initiative, but in service not just to oneself but to others; relationship encompasses the importance for the individual of ties to family, community, nation, and world; respect allows individuals to relate themselves to all people and all life.

Toqueville, a visitor from France to the United States in the 19th century, found Americans to be resourceful, civic-minded, and individualistic, yet hopeful about the creation of a new society through the power of education:

> The majority of [Americans] believe that a man by following his own interest, rightly understood, will be led to do what is just and good. They hold that every man is born in possession of the right of self-government, and that no one has the right of constraining his fellow creatures to be happy. They have all a lively faith in the perfectibility of man, they judge that the diffusion of knowledge must necessarily be advantageous, and the consequences of ignorance fatal; they all consider society as a body in a state of improvement, humanity as a changing scene, in which nothing is, or ought to be, permanent; and they admit that what appears to them today to be good, may be superseded by something better tomorrow. I do not give all these opinions as true, but as American opinions. (1945, p. 393)

Americans, as Toqueville realized, have ever embraced change and the promise it held for a better world. At our best, we have sought to make that promise a reality for all of our citizens, not just for a chosen few. Bellah et al. (1991) has argued that in order to create a *good society*, Americans must learn to attend to, and care for, their families, their communities, their nation and their world; that by taking responsibility for themselves and each other, Americans can build bridges of trust across the barriers that often divide people of different economic levels, ethnicities, religions, or genders; that through a politics of generativity, Americans can acknowledge their respect for both those generations who have come before and provide for those generations that will follow. Resourcefulness, relationship, and respect, when taken seriously as part of the moral education of all Americans, can be steps on the road to a good society.

LEARNING FROM A LIFE

Through stories, dialogues, and lived example, Shou Cha has educated me in a variety of ways: I have learned about the importance of history, and how the arrival of a refugee in the United States is but the latest chapter in a relationship where the loyalty of the Hmong people came into contact with the geopolitics of the American nation. Learning about Shou's life has taught me that religion and literacy can be a powerful combination, and has reminded me of the traumatic change a new religion can bring to a family and community relationship. As a father of two small children, Shou's stories have encouraged me to reconsider my role as a parent, and to learn from my memories as a child. I have been educated about the tremendous store of knowledge and wisdom that can be found in new Americans like Shou Cha. Finally, Shou Cha has shown me through his life that one can make peace with other Americans by listening to, and respecting, all of their histories. In a way, I, too, have become a *new American*, with new hopes for a nation that contains persons with the wisdom of Shou Cha.

Because of their potential for representing life experiences, deepening understanding and connecting the individual story to societal contexts, I believe that narratives such as Shou Cha's have powerful lessons for us all. In the paragraphs below I would like to talk about some possible lessons from this life history for researcher, educators, policymakers, and all Americans.

FOR RESEARCHERS

How does one approach the authenticity of autobiography in the writing of the life of another? Writing the life history of Shou Cha has caused me to reflect deeply on this question. So many differences of culture, language background, religious conviction, and income (to name a few) could potentially separate us, and prevent me from understanding his life and its meaning. Yet, I felt that if we approached this writing of a life as a dialogue in search of common ground—as fathers, as educators, as Americans—the authenticity would arise from our reflections together.

This dialogue is often represented in the text by presenting a story by Shou, followed by my commentary. Yet, my commentary has been influenced by Shou's reading of drafts of this work, just as his stories are influenced by my questions. In short, the prose, poetry, and interpretation of this text are products of our research relationship. Researchers must show their value for the relationship that they establish with informants by respecting their words, their interpretations and their theories. In this way researchers have the opportunity to reexamine their own theories as well as their own voice. By going over drafts of this work with Shou Cha, I not only was able to clarify words, themes, and theories, but I was also able to get a sense of the respect that Shou Cha has for the process of sharing a life history, and for the importance he finds in passing along this story of himself, his family, and his Hmong community to a wider audience.

To represent the emotive power of Shou's narrative I have rendered it at times as poetry:

> *Black, white, brown, yellow*
> *we are the same people.*
> *We are different in skin only,*
> *but we are all human.*

We are the same, created by God,
one creator,
and it is very beautiful.
Different colors, and very beautiful.

I believe that researchers must learn to value the artistry in the voice of the informant, and to show that value in the way that they represent voices of others in the content and form of the text. This life history of Shou Cha has been in part a search for ways to bring the vitality and the aesthetic quality of oral narratives into the written form. Brunner (1994) has called for such a return to the aesthetic:

> We need a new vision, and I believe as others that part of that vision can oc-
> cur through the systematic use of aesthetic materials—materials that al-
> low for an opening onto educational theory, social theory, and critical
> practice, materials that allow for imagining our world as it could be other-
> wise. (p. 236)

Researchers who wish to add authenticity to their work and broaden its scope and audience should consider alternatives to the dry prose of many social science texts which squeeze the life out of words.

Moreover, this research has illustrated ways in which narrative inquiry can contribute to the building of theory. By reconceptualizing the self as resourceful, respectful and relational, this work offers a new, wholistic perspective through which to examine immigrant (and American) identity. Moreover, this work suggests an understanding of culture that is both a *movement* between the beliefs and traditions of the past, the exigencies of the present, and the hopes and dreams of the future; and a set of tools needed to reinvent traditions in a new setting, much as the Hmong and Christian traditions are reinvented through Shou's Hmong church.

Through this life-history research, the voice of a member of the Hmong community could be brought into the public discourse about education. Of course, such an approach to educational life history could also be of research relevance to other people in American society whose voices need to be heard. Lincoln (1993) suggests that by writing narratives of the *"silenced,"* new avenues can be opened for social scientists. The study of lives can lead to developments in grounded theories. Moreover, by including the protagonists in the construction of their own narratives, narrative inquirers can gain multivocality and authority of voice. Such multivocality is needed in educational circles, as many teachers and policymakers have little personal experience of the daily struggle faced by poor students and their families, and the voices of such families and students are rarely heard when educational policy is being formulated. Narratives have the power to bring these voices to the attention of educators and policymakers.

FOR EDUCATORS

Shou Cha has no teaching certificate, no college degree, no high school diploma. Yet, he is a valued member of a teaching staff at an elementary school that is noteworthy for its work with diverse children. His educational expertise comes from life experiences: Into his work as a bilingual assistant he brings knowledge of four languages, Hmong, Laotian, Thai, and English, and a lifetime of moving between cultures. In the classroom and in his work as a community liaison, he brings years of experiences teaching and working with a Christian ministry, and values of hard work, responsibility to community, and respect for all people that reflect both his religious convictions and Hmong traditions.

Cultural identities can and must change, but, as Ogbu (personal communication, May 10, 1996) noted at the Michigan Bilingual Education Conference, we need not leave these identities at the schoolhouse door. Shou Cha's narrative reminds us that tremendous cultural resources exist in the homes and communities of diverse students. Through his work in the school and community, Shou has entered the cultural conversation, and America is renewed by his contribution to our ongoing dialogue. Parents and community members such as Shou are key players in the lives of immigrant children, showing them that learning in the school and in the home is related, and that their identities as children need not be fragmented into public and private spheres. Rather, as Covello illustrated half a century ago, children can learn at school how to respect, and transform themselves and their communities. By acknowledging the rich cultural resources of immigrant parents and children, schools can include them in the American experience, offering a sense of belonging to youths who might otherwise try to find themselves by dropping out or joining gangs.

Teachers can draw on the cultural resources of parents and students, thereby enriching the curriculum and school life. Moll and Greenberg (1990) have shown that extending the "zones of knowledge" from the school into families and communities has definite implications for curriculum and instruction. In their view, the immigrant home can and should be a locus for action research by teaching professionals. By examining the learning taking place in the home, teachers can challenge common assumptions about "cultural deficits." For example, Shou Cha lacks formal education, yet he contributes to his family and the larger community in educationally significant ways. There are thousands of people like Shou Cha who could strongly contribute to the education of all children in schools, and a curriculum that is embedded in community needs and influenced by community strengths can encourage these people to come forward.

In referring to the work of educators, Diana Canek has said, "We are the interpreters of our society." In order to better understand the "circles of meanings" (Rabinow & Sullivan, 1987) reflected in the lives of new Americans, teachers, too, must learn to think and act as interpreters and biographers of and for their students. The study of life stories provides a format for improving teacher—student relationships through awareness of cultural difference, an important component in cultural therapy as practiced by the Spindlers or in "family-based multicultural education" as recommended by Walker-Moffat (1995). Narratives of lives also provides a format for teachers to interpret the dominant culture to all students, and especially those who come to school with different cultural understandings. Finally, the work of narrative construction and interpretation provides an ongoing format for the continual personal and professional growth of teachers who are mired, all too often, in curricula that is not of their own creation and removed from the life experiences of their students.

Poetry, of course, is one form of interpreting life experience that resonates across cultures and across time. The poetry in this book represents the thoughts and experiences of Shou Cha, yet its form is based on our collaboration. This poetry influences our understanding of Shou's life in all of its psychological, sociological, and historical dimensions. Poetry offers an avenue to transform the way that arts and humanities are addressed in public schools. Teachers across disciplinary boundaries should have the opportunity to engage students in the poetic representation of the life around them, and to collaborate with them in transforming their living poems onto the printed page.

Finally, teacher education must expose not only preservice and continuing teachers to the lives of new Americans, but must provide them the conceptual and methodological tools to better understand those lives. Principles and practice of ethnographic and narrative inquiry should be a part of teacher preparation programs. As suggested by Zeichner (1993), preservice teachers should be encouraged to address their own sense of cultural identity as well as participate in direct intercultural experiences in the wider community. The use of ethnographic techniques such as participant observation and field notes can help students document these experiences for later reflection with colleagues (Moll, 1992).

Witherell and Noddings (1991) suggest that narratives are central to the work of teachers and counselors, allowing one to penetrate cultural barriers, discover one's "self" and the "other," and deepen understanding. Critically examining the autobiographies of immigrants and their children within the context of a discussion group is one promising way of increasing the cultural understanding of teachers from both majority and minority cultures (Florio-Ruane & DeTar, 1995; Galindo & Olguin, 1996). Another example comes from my own use of Kotlowitz's (1991) *There Are No Children Here*, the story of two African-American boys growing up in Chicago's housing projects, with classes of preservice teachers who are largely European-American and who grew up mostly in small towns and suburbs. Students usually find Kotlowitz's well-documented "story" very meaningful, and challenging to some of their preexisting ideas about race, class, and educational opportunity.

Moreover, works such as *There Are No Children Here* moves the reader to raise ethical questions: Why does the drug trade appear to be one of the few economic alternatives in many poor urban neighborhoods? Why must children dodge bullets on a school playground? Why do many members of our society want to demonize "welfare mothers" and their children rather than address the social and economic reasons for their poverty and marginalization? Similarly, moral questions arise from Shou Cha's narrative. What responsibility does the American government and society have for refugees, many of whom are here as a direct result of American military activity abroad? As educators of all children, what responsibility do schools have for reaching out to all parents, especially those who do not speak the dominant language? What is the place for spirituality in the public schools? How should schools prepare the next generation of citizens for America and the world? Good narratives cause the reader to ask such moral questions. They enable educators to engage students and others in the "realm of practical ethics" on the mutual "quest for goodness and meaning" (Witherell & Noddings, 1991, p. 4).

FOR POLICYMAKERS

Shou Cha has a long memory, and because remembrances of things past help to guide him in his life and work today, his life history contains many stories from the past: How the Hmong people lost their land by the Yellow River or in the mountains of northern Laos, how they lost, and regained, their *books*, how they have ever supported those whom they have trusted, even when this trust was betrayed—such stories from the past provide Shou with a framework for analyzing his world today. The life history of Shou Cha could provide policymakers with a framework for a better understanding of the educational lives of new Americans.

A narrative approach to the study of immigrant education can contribute to an understanding of how historical conceptualizations of immigrants have led to certain educational policies, and how these policies, in turn, have impacted the lives of immigrant families. Narratives of immigrant educational lives in the 1990s offer ways in which to study how changing bilingual, multicultural, and social welfare policies continue to impact immigrant families. The autobiographical writings of Rodriguez and Covello have influenced our understanding of policies ranging from bilingual education to tracking. Policymakers, who often rely on generalized concepts of immigrants and their needs, could use the life history of a Hmong immigrant to become more aware of the individual complexity and variety of the most recent generation of new Americans, and how their needs are changing with the shifting social and economic contexts in American life.

This life history also suggests ways in which school management policies could move beyond the "discipline and punish" metaphor to one of "making peace." Children learn from the examples of role models, and in settings such as Horace Kallen school where many ethnicities and languages are represented, the expanded use of community liaisons can facilitate the peace making process. Policymakers need to think again about the teaching of values in schools. Without the values of resourcefulness, relationship and respect, learned and practiced in schools, we can expect youths to turn elsewhere in their search for understanding—dropping out, joining gangs, and so forth. McLaughlin and Heath (1993) argue that myths about teenagers from inner-city schools—that can't be trusted, that they are lazy, that they are beyond redemption, just to name a few—discourage youths from becoming involved in positive ways in their communities. Instead, such myths "convey disrespect and preclude the empowering strategies essential to youth's productive development" (p. 235). By building relationships between teachers, students and their families, respecting all students and allowing them room to develop their resourcefulness in creative, cooperative ways, schools can teach children from an early age that they are valued members of a community, and that their help is needed in building a better life for all.

One way that this life history suggests of working for peace and social justice through the schools is the use of community liaisons. Clearly, having a person who is an insider in a community and can speak the "*language*" of the community is necessary to foster the holistic growth of children, families, and communities, with the help of schools. According to historians Tyack and Hansot (1982), such was Covello's dream in East Harlem—to use the school as a means for bettering the lives of all members of the community, to truly make it community-centered:

> Covello had no aversion to arguments and disputes. Nor did he interpret the absence of conflict as a sign of progress. East Harlem was a violent

place—the open violence of youth gangs and the *Cosa Nostra*, the more hidden psychological violence of hunger and dark, crowded tenements, the anger of incomprehension between parents and children. Covello wanted to channel this energy of conflict into collective political and social actions that would improve the lives of people, that would give them voices and power. (p. 211)

Through community liaisons Horace Kallen school redistributes the power for decision-making from the front office into the communities. The liaisons contribute their understanding of community needs and politics, and in their turn are being trained in the nuances of the American educational system and civic democracy. As Horton (1990) has suggested, if we value participatory democracy, we must begin teaching this value through the schools by respecting community voices in the process of educational decision-making.

The life history of Shou Cha also challenges educational policymakers to reconsider the individualistic philosophy that often underlies schooling in our democracy. Resourcefulness, relationship, and respect can provide the foundation for building social capital in the United States. Putnam (1995) defines social capital as the human networks, norms and social trust that facilitate coordination and cooperation for mutual benefit. He cites cross-national evidence of the value of social capital for fostering reciprocity and encouraging collaboration, resolving collective dilemmas, and broadening "the participants' sense of self, developing the 'I' into the 'we'" (p. 67). He argues that America suffers from declining social capital, citing declining membership in social and civic organizations and lack of civic participation, and suggests that we must find ways to "reverse the adverse trends in social connectedness, thus restoring civic engagement and civic trust" (p. 77). By focusing on the development of social capital rather than individual achievement, policymakers must find ways to encourage the development of a democratic and cooperative citizenship in schools.

FOR ALL AMERICANS

This life history of Shou Cha began with an episode 2 years ago in which he was shot, and after which he felt a sense of homelessness, that

> *This place belongs to someone else.*
> *It's not my house.*
> *I don't belong to this Earth.*

Through subsequent work with the diverse staff and students at Horace Kallen school, and his own reflections, Shou has come to a different understanding of America and Americans:

> *Many different peoples live in the*
> *same town*
> *black, brown, yellow*
> *if they look a certain way, they have*
> *their own community.*
> *I don't deny it,*
> *it is good to serve your own*
> *community.*
> *Please do your best for them.*
> *But then you should*
> *treat others nicely, too.*
> *black, white, brown, yellow*
> *we are the same people.*

Shou has come to believe that America is a place where groups like the Hmong can find a home, can serve their own community, and yet also be part of a larger, multicolored tapestry.

Walzer (1990) has said that "Americans have homesteads and homefolks and hometowns"—and, we should add, *homeboys*—"but they don't have much to say about a common or communal home" (pp. 592–593). As a newcomer who has engaged in his own personal struggle to find a home in America, Shou Cha offers a lesson for all Americans who would make peace with themselves and their communities. We must reject messages and policies that are founded in fear and mistrust, and learn how to live with all the diverse citizens of our nation and our planet. As Shou Cha's life has demonstrated, one of the best ways to learn this lesson is to work and study in educational settings that value all the languages and cultures that contribute to our changing nation. The values of resourcefulness, relationship, and respect can be tools for constructing a great community out of diverse individuals.

Alongside American individualism, with all of its potentials and dangers, a communitarian spirit also has its place in our society. This spirit has been fostered by generations of newcomers. From the Cherokee call for a *gadugi*, "to help one another," to the American Indian Movement community patrols in urban areas; from African Americans and their supporters who organized the road to freedom along the Underground Railroad, and later, the road to Civil Rights; from Latin American traditions such as the *minga*, or communal working of the soil, to the United Farm Workers, building communities to protect those who work the soil; from Asian Americans such as the Hmong, who organize extensive mutual support networks to take care of the housing, food and employment needs of new members of the community; from European Americans traditions symbolized by the barn-raising, still practiced in many Amish and Mennonite farming communities.

Moreover, the history of the United States is in part a history of diverse peoples coming together to build and support communities across ethnicity and color. Diverse Americans have contributed to the architecture of our cities, and the preservation of our parks and green spaces; they have fought side by side in the union movement and have sought to preserve the livelihood of small farmers; their spirit provides the rhythms for American music, dance, and literature; their commitment to the future has guided the education of our young, the future of our democratic society. Green (1996) has written that the needs, aspirations and contributions of diverse Americans must be recognized, "that a plurality of American voices must be attended to, that a plurality of life-stories must be heeded" if the promise of the American community is to be fulfilled (p. 28).

Walzer (1990) has argued that America is more than a place, or collection and mixture of cultures, but an idea of unity rising out of plurality:

> If there are cultural artifacts, songs and dances, styles of life and even philosophies, that are distinctively American, there is also an idea of America that is itself distinct, incorporating oneness and manyness in a "new order" that may or may not be "for the ages" but that is certainly for us, here and now. (p. 608)

Shou Cha's values of resourcefulness, relationship, and respect represent the best of Hmong and American traditions and offer us a pathway to unity. These 3 R's, if taken seriously in school and society, offer hope for making peace in a diverse nation, a peace founded in tolerance and justice. By listening to, and valuing, the voices of newcomers like Shou Cha, America renews herself, and moves forward toward the realization of a dream: *e pluribus unum*, out of many, one.

8

From One Life to Many: Rediscovering America Through Autobiography

> In the morning they again gave us fish and roots, and treated us so well that we became reassured, losing somewhat our apprehension of being butchered.
> —Cabeza de Vaca (1527, p. 61)

Shou Cha's story is unique, and at the same time one of many millions of stories of newcomers to America. Most of these stories are passed on as family oral history, but remain largely unwritten. However, a growing body of work exists concerning the lives of newcomers to the United States and their children. Reading these lives, we can rediscover America through the diverse perspectives of our people.

I have chosen three autobiographical works to profile in order to continue this process of rediscovery: Hoffman's (1989) *Lost in Translation: A Life in a New Language*, Kingston's *The Woman Warrior* 1976), and Colon's *A Puerto Rican in New York and Other Sketches* (1975).[1] Each of these works are connected to larger themes of uprootedness, struggle to define, and redefine oneself in a new land, and the search for common ground among disparate peoples. Weaving together these thematic strands is the traveler's tale of Alvar Nunez Cabeza de Vaca (1527/1964), a castaway who, in 1527, began a journey on foot from Florida to Mexico, his writings address many of the themes that are the focus of later autobiographies of newcomers, and he provides a glimpse of light during the long night of the conquista. In his 8-year struggle to find a way home,

---

[1]For other autobiographies of immigrants, see Antin (1912), Capra (1985), Galarza (1971), Houston (1978), Riis (1901), Carnegie (1920), Bok (1922), and Anderson (1951).

Cabeza de Vaca finds himself, and comes to recognize his common bond with the peoples of the new world.

A GREAT EMPTINESS

Shipwrecked in Florida, Cabeza de Vaca spent years living and working with a number of tribes. Of one of these groups, he writes: "They have the custom, when they know each other and meet from time to time, before they speak, to weep for half an hour. After they have wept the one who receives the visit rises and gives to the other all he has" (Cabeza de Vaca, 1527/1964, p. 72).

In *Lost in Translation: A Life in a New Language* (1989), Hoffman describes her journey to a new life and a new language in Canada and the United States. She was 13 years old when her family emigrated from Poland in 1959. On board the ship in the harbor of Gdynia, Hoffman suffers her first attack of nostalgia:

Tesknota—a word that adds to nostalgia the tonalities of sadness and longing. It is a feeling whose shades and degrees I am destined to know intimately ... Looking ahead, I come across an enormous, cold blankness—a darkening, an erasure, of the imagination, as if a camera eye has snapped shut, or as if a heavy curtain has been pulled over the future. (p. 4)

Her parents, who grew up in a small Jewish enclave near Lvov, had lost most of their families and friends to the extermination camps of the Holocaust. Hoffman is named for both of her grandmothers, as "my parents have no lack of the dead to honor" (p. 8). Having lost so much, they were left with "a deep skepticism about human motives, and a homegrown version of existentialism ... with its gamble that since everything is absurd, you might as well try to squeeze the juice out of every moment" (p. 16). In Cracow, where they settled after the war, Hoffman's father augments a meager income in an import–export store with a brisk trade in "forbidden dollars" and smuggled goods. He was involved, like so many others, in an "ongoing game of outwitting the System" (p. 14). Thus, the family was able to live comfortably, and, more importantly, save in secret hiding places the foreign currency they would need to leave the country.

After a long journey Hoffman and her family arrive in Vancouver, where the family finds a room in the home of an elderly Polish Jew for whom they do housecleaning. Ewa and Alina become Eva and Elaine on their first day at school: "We walk to our seats, into a roomful of unknown faces, with names that make us strangers to ourselves" (p. 105). As the two sisters begin to adapts to the ways and language of the school, they become further isolated from the life of their parents. Eva doesn't like to see the bonds that hold her small family together breaking down, and is hurt when her mother tells her she is becoming "English": "I know she means I'm becoming cold. I'm no colder than I've ever been, but I'm learning to be less demonstrative" (p. 146).

After completing her studies in Vancouver, Hoffman was encouraged to attend university, this time in the United States. She found the people in her new environment at Rice University in Houston to be puzzling. She writes that she felt like a "naturalist trying to orient myself in an uncharted landscape, and eyeing the flora and fauna around me with a combination of curiosity and detachment. They might be upset if they knew the extent to which I view them as a puzzling species" (p. 174). As an English major she began to discover an *American* spirit in the literature she read:

> At this point in my education, I can't translate backward. Literature doesn't yet give me America in its particulars—though as I read Emerson and Thoreau and Walker Percy, I feel the breath of a general spirit: the spirit, precisely, of alienness, of a continent and a culture still new and still uncozy, and a vision that turns philosophical or tortured from confronting an unworded world. (p. 184)

This spirit of alienness she found reflected in the lives of her American friends and lovers as well. She was surprised to find that her Texan boyfriend harbored feelings of emptiness behind his strong, smiling exterior:

> How do you talk to an alien? Very carefully. When I fall in love with my first American, I also fall in love with otherness, with the far spaces between us and the distances we have to travel to meet at the source of our attraction. My fair-haired Texan is tall and blue eyed and has a sweet smile meant to be well liked ... What does he tell me about? Emptiness. There is a great emptiness, a vacuum within him and there's nothing with which to fill it up. (p. 187)

Hoffman's years in college coincided with the social and political upheavals of the 1960s, when universities became sites for protests against the war, against social policies, and, more generally, against accepted middle-class values. As Hoffman struggled to become fluent in the formal English of the academy, she found her classmates rejecting formal rules of language:

> Ironically enough, just as I'm trying to fill myself with the material of language, my fellow students begin to cultivate willed inarticulateness, as if

strings of complete sentences showed a questionable investment in a sick civilization. (p. 191)

In later years, as a graduate student at Harvard, and as an editor for the *New York Times Book Review*, Hoffman pondered the qualities she shared with the generation of Americans with whom she came of age in the 1960s. Perhaps mostly what they shared was an uprootedness, a refusal to assimilate:

> In a splintered society, what does one assimilate to? Perhaps the very splintering itself ... I share with my American generation an acute sense of dislocation and the equally acute challenge of having to invent a place and an identity for myself without the traditional supports. It could be said that the generation I belong to has been characterized by its prolonged refusal to assimilate—and it is in my very uprootedness that I'm its member. It could indeed by said that exile is the archetypal condition of contemporary lives. (p. 197)

Cabeza de Vaca and his companions learned half a dozen indigenous languages during their 8 years of wandering from Florida to Mexico, and they found ways to communicate with their hosts when oral language failed:

> We came across a great variety and number of languages, and God our Lord favored us with a knowledge of all, because they always could understand us and we understood them, so that when we asked they would answer by signs, as if they spoke our language and we theirs; for, although we spoke six languages, not everywhere could we use them, since we found more than a thousand different ones. (pp. 158–59)

Mutual understanding is not taken for granted by Hoffman. She illustrates in a number of ways in her autobiography that, even when two people share the same language, they do not necessarily share the same meaning. Perhaps the vast distances of America, coupled with the continuous movement of its people, contributed to this sense of uprootedness. For Hoffman, when Americans are unsure of their own identities and their own sense of place, difference becomes a potential threat, and strangers are as likely to be shunned as to be welcomed:

> In the distended and foreshortened perspectives of the American spaces, others tend to become puzzling Others—and so do our own selves, which grow in strangeness and uncertainty in direct proportion to the opaqueness of those around us. There are so many strangers, in America. How can we take for granted that, surely, we understand each other? (p. 267)

Lost in Translation is at once a very personal journey as well as a chronicle of a generation growing up in the 1960s. Yet, like the story of millions of other Jewish immigrants to America, Hoffman's story begins with persecution. For centuries the targets of discrimination and periodic pogroms, the Jews of Europe and Russia came under increasing attack in the late 19th century, in large part to deflect attention from the failures of local regimes. "Almost everywhere, government officials encouraged acts of violence against Jews," and by 1900 one third of all Jews in Eastern Europe and Russia had emigrated, mostly to America (Takaki, 1993, p. 277). Many settled in New York City's Lower East Side, a ghetto that soon contained more than 500 people per acre (Howe & Libo, 1979). For many Jewish writers, "the world of culture and ideas was a liberation" from the overcrowded conditions of such ghettos (Rubin, 1992, p. 198).

The lasting impact of the Holocaust can be seen in the writings of Hoffman and many others. Meyer Levin (1950) writes: "It isn't a fourth of the Bulgarian Jews and a fifth of the Polish Jews and a third of the French who survived; they all have death inside" (p. 175).

Alfred Kazin (1951) describes the first newsreel he saw from the Belsen concentration camp: "Sticks in black-and-white prison garb ... shuffled about, or sat vaguely on the ground, next to an enormous pile of bodies, piled up like cordwood." He also describes the audience reaction: "People coughed in embarrassment, and in embarrassment many laughed" (p. 166). For these writers, and for millions of others in America and elsewhere, the Holocaust would lead to a reconsideration of what it meant to be Jewish.

The great emptiness that Eva Hoffman senses in the American spirit, then, reflects also the great emptiness behind her: As part of the generation growing up after the Holocaust, continuity and community would need to be redefined, like words of a new language.

GHOSTS IN THE MACHINE

Cabeza de Vaca (1527/1964) saw a number of childrearing practices among the peoples with whom he lived. Those of a tribe known as the Mariames were most disturbing: "It is a custom of theirs to kill even their own children for the sake of dreams, and the girls when newly born they throw away to be eaten by dogs" (p. 88).

The Woman Warrior: Memoirs of a Childhood Among Ghosts (Kingston, 1976) considers the life of a girl growing up between the Chinese "talking stories," values, and restrictions of home and the realities of life at school and work in America. There are many targets for Kingston, whose words pierce like swords: Her family and the Chinese immigrants, for their treatment of girl children; an early school experience that left her feeling miserable in her silence; and American *ghosts*[2]—beings who might alternatively discriminate against the Chinese, destroy their livelihoods, or deport them.

Kingston's mother and father had immigrated to the United States from China during World War II. Though Kingston was born in America, the world of her childhood was still governed in many ways by Chinese tradition. One of the most apparent of these traditions was the secondary status of girls within a family. Girls were raised to keep a house and raise the children for men. Through marriage, they were destined to become part of the husband's family.

Refusing to do well in school, to cook, and to clean, Kingston found ways to rebel against the restrictions and limited expectations for girls:

> It was said, "There is an outward tendency in females," which meant that I was getting straight A's for the good of my future husband's family, not my own. I did not plan ever to have a husband. I would show my mother and father and the nosey emigrant villagers that girls have no outward tendency. I stopped getting straight A's ... I refused to cook. When I had to wash dishes, I would crack one or two. "Bad girl," my mother yelled, and sometimes that made me gloat rather than cry. Isn't a bad girl almost a boy? (p. 47)

Although her parents expected her to follow the model of a traditional Chinese female, Kingston felt the need to become more talkative and more independent, like the American girls: "All the time I was having to turn myself American-feminine, or no dates" (p. 47).

Yet, her mother also provides her with alternative female models through stories of the woman warriors of China. These women were strong, fearless, and cunning, ever ready to lead oppressed peasants to victory over the warlords who rob them of their harvests. When confronting the injustices of life in America—the destruction of her family's laundry business as part of urban renewal, the discrimination against the Chinese and others, the constant threat of deportation—Kingston fantasizes of her own role as the woman warrior in America: "From the fairy tales, I've learned exactly who the enemy are. I easily recognize them—business-suited in their modern American executive guise, each boss two feet taller than I am and impossible to meet eye to eye" (p. 48).

Referring to a racist boss who had fired her for questioning his planning of a banquet at a restaurant being picketed by the NAACP, she says, "If I

---

[2]Kingston has been criticized for translating the Cantonese *kuei* as "ghost." Some have suggested that the character more frequently is used to express "demon." For a wide-ranging critique of Kingston's work see Wong, 1992.

took the sword, which my hate must surely have forged out of the air, and gutted him, I would put color and wrinkles into his shirt"(p. 49).

Language added complexity to Kingston's relationship with her family, society and herself. Her mother liked to tell her how she had cut Kingston's tongue when she was born. In spite of the evidence to the contrary, Kingston insisted on asking her about it, so her mother explained:

> I cut it so that you would not be tongue-tied. Your tongue would be able to move in any language. You'll be able to speak languages that are completely different from one another. You'll be able to pronounce anything. (p. 164)

Nevertheless, when she entered kindergarten and was asked to speak English, Kingston became silent, like many of the Chinese and many other minority language children. Not only the language, but the rules of expected behavior were quite different. Assimilation-minded teachers failed to cross the cultural and personal borders to get a glimpse of the world through Kingston's eyes:

> At first it did not occur to me that I was supposed to talk or to pass kindergarten ... It was when I found out I had to talk that school became a misery, that the silence became a misery. I did not speak and felt bad each time that I did not speak. I read aloud in first grade, though, and heard the barest whisper with little squeaks come out of my throat. "Louder," said the teacher, who scared the voice away again. The other Chinese girls did not talk either, so I knew the silence had to do with being a Chinese girl. (pp. 165–166)

Kingston's account dramatizes the shame and discomfort of this *silent period,* a time needed by many language learners to process a new language without having to produce it (Krashen & Terrell, 1983). What she did produce were elaborate paintings of life scenes hidden behind a black veil:

> I painted layers of black over houses and flowers and suns, and when I drew on the blackboard, I put a layer of chalk on top. I was making a stage curtain, and it was the moment before the curtain parted or rose. (p. 165)

Perhaps she, like the figures in her paintings, was waiting for the black curtain to open on her existence in order to realize her full potential.

Her classmates in the public schools represented many of the diverse groups which call San Francisco home. Interestingly, she was attracted to the African-American students, so unlike herself in their talkativeness. These students were also her protectors:

> I liked the Negro students (Black Ghosts) best because they laughed the loudest and talked to me as if I were a daring talker too ... Some Negro kids walked me to school and home, protecting me from the Japanese kids, who hit me and chased me and stuck gum in my ears. (p. 165)

Kingston also realized that the tough Japanese students had endured their own share of the underside of the American experience, having been interned for a long period during the war: "The Japanese kids were noisy and tough. They appeared one day in kindergarten, released from concentration camp, which was a tic-tac-toe mark, like barbed wire, on the map" (166).

For her mother, Americans were *ghosts,* not quite real like the Chinese. Americans worked all the time, and poor immigrants such as Kingston's mother would not have a moment of rest:

> "This is a terrible ghost country, where a human being works her life away," she said. "Even the ghosts work, no time for acrobatics. I have not stopped working since the day the ship landed. I was on my feet the moment the babies were out. In China I never even had to hang up my own clothes." (p. 104)

Individual ghosts would reinforce her mother's impressions of Americans when they brought their business to the family laundry:

> "No tickee, no washee, mama-san?" a ghost would say, so embarrassing.

> "Noisy Red-Mouth Ghost," she'd write on its package, naming it, marking its clothes with its name. (p. 105)

Cabeza de Vaca observed how disagreements and arguments were handled within one of the tribes:

> *After they have fought and settled the question, they take their lodges and women and go out into the field to live apart from the others until their anger is over, and when they are no longer angry and their resentment has passed away they return to the village and are as friendly again as if nothing had happened." (p. 118)*

Woman Warrior is a book in which the discrimination and bigotry faced by Chinese immigrants are addressed head on. Kingston (1976) couches her own talking story within a larger history of mistreatment of Chinese workers and exclusionary immigration policies that continue into the present. She speaks of the ever-present fear of being deported, the rumors that, not only adults who had entered the United States illegally, but their American-born children might be sent packing. The answer was to avoid dealing with authorities, and to obfuscate:

> Lie to Americans. Tell them you were born during the San Francisco Earthquake. Tell them your birth certificate and your parents were burned up in the fire. Don't report crimes; tell them we have no crimes and no poverty. Give a new name every time you get arrested; the ghosts won't recognize you. Pay the new immigrants twenty-five cents an hour and say we have no unemployment. And, of course, tell them we're against Communism. Ghosts have no memory anyway and poor eyesight. And the Han people won't be pinned down. (p. 184–185)

At the same time, Kingston is Chinese born in the United States, almost ghost-like herself in her mother's eyes. Moving beyond anger, she claims America for her own. This was the only home she knew and the stories of the excesses and atrocities of the Cultural Revolution in China solidified her determination to stay in the United States:

> So while the adults wept over the letters about the neighbors gone berserk turning Communist ... I was secretly glad. As long as the aunts kept disappearing and the uncles dying after unspeakable tortures, my parents would prolong their Gold Mountain stay. We could start spending our fare money on a car and chairs, a stereo. (p. 190)

Like the woman warrior captured by barbarians in her talking story, Kingston still, at times, feels like a stranger in the land of her birth. Yet she has a song to play, and she has found the language in which to make others listen.

When Kingston's family arrived in the United States, there had been established Chinese communities on the West Coast for at least 90 years. Chinese began arriving in California in the 1840s and 1850s, leaving behind harsh economic conditions that were the result, in many respects, of the intervention of western powers in Chinese affairs: Britain's attempt to force opium imports, China's defeat in the Opium Wars that followed, and the need to pay large indemnities to England and her allies led to heavy taxation of Chinese peasants. Most of those who left for *Gold Mountain*, as California was called, were men, and they often left wives and children behind. By 1870, there were 63,000 Chinese in the United States, engaged in pursuits as varied as mining, railroad building, agriculture and urban manufacturing (Takaki, 1993).

The Chinese increasingly became the targets of resentment, especially during hard economic times such as the Panic of 1873. In 1882 the Chinese Exclusion Act was signed into law, ending for a time immigration from China during a period of massive immigration from Europe. Those

who had made it to the United States were forced into operating laundries and other forms of self-employment because of ethnic antagonism
(Ong, 1983).

The Chinatown of Kingston's youth was created as much by discriminatory employment and housing practices as by the wish of Chinese people to keep together. Kingston's own journey from this world to the
academy and career suggests both the struggles and the possibilities of an
immigrant child redefining her America.

WE THE PEOPLE

*As Cabeza de Vaca and his band of survivors journeyed on foot across
America, their fame as healers went on before them. Native peoples would
greet them at each village with food, clothing and other gifts. Most of this
was distributed among the multitudes who accompanied them: "We par-
took of everything a little, giving the rest to the principal man among those
who had come with us for distribution among all ... Often we had with us
three to four thousand persons" (Cabeza de Vaca, 1527/1964, pp. 143–144).*

A *Puerto Rican in New York and Other Sketches* (Colon, 1975) chronicles Colon's life from his youth in Puerto Rico through 40 years as a
worker, organizer, and writer in New York. In San Juan, his education
came as much from the life around him as from school. He learned one of
the most important lessons of his school days when he observed, through
the slats of his classroom window, a police attack on striking
dockworkers. He would listen to "el lector," who would read from works
of literature, philosophy, and politics to the workers at the local factory.
Later in life he would describe his education:

> All the learning, so-called, that I had was acquired listening to the tobacco
> workers from outside one of the tobacco factory windows when I was a boy
> in my hometown in Puerto Rico ... This was followed by an unorganized, if
> abundant, reading at public libraries ... plus a few books, pamphlets and pe-
> riodicals of serious reading in the social sciences. (p. 177)

Realizing the economic limitations of life in Puerto Rico, at the age of
17 Colon stowed away on a ship bound for New York. He held a variety of
jobs, from dangerous work on the docks to dishwashing and busing tables
in restaurants, where he was "to be appropriately humble and grateful
not only to the owner but to everybody else in the place"(p. 41). Everywhere he learned of discrimination against people of color:

> The conversations among the Puerto Ricans on the large wooden benches
> in the employment office were always on the same subject. How to find a

decent place to live. How they would not rent to Negroes or Puerto Ricans. How Negroes and Puerto Ricans were given the pink slips first at work. (pp. 40–41)

Though he looked tirelessly for work, his sense of injustice, developed in his early educational experiences in Puerto Rico, would not allow Colon to keep silent when confronted with oppression, even when he desperately needed a job:

> The weeks of unemployment and hard knocks turned into months. I continued to find two or three days of work here and there. And I continued to be thrown out when I rebelled at the ill treatment, overwork and insults. (p. 41)

On one occasion Colon got some work doing Spanish translations for silent movies that were being marketed to Latin America. He would type the translations at home, send them in, and receive a check in the mail. After a particularly satisfactory translation of Longfellow's "Song of Hiawatha," Colon was invited to come down to work at the film agency in a salaried position. He put on his best clothes, went up to the office on top of a tall building, and asked to see the man who had sent him the invitation.

> The minute I told him who I was and showed him the letter he himself had signed offering me steady work as a translator, he assumed a cold and impersonal attitude. He made it short and to the point. "Yes, I wrote that letter. I invited you to come translate for us here at the office." And pointing to the other side of the room he added "That was to be your desk and typewriter. But I thought you were white." (pp. 50–51)

One of the strengths that Colon and other Puerto Ricans in New York could rely on was family. This sense of family extended across generations and included members whose exact blood relationship was forgotten:

> The family came: mother, father, sisters, brothers, cousins, and just friends who, because of living with us so many years, had become part of the family. An old Puerto Rican custom. Many times we asked mother about someone who had been living with us for years. "In what way is Jose related to us?" And my mother, after a lot of genealogical hemming and hawing in which the more she explained the more she got involved and confused, would end with a desperate whimsical gesture: "He is just part of the family." And there it ended. (p. 44)

This inclusive conception of family was an important base from which Colon would build his ideas of socialism, and the brotherhood and sisterhood of all working people. He met with failures in his effort to work for the good of all. Despite the value placed on courtesy in Puerto Rican culture, Colon failed one night to help a White woman with two small children, a suitcase, and a baby in her arms, descend the subway stairs:

> How could I, a Negro and a Puerto Rican approach this white lady who very likely might have preconceived prejudices against Negroes and everybody with foreign accents, in a deserted subway station very late at night?

Fearful of a prejudicial response, he forgot his upbringing and fled by:

> Like a rude animal walking on two legs, I just moved on half running by the long subway platform leaving the children and the valise and her with the baby on her arm ... This is what racism and prejudice and chauvinism and artificial divisions can do to people and to a nation! (p. 116)

As an activist within the communist party, there were other moments when the whole world seemed to be coming together. One night when Colon was at a worker's vacation camp, a spontaneous musical celebration occurred during a thunderstorm:

> Someone shouted, "How about going onto the highway in our swimming suits to take a shower?" Nobody answered but in a matter of minutes the highway was covered with young and old—Jews, Italians, Negroes, Mexicans, Spaniards, Cubans, Chinese and Puerto Ricans. We joined arms in twos, fours and sixes and started to sing and sing at the top of our voices to our hearts' content ...
>
> > Avanti popolo
> > Alla riscossa
> > Bandiera rossa
> > Bandiera rossa ...

When I remember that night on the highway I feel young and happy, and full of hope and optimism again. (p. 146)

By the 1950s, New York was home to over 600,000 Puerto Ricans. When government officials and others raised the question of reaching these thousands, of opening channels of communication to them, Colon had an answer. The first part of the answer was to recognize the effects of hundreds of years of exploitation on the Puerto Rican people. Too often had they been taken advantage of by Spanish, French, and American visitors to their island:

So when you come to knock at the door of a Puerto Rican home you will be encountered by this feeling in the Puerto Rican—sometimes unconscious in himself—of having been taken for a ride for centuries ... That is why you must come many times to that door. You must prove yourself a friend, a worker who is also being oppressed by the same forces that keep the Puerto Rican down. Only then will the Puerto Rican open his heart to you. (p. 148)

As a cultural critic Colon was concerned with the representation of Latin American history in the United States. The paucity of information that children received in schools was accompanied by simplistic misinterpretations of history presented in the movies:

As far as instruction in the most elementary knowledge of Latin America is concerned, we are forced to state that what our children receive is a hodgepodge of romantic generalities and chauvinistic declarations spread further and wider by Hollywood movies. (p. 57)

For Colon, such films as *Santiago*, wherein "the heroic deeds of the Cuban people ... are dumped into the Hollywood ash can and replaced by the most fantastic, flashy, super-colossal misinterpretation of Cuban history," were recipes for further bigotry and misunderstanding of Cubans, Puerto Ricans, and other Latin Americans living in the United States. Reaching out to such people would mean listening to their stories and learning their history.

We traveled over a great part of the country, and found it all deserted, as the people had fled to the mountains, leaving houses and fields out of fear of the Christians. This filled our hearts with sorrow ... (The Indians) told us how the Christians had penetrated into the country before, and had destroyed and burnt the villages, taking with them half of the men and all the women and children, and how those who could escaped by flight (Cabeza de Vaca, 1527/1964, p. 163).

While still in Puerto Rico, Colon had come face to face with the inequities of the American experience. He observed the social and economic disparities in San Juan, and would later ask, "In this 'we the people' phrase that I admired so much, were there first and secondary people?" (p. 198). He described a colonial relationship in Puerto Rico that forced workers such as himself to migrate to the United States, adding that "colonialism with its concomitants, agricultural slavery, monoculture, absentee ownership, and rank human exploitation are making the young Puerto Ricans of today come in floods to the United States, if only for a few months, to work in the equally exploited agricultural fields"

(p. 201). Once in New York, Puerto Ricans faced discriminatory, divide-and-conquer strategies employed to keep a diverse group of workers isolated from one other:

> I came to New York to poor pay, long hours, terrible working conditions, discrimination even in the slums and in the poor paying factories where the bosses very dexterously pitted Italians against Puerto Ricans and Puerto Ricans against American Negroes and the Jews. (p. 200)

Colon sought for a solution through a political and social movement. This meant moving in circles beyond the Puerto Rican community, forging relationships with immigrants, and long-time residents of the United States, and engaging in struggle with others. By the 1950s he would see such efforts increasingly hampered by the anticommunist furor of the McCarthy Era. Nevertheless, social movements in succeeding decades would echo his words for a transformation of the American experience: "We are ready to fight for lower prices, more housing, for a progressive people's government and for peace for 'We the people of the United States in order to form a more perfect union'" (p. 201).

Puerto Rico came under the control of the United States in 1898, one of the "fruits of victory" following the Spanish-American War. As America's imperial expansion extended from the Philippines to the Caribbean, the "the old rhetoric of freedom and equality" in the United States "gave way to race, language, empire" (Crawford, 1992, p. 49). The people of the Puerto Rico, descended from Native, African, and Spanish roots, had lived under Spanish colonial rule for centuries; Spanish was their language. Yet, under American control, by 1909, 80% of Puerto Rico's grade schools had English as their medium of instruction. As children generally had no use for the language in their life outside of class, studies were neglected, and most students dropped out by third grade. In effect, the subordination of the Spanish vernacular denied "an education to all but a few native elites" (Crawford, 1992, p. 51). This official English policy for Puerto Rican schools remained in effect until it was scrapped in 1949.

One hundred years later, in 1998, Puerto Ricans are reconsidering their territorial status. Though its future statehood is still to be decided, the many personal connections between the island and the United States are clear. According to the 1990 census, approximately 3 million Puerto Ricans reside on the mainland. There struggle for equitable treatment continues, and this struggle often focuses on language issues: Soto's (1997) study of a Puerto Rican community's fight for bilingual education for its children illustrates both the obstacles still to be overcome, as well as the strength of a community.

Perhaps Colon understood that the struggle for equality and justice could only be effectively waged once Puerto Ricans joined with others to find common ground and form a common agenda.

A group of mounted, armed conquistadors told the native peoples accompanying Cabeza de Vaca that they were the real Christians, and the lords of the land, whereas Cabeza de Vaca and his companions were "people of no luck and little heart." However,

> *the Indians ... parleyed among themselves, saying that the Christians lied, for we had come from sunrise, while the others came from where the sun sets; that we cured the sick, while the others killed those who were healthy; that we went naked and shoeless, whereas the others wore clothes and went on horseback with lances. Also, that we asked for nothing, but gave away all we were presented with, meanwhile the others seemed to have no other aim than to steal what they could, and never gave anything to anybody. (Cabeza de Vaca, 1527/1964, pp. 171–172)*

IN SEARCH OF EL DORADO

Within the autobiographical narratives of Hoffman, Kingston, and Colon we can recognize again the themes of rootlessness, changing identity, and the struggle to find common ground with others that characterized much of the life history of Shou Cha. Like him, Hoffman, Kingston, and Colon are all castaways of a sort in century marked by vast migrations of economic and political refugees. For Hoffman, vast emotional spaces separate Americans as much as the long distances traveled on the map. Kingston's work suggests the ultimate sacrifices made when trying to form a personal identity as a person living in two worlds, each containing its flaws. Colon uses his personal life story to highlight issues in the social struggle to which he is committed. Yet, like Cabeza de Vaca, the nature of his journey of rediscovery causes him to bridge more readily the differences that separate him from diverse others. Though personal and individual, these autobiographies give us a sense of the struggle of people of many cultures as they encountered life in a new world.

The *America* to be discovered lies within our people, our stories and our dialogues together, and autobiographies and life histories provide a point of departure. Through autobiography we can take a dual journey, inward toward the life of the individual, and outward to encompass the relationships that tie each of us to culture, society, and history. Like the explorers of the 16th century we still search for *el dorado;* yet, the *el dorado* for which we search is not a place on the map, but a terrain of the heart.

Epilogue:
Research as an Opening

> For now we see in a mirror dimly, but then face to face;
> Now I know in part, but then I shall know fully, just as I
> also have been fully known.
> —1 Corinthians, 13:12

The gales of November have returned to Windigo. Brown oak leaves, the last to fall, go clattering along the gutters. The clouds have blown by and, low in the southwest, Jupiter and the crescent moon can be seen peeping through the bare branches of the trees. It is a good night for gathering close, fighting off the chill of the season and of the times with a rare tale.

Shou and I are on our own tonight: He has a full house at home, as half a dozen relatives have just arrived from the Thai camps, and, until Shou helps them find their place to live, they will be staying with him and his family. My house will soon be filled with the sounds and exuberance of a 2-year old's tea party with his favorite neighbors. So Shou and I drive out to a 24-hour breakfast joint that lies along a strip of flea-bag motels at the north entrance to Windigo. Out there on the edge of the city we talk about what we have learned during our time together.

Don: "Has this been a process that you have found to be valuable for yourself, personally?"

Shou: "Yes. There are a couple of things. One is to recall my past life, and even recall the culture I grew up with, and any major events or points in my life—you know, if you don't talk back, then you just can't recall. You don't have someone to talk to about your past life. So it is to recall those events in my past life. I also am interested in having a copy of the story for myself. Also, I know that my life might have lessons for others; I can provide my life for anyone else who might be interested. The other thing is when we study together, when we say it, record it, and write it down, it gives me a big lesson: I have probably made many mistakes in my past life, and I can learn many things from my previous life, too. Also, my son and the young people, how do they think about the old people, the parents. Parents and children, how do they think. That also corrects me—the way that I live, the way that I am a father, the way I correct my children."

Don: "You talk about how you see your children differently when you share these kinds of things. One thing I notice is when you tell a lot of these stories, you talk about your relationship with your children, but you use examples of your relationships with your father and your parents. Maybe another interesting part of remembering these stories is that you remember how you were: Maybe it was not exactly the same, it was a different country and a different time, but a similar age."

Shou: "Yes, that's right. I know my childhood was somewhat different than my children's. How I acted toward my father and how my children act toward me is somehow different. Yet, I can still adapt something from it. What I did towards my father I thought was good, but *I did not know how my father thought about me.* Did he think I was a good boy, or not good? Sometimes I think that my children are quite naughty or they don't really obey my directions; but, to compare them with other children, my children are in some way even better. My children are satisfactory, not excellent, but we are only human. I can say that I made mistakes when I was a child, and I can see that my children make mistakes when I am a father."

Don: "You've given some good reasons for people to read about a life—your life, or other people's lives. I mean, every one of us has done things that other people can learn from. Do you think that this is also a story about the Hmong people—certainly your perspective of them, and not the whole story—but it does deal with some of the issues of the newest Americans who have come here. Do you think the story has an importance for other Americans to read, in terms of coming to understand each other?"

Shou: "Yes. I think it is important. They might think back to their young life, compared to my young life. They also might think about I as a father, compared to my children. It is good to compare the stories. The way I lived, when I was a young boy, I may never go back to live like that again. But it is in my brain."

Don: "One of the things about talking to someone like you or reading about your life is how it might influence people in schools—teachers, students, and other people. You are a member of the community. Right now you are working for the school, not because you have a degree, not because you have a certificate of some kind, but because you have a life experience and a lot of skills and knowledge that are beneficial. I think one thing I've learned from doing this project with you is just how much someone like you, who has a lot of knowledge, but not necessarily from the school—how much the school can learn from someone like you, or can benefit from having someone like you work with the kids, or even just to know about your life. If teachers knew about that, it might help them when they have people come into the classrooms who are Hmong or other kids who are different. You are with a school that recognizes those things, but do you think that is something that all schools need to be more aware of, that there are people in the community who know a lot, and it would be good for them to get to know them a little bit better, or use them as resources for the kids."

Shou: "I would think that even if you establish a very good school, and you exclude the community, I think that is not a very good idea. To my knowledge, it is good to know the people. They are somewhere outside the school. They could have a better idea, or they could just support you. I myself never went to school when I was a boy. To me, anyone in the community might know something that the educator does not know. And we need one another. If you open your mind to your community, there will be formed knowledge. If any school opens their mind to their community, it will help very much."

Don: "I really have benefited a lot from this project. I have learned a lot, not just about you, but about spiritual things, about parenting, about what it means to be educated—is that just school education, or what else does it mean?—a lot of different things. One thing I wonder about, as you think about doing this project, working with me in the role of a researcher, someone who is trying to find things out, do you have any particular advice that you would give to other people such as myself, maybe who haven't done this kind of thing, but who want to understand the community better, or who want to understand education in a way that honors what the community knows? Do you have any advice for researchers, say, who might work with other people in the Hmong community or other people in the community, or to study other people's lives like yours? What would you suggest that they do?"

Shou: "I would think that asking the particular person whom you want to research about, make a special request: Can I do this? I will appreciate how important you are to me if I could do it. I think most people will accept the research. I do not know if other people will agree with me, but since you are asking a big favor, they would try to support you. I know working with someone who might not benefit you right away, it might not be a very good idea for you to say yes. But I myself, I am a generous person who will provide my own life to anyone who wants to hear it. Anyone who wants to do this kind of research, I think it is important to ask it as a big favor, and then be honest to the person, like what we are doing here today, and appreciate the job. I think that is the most important. Just spending time together like this is good. One thing I do not know for sure if they could share their own personal lives, like what I share. If I am open, they should be open, too."

Don: "So, you are suggesting that the researchers, too, must be willing to open their lives."

Shou: "Yes. There is something we might avoid, which is not to hurt one another."

Don: "I thought about that, and decided I should put in the story about my letter to my brother. I thought, this story about your father's death is a very personal story from you. It hurt. It hurt a lot then, and it probably still hurts. For me to not share a story of mine, which maybe is not as dramatic, but it certainly was a hurtful thing, certainly for my brother, what I did. And not putting that in, I would feel like I hadn't participated fully."

Shou: "I think we have been very, very open, and I believe that it is worthwhile doing that. For me, I wanted to share."

Appendix:
Narrative Inquiry
and the Life History
of a New American*

> Interpretation is an art; it is not formulaic or mechanical. It can be learned, like any form of storytelling, only through doing.
>
> —Norman Denzin (1994, p. 502)

In *Keeping Slug Woman Alive* (1993), Sarris reflects on the difficulties he experiences and the insights he gains from doing the life history of Mabel McKay, a Pomo medicine woman whom he has known since childhood. He concludes that such work is best envisioned as a dialogue of discovery of the self and the Other:

> In understanding another person and culture you must simultaneously understand yourself. The process is ongoing, an endeavor aimed not at a final and transparent understanding of the Other or of the self, but at continued communication, at an ever-widening understanding of both. (p. 6)

In this chapter I argue that narrative inquiry offers unique possibilities for fostering such "continued communication" between the self and Others, and that engaged in a narrative dialogue with diverse Americans, we gain a deeper understanding of who we are, and who we would become. In the first part of this chapter I provide an overview of current trends in qualitative research and particularly, of narrative as a mode of inquiry across disciplines, outline the distinctions between narrative and paradigmatic ways of thinking, describe issues in story reconstruction, address representational dilemmas arising in personal narratives, and discuss methods and issues involved in narrative interpretation. In the

---

*An adapted version of this appendix appears in D. Hones, "Known in Part: The Transformational Power of Narrative Inquiry," *Qualitative Inquiry*, 4(2), 225–248.

second part of this chapter I describe how I used narrative inquiry in writing the educational life history of Shou Cha.

CURRENTS IN QUALITATIVE RESEARCH

Qualitative research is comprised of a broad array of traditions and assumptions that include positivism, poststructuralism, and various perspectives and methods of cultural and interpretive studies. Denzin and Lincoln (1994) write that "qualitative research is difficult to define clearly," as it privileges no methodology, and has "no theory, or paradigm, that is distinctly its own" (p. 3). Denzin and Lincoln do, however, identify five viewpoints shared by many qualitative researchers: Qualitative researchers may be influenced by positivist and postpositivist traditions, but they are less likely to rely on statistical measurements in their interpretation of events; they tend to accept a postmodern position which argues for many different ways of explaining the social world; they are generally interested in representing the perspective of individual subjects; they acknowledge that the social world is in movement, and that this movement constrains their work in various ways; and they favor rich descriptions of people and events.

Like a great river, qualitative research contains many currents, and the waters of these currents often intermingle and influence the flow of the stream. In the following I briefly describe some of the important theoretical trends and modes of inquiry that are influential in qualitative research today. This is not meant as a comprehensive list, but merely a few highlights along the evershifting course of the great river.

Constructivist. For constructivists, knowledge and truth are created, not discovered. A particularly attractive form of constructivism among educational researchers is social constructivism, which assumes that the terms by which the world is understood have been created socially and dialogically (Gergen & Gergen, 1991; Guba & Lincoln, 1989). By arguing that knowledge comes through dialogue with others, constructivists suggest that researchers will come to understanding by exchanging points of view with informants, and testing competing viewpoints "not against predetermined standards of rationality but against the immediate exigencies of life" (Jackson, 1989, p. 14).

Interpretivist. Interpretivist theory is derived from the German intellectual tradition of hermeneutics, phenomenology, and critiques of positivism. Rather than provide scientific explanation, the goal of the natural sciences, interpretivists seek to understand the meanings of phenomena in the social world. One paradox faced by interpretivists is how to give primacy to the subjective experience of informants, and at the same time, create an objective interpretive science. Rabinow and Sullivan (1987) address this paradox by arguing that interpretation is not merely a method, but part of the human condition. The study of the human condition is profoundly interpretive, in Schwandt's (1994) words, because "we do not simply live out our lives *in* time and *through* language; rather, we *are* our history" (p. 120).

Critical.   Critical theory, with its roots in the work of Frankfurt school philosophers such as Herbert Marcuse, examines forms of socially constructed domination, injustice, and discourses of power. Critical theorists seek to question that which appears obvious, to engage in a transformative praxis with disempowered persons and groups, and one of their goals, according to Kincheloe and McLaren (1994), should be "the alleviation of suffering and the overcoming of oppression" (p. 154). Less deterministic than Marxists scholars, critical theorists such as Giroux (1988) argue that schools are not merely means of social reproduction, but are potential sites for resistance and critical empowerment.

Feminist.   The variety of feminist approaches to inquiry share an outlook that centers on the diverse experiences of women, problematizes the social and institutional construction of those experiences, and utilizes research to influence theory, practice and policy to address issues of social justice (Olesen, 1994). Feminist theory is marked by a special attention to subjectivity, relationships, and interactions. Feminist theory thus shares a constructivist concern for dialogue, an interpretivist concern with meaning-making, and a critical concern for research as a means for addressing issues of power in society.

Ethnography.   Ethnography has its roots in the fieldwork of anthropologists such as Malinowski (1922). Generally, it refers to a mode of inquiry characterized by participant observation, the study of a small number of cases, work with "raw" data such as field notes and audio transcripts, and an emphasis on the particular that encourages an interpretive analysis that relies more on rich description and explanation than on statistical data (Atkinson & Hammersley, 1994). Questions facing contemporary ethnographers include: Can the research text represent reality, or should it be treated as fiction? To what extent do informants author the text? Do research texts adequately represent the lives and conditions of those studied? As with other modes of inquiry, such questions are both methodological and ethical in nature.

Phenomenology and Ethnomethodology.   Phenomenology is concerned with the way in which the *"life world"* is experienced, made, and remade by members of society in subtle ways on an everyday basis. Humans have a commonsense *"stock of knowledge"* that they draw on and tend to share, *intersubjectively* (Schutz, 1964). Sharing phenomenology's concern for how people experience their world, ethnomethodology focuses attention on how the daily interpretations of reality by members of a group produces and organizes social life. Thus, ethnomethodologists are interested in natural discursive practices of informants, and how their *"talk"* constitutes or reconstitutes a local reality.

Grounded Theory.   This is a methodology for generating theory from data that has been systematically gathered and analyzed. Grounded theorists such as Glaser and Strauss (1967) argue that theory emerges from the doing of actual research, and that theories grounded in data can be modified and extended as new data is gathered and analyzed. This emphasis on theory development differentiates grounded theory from other approaches to qualitative research. Grounded theory is also noted for systematic questioning and coding procedures, theoretical sampling, and conceptual integration (Strauss & Corbin, 1994).

Historical and Biographical Inquiry.   Historians and biographers are concerned with the story of lived experience. They each see the study and writing of lived experience as work of interpretation. The data gathered in these approaches might include written records of the past, such as letters, diaries, newspapers, and popular literature, or, in the case of living informants, and oral interviews. Historians focus attention on a given period of time and how "we all live history," both in larger events such as wars and recessions, as well as in "the most mundane aspects of our daily lives" (Tuchman, 1994). Biography is the history of a person's life, and biographical inquiry moves beyond disciplinary boundaries to explore a life's many contexts.

Participatory Research.   Participatory and action research seeks to make the research process and research findings more accessible, and relevant to the lives of those studied. Influenced by feminist and critical theory as well as new spiritualities and theories of science, participative researchers tend to see humans as cocreators of reality through participation (Reason, 1994). There is an emphasis on experiential knowing, dialogue, and reflective action by persons and communities, with knowledge arising from this action (Freire, 1968). Data in participative inquiry can range from formally transcribed conversations to expressive forms such as song, dance, and theater. This type of inquiry attempts to create authentic dialogue between researchers and the people whom they wish to study (and serve). One particular strand, Participatory Action Research (PAR), encourages the development of research projects that develop leadership potential within the community studied for further research and action efforts.

NARRATIVE INQUIRY

There is an increasing use of narrative inquiry within the broader field of educational research. Phillips (1994) traces the history of educational inquiry from naturalistic social science to hermeneutics to narratives, a history marked by "the gradual erosion of the positivist model of man ... and the struggle to replace it with a model that more adequately reflects what we humans take to be the nature of ourselves as thinking, feeling, and sometimes rational creatures"(p. 14). Much importance in qualitative research today is placed on meaning-making and folk psychology (Bruner, 1990). Bellah et al. (1985) suggest that social science, when utilizing interpretive methods, can become "a form of self-understanding or self-interpretation" as it "seeks to relate the stories scholars tell to the stories current in the society at large" (p. 301) The integration of historical, sociological, psychological and cultural perspectives to describe the lives of others allows for what Rabinow and Sullivan (1987) call the return to the hermeneutical circle, or "circle of meaning" that is a goal of interpretive social science.

Narrative research takes hermeneutics one step further by arguing that people understand their lives and explain their lives through stories, and these stories feature plots, characters, times and places. Polkinghorne (1995) argues that the narrative is "the linguistic form uniquely suited for displaying human existence as situated action" (p. 5). Clandinin and Connelly (1994) suggest that the reconstructed stories of people's lives are a fundamental educational tool: "People live stories, and in the telling of them reaffirm them, modify them, and create new ones ... Stories ... educate the self and others, including the young and those, such as researchers, who are new to their communities" (p. 415).

Moreover, noted scholars in many fields have suggested that the study of individual lives over time is indispensable for social inquiry (see, for example, Clausen, 1993; Cremin, 1988; Gardner, 1994). In anthropology, Rabinow (1977) and Crapanzano (1980) have explored the difficulties and possibilities of combining life histories with cultural analysis; in psychology, life history has often been part of the study of personality development over time (Erikson, 1962; White, 1952); and in sociology, individual life histories have been woven into community mosaics

(Becker, 1970; Terkel, 1972). Such biographical work encompasses Mills' (1959) contention that "Man is a social and an historical actor who must be understood, if at all, in close and intricate interplay with social and historical structures" (p. 158).

In her extensive survey of narrative research in the field of education, Casey (1996) suggests several reasons why this mode of interpretive inquiry has wide appeal at the end of the 20th century: Narrative research reverses "the academic trend toward deterministic economic analysis and reproductive cultural studies of schooling" by focusing on human agency, and the ability of individuals to creatively construct their lives within social and historical contexts (p. 214). Much current narrative research focuses on the lives of ordinary people, individuals whose lives are in part defined by racial, class and gender boundaries constructed by the dominant culture. By "celebrating" the lives of diverse individuals and diverse histories, such narratives offer an alternative to a traditional canon shaped by a history of "great White men" (p. 215). Moreover, narratives offer contrasting ways in which to address the social and psychological disruptions that characterize the postmodern era. At the level of the TV talk show, "telling one's story becomes exhibitionism, and listening to another's becomes voyeurism." However, narrative also offers a "way to put shards of experience together, to (re)construct identity, community, and tradition, if only temporarily" (p. 216).

What is narrative research? Polkinghorne (1995) notes that although the term *narrative* has been used extensively in research reports to describe any prosaic discourse (e.g., field notes, written transcriptions), used more specifically, *narrative* refers to a story (or "emplotted narrative"). Clandinin and Connelly (1994) distinguish between the narrative phenomenon, or *story*, and the narrative method, *inquiry*. In narrative research stories are what the inquirer collects, retells, and writes. Central to the construction of a narrative are time, place, character, and multiple researcher "I's": "The 'I' who speaks as researcher, teacher, man or woman, commentator, research participant, narrative critic, and theory builder." (p. 416)

Narrative Thought

The term *narrative* can describe a form of cognitive organization. In recent years, psychologist Bruner (1985) and others (Polkinghorne, 1995; Ricoeur, 1983) have argued that narrative knowledge, rather than a mere emotional response, is a form of reasoned knowing. Bruner suggests that there are two types of cognition, one paradigmatic, and the other narrative. Paradigmatic cognition involves classifying by category or concept, and has traditionally been held as "the exclusive cognitive mode for the generation of trustworthy and valid knowledge" (Polkinghorne, 1995, p. 9). Paradigmatic thought guides much of contemporary scholarly work, as it provides a way to bring order to individual items through categorization. Narrative cognition, on the other hand, involves understanding human action by noticing the differences, and the diversity of human behavior. Experiences are translated into specific, "storied" episodes. The object of narrative inquiry is not to find instances of a general type, but to find analogies to a similar remembered episode (Polkinghorne, 1995). Thus, inherent to the method of narrative inquiry is the use of narrative cognition as a way to organize life events. Table A.1 presents some of Bruner's (1985) contrasts between paradigmatic and narrative modes of thought in a more "paradigmatic" fashion:

TABLE A.1
Modes of Thought and Understanding in Science and Scholarship[1]

	Paradigmatic (Logical/Scientific)	Narrative (Literary/Historical)
Goals, ideals of inquiry	Formal, mathematical system of description and explanation of causality; knowledge of universal truths; certainty, predictability	Expressive representations of human intention, thought, and action, and of relations between events and human meaning making; verisimilitude or life-likeness, representativeness
Form	Categories and systems; abstract argument; timeless	Narratives and stories; particular, concrete; temporal
Language	Consistent and noncontradictory; neutral; minimizes voice of inquirer	Multiple and many leveled meanings; figurative; recognizes, sometimes maximizes, voice of inquirer
Verification	By appeals to procedures; reflects established methods	By appeal to representational effectiveness; conveys meanings

Note. Based on the work of Bruner (1985), this table illustrates that paradigmatic and narrative modes are distinct ways of knowing, with different goals, forms, language and ways of verification. Bruner and others have argued that each mode of thought has value for empirical research.
[1]From Huberman, Thompson, and Weiland (1997, p. 17).

Retelling a Life, Reconstructing a Story

Narrative inquiry can be distinguished from other types of qualitative research by its focus on the individual, the personal nature of the research process, its "practical" orientation and its emphasis on subjectivity (Hatch & Wisniewski, 1995). Focusing on the central moments in individual lives allows life history and narrative researchers to bring more complexity and ambiguity to the reality of human interaction in the world, with characters who are "more 'rounded' and believable ... than the 'flat,' seemingly irrational, and linear characters from other forms of qualitative inquiry" (Sparkes, quoted in Hatch & Wisniewski, 1995, p. 116).

Related to this focus on the individual is the personal nature of the narrative inquiry. To be effective, this type of inquiry requires the researcher and the subject to work toward a shared understanding of the subject's story, and their relationship is built on dialogue and subject collaboration in the design, conduct, and analysis of the research. The focus on individual lives enables narrative research to place social theory in a practical light, as well as to connect an individual's personal history with the social history of his or her life span. Finally, narrative research is marked by subjectivity. The focus on the subject's "voice" and story are seen as a positive contribution of the narrative genre to social science research. This feature of narrative research has been utilized by writers who seek ways to let their informants speak for themselves, especially those informants who, by nature of their race, class or gender, have mostly lived on the margins of the dominant society (e.g., Belenky, Clinchy, Goldberger, Tarule, 1986; Gwaltney, 1980; Kotlowitz, 1991; McLaughlin & Tierney, 1993).

Smith (1994) contends that the life history writer must identify a hero or heroine, even if the larger society does not recognize the person as such. Moreover, the writer must attempt to find the "essence" of the protagonist, the inner person behind the outer veneer. Finally, life history writers must acknowledge their own inability to ever completely understand the "other." The anthropologist Geertz (1983) contends that, at best, one's understanding of the "other" is more "like grasping a proverb, catching an allusion, seeing a joke or ... reading a poem—than it is like achieving communion" (p. 70).

Narrative inquiry shares much in common with other forms of qualitative research in its methods of collecting and processing data, yet there are important differences. As with ethnography, narrative inquiry involves data from both "outside" research, such as interviews, oral histories, and field notes, and "inside" research, with letters, documents, and library materials (Clifford, 1970; Smith, 1994). Perhaps more than with other qualitative methods, narrative inquiry is concerned with the way in which a subject's life and thoughts are represented through field and research texts. Clandinin and Connelly (1994) suggest that this collected data, or "field text", gains its meaning through the relationship between the researcher and the subject. Between the field experience and the field text are various levels of subject collaboration, interpretation, and researcher influence. Some narrative researchers are inclined to present powerful passages from oral histories, interviews, and other field texts without comment, letting them "speak for themselves." However, Clandinin and Connelly argue that the field text must be reconstructed as research text, by probing for meaning and social significance, and developing patterns, themes, and narrative threads in the subject's story.

Drawing on the work of Dollard (1935), Polkinghorne (1995) suggests several criteria for the development of life narratives. These include the description of the cultural context; the physical, mental, and psychological nature of the protagonist (subject); the social relationships of the protagonist (family, friends, coworkers); the choices and actions of the protagonist moving toward a goal; consider the historical background of the protagonist; the construction of a coherent story with marked beginning and point of denouement; the development of unique characters and plot; and the writing of a storyline that is plausible, understandable, and consistent with the data. Polkinghorne suggests that these guidelines "advance the ideal of an integrated plot that synthesizes the cultural, biological, historical and individual aspects of the person into a unified story" (p. 32).

The narrative inquirer recognizes the primacy of writing in the research process. Denzin (1994) argues that "fieldworkers can neither make sense of nor understand what has been learned until they sit down and write the interpretive text" (p. 502). He suggests four interrelated problems that the writer of narratives must address in moving between the field and the text: This interpretive movement involves *sense making*, wherein the researcher decides what from the field notes and transcripts shall be included in the research text, and how the story will be represented; *representation,* wherein the researcher grapples with how best to represent the voice of the Other, and recognizes that "representation ... is always self-presentation" by positioning him- or herself in the story (p. 510); *legitimization,* wherein the researcher must decide what type of authoritative claims to make about the public text; and *desire,* which involves the creation of a text that is vital, engaging, and an adventure for both the writer and the reader.

Representational Dilemmas in Personal Narratives

Narrative researchers surveyed by Hatch and Wisniewski (1995) suggested that there are strong ethical concerns to be addressed in relationships with research participants. How can a narrative inquirer retell another's life in a way that avoids distortion and disempowerment? Researchers must recognize the vulnerability of subjects, and addressing issues of authorship, ownership, and voice in texts. One of the respondents, Lisa Smulyan, asks: "How do we carry out a collaborative, mutually beneficial project while working through issues of knowledge, power, control, and privacy; how, as a researcher, can I contribute as much as the subject of my work is giving" (p. 119)?

Recognizing that the story reported will not be the same as the story told, Grumet (1991) nonetheless argues that the narrative inquirer must give a fair representation of the story back to the teller: "So if telling a story requires giving oneself away, we are obligated to devise a method that returns a story to the teller that is both hers and not hers: that contains her self in good company" (p. 70).

By sharing manuscripts with informants and involving them in the analysis and interpretation of their life narratives, researchers can combat a long social science tradition of paternalism toward "natives" that has accompanied cultural, economic and political colonialism. An example of such a collaborative approach is found in the work of anthropologist McBeth with informant Burnett Horne (McBeth & Burnett Horne, 1996). Their joint analysis and interpretation of Burnett Horne's life history is presented to the reader as a dialogue. Such dialogues between the worlds of the researcher and those of the informants, according to Tedlock (1983), "will stand or fall on their own merits ... not on the basis of whether the investigator got what he claims he had been looking for" (p. 333). Thus, the representation of the informant and the researcher in the text is a major concern of narrative inquiry. Tierney suggests that "how we present that life, who is 'author' and how subject-researcher gets defined are issues that go to the heart of doing qualitative work in a postmodern world, and they are best dealt with in life history work" (quoted in Hatch & Wisniewski, 1995, p. 121).

A possible form for representing the interplay between researcher and informant is suggested by psychologist Coles. In *Children of Crisis: A Study of Courage and Fear* (1964), Coles presents in narrative form his interactions with several participants on both sides of the movement to desegregate the South. Coles chose to represent long stretches of informant "voice," interspersed with his contextual comments, without using indentations, single spacing, and other traditional means of differentiating between the voice of the researcher and that of the informant. Here is a sample from his narrative of "Larry", a student from the north who was finishing his "Freedom Summer" sojourn in Mississippi:

> Larry left very early in the morning, and he left quickly. The goodbyes were kept down to a minimum. They all pretended—or believed—he would soon be back. As he drove north he never doubted that he would see the Johnson's again, but he did doubt his capacity to resume life at college. "I kept on wondering how I could face it: the silliness and emptiness; the instructors who think they're God because they've read a few books and can sit and talk about 'ideas'; the ivy that doesn't only climb the buildings but grows up the legs and into the brains of both teachers and students. What would a football game mean to me? A spring riot over nothing? A rule about wearing a tie at breakfast?" (p. 202)

Coles was able to present the voice of both researcher and informant within the context of a life narrative by combining his contextual descriptions and interpretations with direct quotes from informants. This form of arranging the narrative allows Cole to "give prominence to the lives of those people, to their involvements with the world—but there has to be the qualification: as I have seen and known those lives and involvements" (p. 34). Moreover, Coles uses this form to "convey to the reader what about that person ... sheds light upon the central (and vexing) issue this book aims to examine: the relationship between individual lives and the life of a nation—where crisis has come upon them both" (p. 33).

Anthropologist Sarris (1993, 1994) offers another viewpoint on how to represent the interaction and dialogue between a researcher and a protagonist. Sarris found that the ethnographic interviewing methods in which he was trained at Stanford University were inadequate in representing the life of Mabel McKay, a Pomo Indian medicine woman whom he had known personally since childhood. Once, when driving McKay back to the Rumsey Reservation after her lecture at Stanford, Sarris sought her help in identifying a major theme for her life history:

> "Mabel, people want to know about things
> in your life in a way they can understand. You
> know, how you got to be who you are. There has to
> be a theme."
> "I don't know about no theme."
> I squirmed in my seat. Her hands didn't
> move. "A theme is a point that connects all
> the dots, ties up all the stories."
> "That's funny. Tying up all the stories.
> Why somebody want to do that?"
> "When you write a book there has to be a

story, or idea, a theme ... "
"Well, theme I don't know nothing about.
That's somebody else's rule." (Sarris, 1994, p. 5)

Sarris reflects on what McKay's stories taught him about life and about himself, and he suggests that the goal of his work is to "chart dialogues that open and explore interpersonal and intercultural territories" (1993, p. 5).

Truth or Fidelity

Should truth be a criteria in judging personal narratives? Various narrative researchers have argued that such interpretive work be guided, not by concerns for "validity," but rather by concern for believability, fidelity, and plausibility (Blumenfeld-Jones, 1995; Bruner, 1985; Polkinghorne, 1995). Bruner argues that "narrative accounts can be lifelike and exhibit verisimilitude even when they contain demonstrable falsehoods." Citing psychoanalytic theory, Bruner contends that "human adaptation to life itself depends upon (one's success) in generating a believable narrative, one that ... weaves in but does not necessarily mirror the historical truth" (p. 99). Erickson (1992), on the other hand, suggests that thickly described narratives that involve close analysis of elements of social interaction can achieve a descriptive validity.

Phillip's (1994), however, argues that the issue of truth in narrative accounts must not be overlooked. Phillips suggests that, when seeking to explain events, subjects may offer stories that they mistakenly believe to be true. At other times, narratives are offered as justifications or rationalizations of actions taken. Phillips adds:

> Unfortunately, human nature is such that we have a pronounced tendency to readily believe that the considerations we offer by way of justification of our own actions were the factors that actually led us to act that way, and it might take a very refined degree of self-understanding for some of us to realize that we have become victims of self-delusion. (p. 20)

Several other aspects of personal stories influence the "truthfulness" of narrative accounts: Stories are grounded in culture, and a cultural understanding of "truth;" they come in multiple, ever-changing versions; and the story told differs from the story heard. Each of these aspects will be explored further to follow.

Stories of individual lives are grounded in culture, and cultural criteria for understanding "truthfulness." Denzin (1989) contends that "autobiographies and biographies are only fictional statements with varying degrees of 'truth' about 'real' lives. True stories are stories that are believed in" (p. 25). Crapanzano's (1980) work with Tuhami, a Moroccan tile worker, illustrates this complex relationship between "truth" and believability. Tuhami's account of his life is full of events that probably never took place, and yet these events contain "truths" that Crapanzano calls "autobiographical":

> It was Tuhami who first taught me to distinguish between the reality of personal history and truth of autobiography. The former rests on the presumption of a correspondence between a text, or structure of words, and a body of human actions; the latter resides within the text itself without regard to any external criteria save, perhaps, the I of the narrator. Their equivalence is, I believe, a Western presumption. (p. 5)

"Truth" in personal narratives comes in multiple versions and is ever-changing. Subjects reporting on the same events or experiences may not concur with each other on the "truth" of what happened; furthermore, versions of events offered by individual subject's may change. Freeman (1993) contends that in the study of lives, truth is ever-changing, as former ideas are challenged, and complexity and comprehensiveness are added. Furthermore, the process of understanding, like the process of development, has no endpoint. Narrative inquirers could use ever-changing, multiple versions of the "truth" to build a more meaningful, believable life history account, much as Kurasawa used several characters' versions of events to give deeper meaning to the story of "Rashomon." Certainly the reports of more than one participant in a given event could be represented in the text, allowing the writer to triangulate sources to create a more believable story.

"Truth" in narratives is further problematized by the nature of the subject–inquirer relationship. As Denzin (1989, p. 77) suggests, "the stories told are never the same as the stories heard." Blumenfeld-Jones (1995) notes that many layers of intention and reconstruction are present in the process of telling life stories: The subject has purposes for telling particular stories, which causes him to reconstruct his own life narrative. In addition, the narrative inquirer has his or her own purposes in mind for the story heard, and is also reconstructing the narrative. For this reason, Blumenfeld-Jones argues that a narrative inquirer must maintain "fidelity" to both the storyteller and the story, much as an artist would maintain fidelity with his or her subject. Rather than the objective truth of science, then, narrative inquirers could pursue the subjective beauty of art: "Narrative inquiry is an artificial endeavor existing within layers of intention and reconstruction. This artificiality brings fidelity and narrative inquiry into the arena of artistic process" (p. 28).

Perhaps through the artistry of this subjective relationship the inquirer remains more "true" to his or her subject and his or her subject's story than through the objective methods of positivist science. Miller (1996) suggests that one can reject both absolutist claims to the truth, as well as cultural relativism, arguing instead that reality is negotiated through social interactions:

> As anthropologists, as educators, as individuals, we must not presume to have an edge on the nature of reality. The life stories told us can provide insight into other worlds which we ourselves have not experienced. If we respect the narrator and the story, then perhaps we can invent a reality which includes both perspectives and fosters understanding. (p. 116)

Narrative Interpretation

Denzin (1994) identifies several major research paradigms that influence the interpretation of narrative texts. One popular postpositivist interpretive style involves the use of grounded theory. As developed by Glaser and Strauss (1967), grounded theory does not seek to force data to conform with existing theory, but rather develops theory and interpretive categories that are "grounded" in the data itself. For example, Ruth and Oberg (1992) used grounded theory to analyze the collected life stories of several women, grouped qualitatively similar life stories together into categories, and then labeled the categories by their dominant qualities. Thus, commonalities existing across life stories were uncovered. A constructivist interpretive style makes use of grounded theory as well as inductive data analysis and contextual interpretation. The goal of constructivist interpretation is to triangulate various data sources that are credible, transferable, dependable, and confirmable. Critical theorists use an interpretive style that seeks to engage the voices and collaboration of oppressed groups of people within the framework of a neo-Marxist cultural critique of social structures. Poststructural interpretive styles are varied, yet have certain tenets in common. Denzin makes an important distinction between positivist and postpositivist types of analysis and the analytical frameworks employed by poststructuralists. Unlike the former, poststructuralists do not rely on preconceived categories, and do not seek to impose their theoretical frameworks. Rather, their goal is to let "the prose of the world speak for itself," and they highlight multivocality and multiple perspectives (p. 511). Denzin's interpretive style of choice involves the organizing of life histories around "epiphanies," important, life-shaping events, using a poststructuralist interpretive framework he calls *interpretive interactionism*. This style "begins and ends with the biography and the self of the researcher," and encourages personal stories that are thickly contextualized, and "connected to larger institutional, group and cultural contexts" (pp. 510-511). Moreover, the stories presented in the text "should be given in the language, feelings, emotions, and actions of those studied" (p. 511).

WRITING THE LIFE HISTORY OF SHOU CHA

In the life history of a Hmong American that follows, I have chosen the following methods drawn from narrative inquiry: Following the advice of Polkinghorne (1995), Smith (1994), and others, I have chosen a single protagonist and sought to develop a plot, and describe fully the setting and characters. Like Grumet (1991) and McBeth (1996), I am concerned with representing my informant's story in a respectful manner, and with including him in the process of analysis and interpretation. Furthermore, like Coles (1964), and Sarris (1994), I seek a form for this story that allows for the representation of the dialogue between myself and my informant, and for substantial passages of my informant's "voice." Moreover, I wish to use narrative forms that are engage readers aesthetically as well as critically (Brunner, 1994). My interpretation of this life history narrative encompasses four dimensions: First, through the arrangement of the story itself, punctuated by epiphanies experienced by my informant (Denzin, 1994; Polkinghorne, 1995); secondly, through the contextualization of my informant's life within history, culture, and the social milieu; third, through the identification of emergent themes, drawing on a combination of grounded theory (Glaser & Strauss, 1967) and Denzin's (1994) interpretive interactionism; and finally, through a search for significance that both shapes, and is shaped by, the story itself.

Education comes from the Latin *educere*, "to lead out." Through the medium of this life history I look to represent or interpret an individual's educational experiences, with *education* understood broadly as a process of leading out: that is, those experiences in the family, in school, in books, in nature, in community, in solitude, material as well as spiritual, which help guide an individual on his or her path in life. Moreover, I seek to place these educational experiences within important contexts of family, community, school, society, and history.

The Protagonist

The writer of educational life histories begins by choosing a protagonist whose life and learning will be explored. Every one of us has stories to tell about our lives, and many of these stories could be of educational interest. Therefore, it is important for the researcher to narrow the quest for potential protagonists somewhat, perhaps by posing questions to oneself: Is there a particular educational problem I would like to explore through biography? Would I like to examine this problem through the life of a teacher, a student, a parent, and/or a community member? Is there a particular subgroup of the general population that is of interest? When I thought about these questions, I realized that the "problem" I was interested in was the role of education in assimilating (or facilitating the adaptation of) new immigrants into American society. Because of my experiences as a teacher of adults and a father, I was interested in doing the biography of a parent who had children in the schools. Finally, a long-standing interest in linguistic and cultural minority communities led to my decision to look for a protagonist among the Hmong refugee community. There is a limited but growing literature about the life experiences of the Hmong in America (e.g., Chan, 1994; Donnelly, 1994; Santoli, 1988; Ungar, 1995). Although I do not speak Hmong and have not visited Southeast Asia, I felt that by exploring the life of a Hmong adult, one of the newest Americans, I would learn more about the Hmong, myself, and the meaning of "being American."

Not being a member of the Hmong community, I was fortunate to have the assistance of a Hmong community liaison who worked at an elementary school where I did research. This liaison talked with members of his community, and came back to me with the name and phone number of a man who had children at the school and who spoke and understood English reasonably well. I called the man, Mr. Lee, arranged to interview him at his home, and began an initial series of weekly visits that would last approximately 3 months. During my visits, I was able to communicate in English without an interpreter with both Mr. Lee and three of his older children. A few months later, as I called to explore the possibility of interviewing additional members of the family, Mr. Lee informed me that he and the rest of the family would be moving north to open a restaurant in a small town. Unfortunately, due to my own family obligations, I was unable to accompany the Lees on this new adventure. Therefore, I called up the liaison again, and he suggested I talk to Mr. Cha, a new member of the bilingual staff at the school. When I met Shou later at his house, I found myself in the presence of someone with a special vitality and warmth. He was a handsome man in his mid 30s, with dark hair, bright eyes, and a lively, expressive face. Shou was delighted to share stories about his life with me, and became an enthusiastic participant in this research.

My research data were comprised largely of audiotaped interviews and observation notes. I interviewed Shou Cha, his wife, some of his children, and his employers, and coworkers at the school. In addition, I observed Shou's interactions with his family, his church, members of the Hmong community, coworkers, and children at the school. Once a protagonist is identified, an educational biographer can prepare an initial interview protocol that allows for open-ended responses, yet, at the same time, focuses on particular issues that may be relevant to guiding questions of the research and the particularities of the informant. My initial interview protocol used with Shou Cha can be found in Table A.2. Of course, once I became engaged in dialogue with Shou Cha, some of these questions became more relevant than others, while new questions arose during the course of our interviews. Other important questions occurred to me later, as I listened to Shou's audiotaped stories or reread transcripts of our conversations.

Gathering Data for the Narrative

My life history of Shou Cha involved collecting and categorizing data through semistructured interviews and participant observation. Over the course of 6 months I spent frequent evenings at the Cha home, especially on Saturdays, the 1 night of the week Shou Cha usually had free. I also spent a few hours each week at Kallen school, interviewing, observing, and volunteering in music activities, and on the playground. In addition, I also spent 1 afternoon as a guest at Shou's church, attending Sunday school and the service.

Interviews were conducted with several informants, principally Shou Cha, the protagonist of this life history; members of his immediate and extended family; members of his church and the Windigo Hmong community, and his coworkers and employers at the Kallen school. Because I am unable to communicate in Hmong, the first language of many of my informants, all interviews were conducted in English. When necessary, Shou Cha, who has strong communication skills in four languages, helped interpret for me, especially when I was a guest at his church.

Participant observation is a key feature of this research, as formal and informal interviews can only reveal part of the life of an individual. Erickson (1992) suggests that through participant observation, "one can test one's theory of the organization of an event by trying out various kinds of participation in it" (p. 209). Participant observation allows for a better understanding of the verbal and nonverbal interaction within the family. I was able to get to know Shou's children, largely through helping with homework, playing chess and checkers, watching them watch television, and doing outdoor activities. I was able to observe Mai Cha as she organized the household, prepared meals, and interacted with the children, Shou, and the many members of the Hmong community who frequented their home. I gained an appreciation for Shou Cha at work, observing him in his interactions with colleagues, parents, and especially children, in his

TABLE A.2
Protocol for Interview With Shou Cha

1. Place of birth, and year. Earliest memories. Stories heard from elders (folktales and Hmong history remembered).

2. Family relationships as child. Number of brothers and sisters; description of father and mother, and their roles in family; activities of the family; games played.

3. Learning at home. Things taught to you by mother, father, siblings, or other relatives—such as farming (techniques, etc.); hunting; fishing; embroidery; traditional medicine; commerce; helping parents, or helping with other children.

4. Favorite activities as a child. Best and worst memories of childhood.

5. Learning in the community. Relationship with extended family, clan, village. Community activities—markets, festivals (e.g., New Year's); describe these.

6. Formal schooling. Describe subjects learned, manner of schooling. Best and worst memories of school.

7. Marriage and parenting. How you met your spouse, how you got married. Why you were interested in marrying this person. Having children—the experience of childbirth. Parenting and child care roles, activities; home medicine; teaching the children—what would you teach them first, and how would you teach them? Best and worst memories of parenting.

8. The war in Laos. Your activities during the war: Father—soldiering? What did they teach you? What did you learn how to do? Strongest/worst memories of being a soldier? Greatest difficulties? Relations with U.S., CIA? Mother—taking care of family and farm? How did you organize the children to help? Did the war come to your village? How did you manage? What did you have to learn how to do? Strongest/worst memories of wartime.

9. Exodus. How did you leave Laos? What were the circumstances of your departure? What dangers did you face on the way to Thailand? What were the strongest memories of this time?

10. Refugee camp life (Ban Vinai?). How long were you there? What did you do to pass the time? How did you organize your family and community? What were the dangers and difficulties of camp life? What are your strongest memories of the time? (to Mother: Did you make any Pan dau (sp) at this time? Do you have any I could see?) How and when did you decide to come to the United States?

11. Coming to United States. Where did you settle first? Where else have you lived, and for how long? What caused you to move from place to place (family, kinship ties)? What were the difficulties faced in adjusting to the new culture, language, and land? What did you need to learn to adapt here? (E.g., language, cultural "rules" of behavior, job skills?)

continued on next page

12. What surprised you most about the United States? About the American people? What are (were) your best and worst impressions of America?

13. Hmong community support. Who helped you when you came to the United States? Who did you stay with? Who helped you find a house? A job? A school for the children? How have you helped other Hmong who have just moved to a new location? Why do you help each other (family, kinship ties—or more extensive ties to all Hmong)?

14. Learning in the United States. What have you learned since arriving here? (E.g., how to drive a car, English, job skills, cultural "rules" of behavior, how to find things that are needed.) Who helps you learn these things? What do you learn from friends? Reading? TV? Your children?

15. Formal education. English classes attended? Other formal education since arrival? Best and worst memories of this schooling? Memorable teachers?

16. Working. What professional learning have you experienced? What jobs have you held? What skills learned? What are difficulties of working in United States? Most memorable work experiences? (Father may be in educational field—sub questions).

17. Parenting in United States. How has your role as a parent changed? How has it remained the same? How has relationship with spouse changed? Relationship with children? Are traditional Hmong values about parent–child relationships changing in your family?

18. What have you taught your children about living in the United States? What have they taught you? (E.g., English expressions, social norms.)

19. What is the role of school in the lives of your kids? Its importance for them? What do you want them to learn? Are there things (e.g., certain behaviors) you do not want them to learn in school? How have your children done with this? Are you happy with their educational experiences?

20. Parent–teacher contact. Do you know your children's teachers? Have you visited their schools? Is this important?

21. What is the importance of Hmong language and culture for your children? What languages are spoken in the home? What traditional cultural practices do you continue to observe (e.g., gender roles, spiritual beliefs, food, etc.). Which Hmong practices do you want your children to continue?

22. What would you like to leave your children, if you could leave them something important from your cultural heritage as Hmong?

23. What does it mean, for you, to be an American? Can you be an American and Hmong, too?

---

role as an intermediary between the world of the Hmong community, and the world of the school.

Interpreting data collected from interviews, participant observation, artifacts, and library research in order to craft an educational life history is always problematic, but more so when one's protagonist has very different cultural and linguistic practices than one's own. My protagonist, and members of his family and ethnic community, must communicate their lives to me through the medium of a second language and culture. It is likely that many of the nuances that they may wish to communicate will be lost in translation or cross-cultural miscommunication. Moreover, some of my informants may have hesitated to speak freely with a researcher who is an outsider to the community. As refugees, they have suffered the calamities of war, loss of homeland, and relocation to a strange new land; their lived experiences and their knowledge of history have given them reasons to distrust people from outside their group.

By taking seriously the dialogical (Bakhtin, 1981) relationship between myself, my informants, and our subject matter, I have tried to overcome some of the initial hesitation on the part of my informants. However, dialogue, encompassing the sharing of stories, information, and interpretation between informant and researcher, raises Clifford's (1988) intriguing question, "Who is actually the author of field notes" (p. 45)? Subjects of ethnographic studies have influenced the direction of research in many subtle or more blatant ways (e.g., Rosaldo, 1980). To what extent will Shou Cha, as well as other informants, author this research? By proposing a life history format, I acknowledge my part in deciding what is included, what is left out, and how the story is arranged on the printed page. However, by regularly sharing relevant sections of my field notes and interview transcripts with Shou Cha, his family, and other informants, I hope to allow them to interpret the text of this life history with me, and to produce vignettes of immigrant life that are meaningful both to the Chas, and to educators and policymakers. In order to create a meaningful life history I seek to document the "circles of meaning," the everyday common sense understanding of the Cha's themselves, what Geertz (1983) calls the "native's point of view."

Through interviews and participant observation I hope to construct a believable narrative of Shou Cha's educational life, and to maintain "fidelity" with my subject and his story. I hope to approach a true record of events, ever-changing as that truth may be, by triangulating the stories of various informants, their letters, and photographs, with the historical record represented in books, articles, video documentaries, and other published research. For example, personal stories about life in a Thai refugee camp can be triangulated with books and videos about such camps.

Finally, I agree with Denzin (1994), that interpretive research is an art, not a science, and something that must be learned through practice. How to best write the tale of the Cha family will be learned through the telling. And, as Van Maanen (1988) suggests, "The magic of telling impressionist tales is that they are always unfinished" (p. 120).

Poetic Representation of the Life History

A number of researchers who work with oral narratives have suggested that one of the best ways to represent the spoken lives of people is through poetry (Conquergood, 1989; Richardson, 1992; Tedlock, 1983). Tedlock (1983) has written:

> If anthropologists, folklorists, linguists, and oral
> historians
> are interested in the full meaning
> of the spoken word
> then they must stop treating oral narratives
> as if they were reading prose
> when in fact they are listening to dramatic poetry. (p. 123)

Sociologist Richardson (1992) takes this concern with aesthetic representation one step further by suggesting the poetic in apparently bland stories of ordinary Americans such as "Louisa May:"

> It was purely chance
> that I got a job here,
> and Robert didn't.
> I was mildly happy.
>
> After 14 years of marriage,
> that was the break.
>
> We divorced.
>
> A normal sort of life. (p. 128)

In seeking to represent lived experience in ways that reaffirm the lives of those being studied, Richardson used poetic structures to engage both the emotions and the critical minds of readers.

Along with the work of Tedlock and Richardson, Conquergood's (1989) life story of a Hmong shaman, presented as an epic poem, has been particularly influential in my decision to occasionally represent the emotive power of Shou Cha's narrative in poetic form. These occasions were few, and tended to come at points where Shou Cha was narrating particular life crises.

In the following pages I give an example of my representation of the "voice" of Shou Cha as I moved between an initial audiotaped transcript and the final form of the research text.[2] I begin at a point in one of our first

---

[2]The full transcript of this episode can be found in Appendix C.

interviews where Shou tells the story that opens this study, recounting how he was shot in the back, outside a convenience store near his home, his recovery in a local hospital, and his feelings when the doctors told him he could go home:

Shou: "But after I came from the hospital the things that I think in my mind—now its quite changed, its changed a lot, but back to that time, the first week, I'm gonna tell you what I think, back to that time. I said,

There isn't any solid place, any place of peace on Earth. There isn't. I stay in the hospital for 2 weeks. I do not, I disown that place. The hospital is not my place. They said, you can go home. And I don't have a home to go. This house I live in which is not my house. Not my home. I live by the money. This place belongs to someone else. It's not my house. I don't belong to Earth.

Besides, I scared. I do not know if next day I get shot again. I don't trust going outside. I do not know how I should live. I do not want to stay by the window. I don't want to sit by the window. I don't want to live in this area. I don't want to live anywhere. I don't belong to this Earth.

These, there were a lot of things in my mind. And a couple, 5 days from the day I got shot, my mother, who stayed with me in this house, she prepared my youngest, my younger, my second youngest daughter going to kindergartner school. And somehow, she does not know why, she fell on the cement walking, sidewalk. And all her face got scratched and bruised, And she does not know why. And that even bring me lower. I said, Why that happen? And she has a problem too, she has a disease sometimes, too. And I said, Why she fall down. And she does not realize how, why, how she fall down. And when I came back her mouth still kind of ..."

Don: "Swollen?"

Shou: "Swollen, her face was still, uh ..."

Don: "Bruised?"

Shou: "Bruised and scratched, and swollen too. And I said, Oh no. Why me? Why me? So my mother also said, this Earth does not belong to us. We do not belong to the Earth. So that's bad, but the only good thing by that time we experienced we say, we don't belong to the Earth. We belong to Heaven, where we should go. And we should go until we are there. That's the feeling back at that time. Very strong."

From the original transcription, various changes were made to craft the story represented in the research text, as the following excerpt from Shou's account illustrates:

But after I came from the hospital, the first week, I'm gonna tell you what I thought. I said:

There isn't any solid place,
any place of peace on Earth.
There isn't.
I stayed in the hospital for two weeks.
I disown that place.
The hospital is not my place.
They said:
You can go home.
And I don't have a home to go to.
This house I live in is not my house.
Not my home.
I live by the money.
This place belongs to someone else.
It's not my house.
I don't belong to this Earth.

Besides, I am scared.
I do not know if
the next day I will get shot again.
I don't trust going outside.
I do not know how I should live.
I do not want to stay by the window.
I don't want to live in this area.
I don't want to live anywhere.
I don't belong to this Earth.

Five days after I got shot,
My mother fell on the cement sidewalk.
And all her face got bruised and scratched.
She does not know why.
And that even brought me lower.
I said,
Why did that happen?
And when I came back
her mouth was still kind of swollen,
her face was still bruised and scratched.
And I said,
Oh no.
Why me?
Why me?
My mother also said,
This Earth does not belong to us.
We do not belong to this Earth.

The only good thing we experienced at that time
is when we said,
We don't belong to the Earth.

We belong to Heaven,
where we should go.
And we should keep going until we are there.

Several issues are apparent in the representation of this episode in Shou Cha's life. First is the issue of language, and whether or not the "voice" of the protagonist is best represented in his exact words. Shou Cha is not a native speaker of English, and he makes occasional grammatical or speech errors. I felt that the meaningfulness of Shou's narrative to an English-speaking audience would be enhanced by correcting such errors. Another issue is the representation of my own voice. For this episode, I made the decision to delete my questions and comments from the research text, and reconstruct it as a longer story in Shou's voice. I made this decision because I felt that, as a major event, or epiphany, in Shou's life, the story had an underlying cohesiveness that was somewhat fragmented by the inclusion of my short questions. Moreover, I felt the meaningfulness of the episode was enhanced when it was reported in Shou's words only, even as he described the dialogues he engaged in with hospital personnel and visitors. Finally, I made the decision to represent part of this episode as poetry. I was moved by Shou's description of his feelings when leaving the hospital, and I felt that, represented as poetry, and set off from the rest of the text by the use of italics, the emotive quality of this passage would be more clearly conveyed in the text than if it were represented as prose.

The representation of Shou's voice in the text has also been influenced by his reading and our discussion of earlier drafts of this life history. Shou, perhaps because of his early training in Hmong song, enthusiastically supported the rendering of some of his oral speech as poetry. Moreover, throughout the text he added additional information or, in some cases, advocated that some information be left out. I would like to discuss two of these instances, as they illustrate both Shou's part in fashioning the research text as well as the importance he places on maintaining strong relationships within his family.

In one of our first interviews, Shou recounted to me a dream he had in Chicago that influenced his decision to go to theological school.[3] After I showed him my initial rendering of this dream as a poem, Shou told me that some of was missing. When I replied that I had transcribed everything on the audiotape, he brought over a marker and a drawing board and explained the dream to me again, diagramming the action from his village in the mountains, along the path through the fields, to the deep, dark jungle. After this initial explanation, he closed his eyes and, speak-

---

[3]For the text of this dream, see pages 98–100.

ing rapidly, retold the dream again, adding quite a few details. When he saw the second draft of this dream, he added one more part that he said was missing: The closing dialogue between he and his wife, as they prepared to be parted until the arrival of the "second ark." Through the additions of these details the text of the dream more than doubled in length.

When I asked Shou if there were parts of the text that he would like to see revised, I thought he might ask me to change sections of the text that might challenge his religious convictions, or his role as a father. Actually, he was not concerned with these parts of the text, but with sections that might reflect badly on members of his family. Sections that he particularly wanted to change involved episodes where his brothers did not measure up to the expectations of their father. Because of Shou's concerns, details in some of the stories concerning the relationships between his father and his brothers have been deleted.

My representation of Shou's voice in the text cannot match the authenticity of an autobiography. Nevertheless, by quoting from him frequently, choosing forms that suggest the emotional power of his speech, and by including him in discussions and revisions of the research text, I feel that this life history of Shou Cha has gained an authenticity of its own.

Three Dimensions of Life History Interpretation

From beginning to end, this life history research is a process of interpretation. Shou Cha begins by interpreting his life to me by means of stories. As a researcher and writer, my retelling of his life history involves three dimensions of interpretation: The story itself as a process of interpretation, the contextualization of individual lives, and the process of finding themes as they emerge from narratives.

Story as Interpretation

The first dimension of interpretation involves organizing the data gathered from interviews, participant observation, and library research into the form of a story. This is what Polkinghorne (1995) refers to as the process of *narrative analysis*, wherein elements of data are configured into a unified, meaningful story. The text that appears in this study has been chosen to present an account that is readable, accurate, and meaningful, and that retains fidelity to the accounts given to me by my informants. In many ways, I follow the model of the "impressionist" *tale* as described by Van Maanen (1988): Dramatic recall, condensed yet vivid contextual descriptions, and the voice of the protagonist are all important elements in such tales. Rather than seeking "correctness," the audience must judge this life history by the standards of "interest (does it attract?), coherence (does it hang together?) and fidelity (does it seem true?)" (p. 105).

Narrative analysis involves the production of an emplotted narrative or story (e.g., life story, case study, life history). The inquirer seeks to configure data elements into a unified, meaningful story. This means discovering and developing a "plot" that reveals the connection between elements of the data. Narrative analysis involves synthesis of data, not categorization. Polkinghorne suggests that in narrative analysis the inquirer must begin with the question, How did this happen? Then the inquirer gathers the data necessary to answer the question. For one form of narrative inquiry, life history, this may include personal diaries, writings of the person, interviews with friends, family, and associates of the person, and interviews with the person herself. This collected data is then interpreted and integrated into a story. Polkinghorne (1995) suggests that "the final story must fit the data while at the same time bringing an order and meaningfulness that is not apparent in the data themselves" (p. 16).

Lives in Contexts

The second dimension of interpretation involves the contextualization of a life within history, culture, and a social milieu. My "inside" research served to deepen my understanding of the varying social and historical contexts of Shou Cha's life. As the research text grew, I found it necessary to become familiar with a variety of literatures, including the cultural history of the Hmong; the historical relations between nations of the West (e.g., France, the United States) and Indochina; religious fundamentalism and missionary activity; and bilingual and multicultural education, specifically regarding the education of new immigrants. Drawing from these and other literatures, I am better able to relate the life of Shou Cha within particular social, historical and cultural contexts, thus making that life more meaningful for a wider audience.

Of course a dilemma faces narrative inquirers who wish to provide a meaningful account of an individual's life, and at the same time, address the larger social, historical and cultural forces that shape that life. Brunner (1994) suggests that a major issue involving narrative form is the question of creating "professional texts that name problems and literary texts ... that illumine those issues and invite vicarious participation" (p. 93). In the same vein Smulyan asks: "How do we place the individual within her social context and demonstrate the powers and forces that shape her experience and also provide a rich description of her story, her shaping of her world" (quoted in Hatch & Wisniewski, 1995, p. 120)?

Representing in some way the "dialectic" between individual lives and societal contexts is one of the major challenges facing narrative inquirers, a challenge Hatch and Wisniewski (1995) argue is essential for narrative research:

> We see the power of life history and narrative accounts in the dialectic between the unique experiences of individuals and the constraints of broad social, political, and economic structures. It may be possible artfully to weave these constraints into life stories so that they are barely visible, but their presence is essential. (p. 128)

A life history of an individual, to be meaningful, must be placed within social, cultural and historical contexts. Such contexts for the life of Shou Cha are developed in the first four chapters of part two, focusing particularly on the intersection of Shou Cha's life with history, community, family and school.

Emergent Themes

The third dimension of interpretation involves the development of themes that emerge from the narrative. The complexity of an individual life should not be sacrificed to an overriding theory, be it positivist, postpositivist, constructivist or critical. In my interpretive work I have chosen a poststructuralist interpretive strategy similar to the *interpretive interactionism* described by Denzin, examining critical epiphanies in the life of Shou Cha, and placing his lived experience within historical, social, and cultural contexts. At the same time I examine emerging themes from the narrative, using grounded theory without the rigid categorization of data, relying rather on the critical encounters with the developing text that I share with my protagonist. Thus, although this life history narrative is punctuated by critical moments in the life and learning of Shou Cha, the arrangement of chapters is as much thematic as chronological.

SUMMARY

Narrative inquiry can offer researchers an intimate portrait of an individual, situated within historical, social, and cultural contexts, yet revealed as an active agent in his or her own life. Through varied narrative forms, writers of lives can bring out the aesthetic in social science texts, and bridge some of the gap that separates the language of informants from that of the academy. Moreover, when narrative inquirers take seriously questions of representation, they can better insure that the stories they retell are given back to informants "in good company," as Grumet advocates.

References

Alliance distinctives and government [Workbook]. (1990). Colorado Springs: Christian and Military Alliance.

Anderson, M. (1951). *Woman at work*. Minneapolis: University of Minnesota Press.

Antin, M. (1912). *The promised land*. Boston: Houghton Mifflin.

Anyon, J. (1995). Race, social class, and educational reform in an inner-city school. *Teachers College Record, 97*(1), 69–94.

Atkinson, P. & Hammersley, M. (1994). Ethnography and participant observation. In N. Denzin & Y. Lincoln (Eds.), *Handbook of Qualitative Research* (pp. 248–261). Thousand Oaks, CA: Sage.

Baca Zinn, M. (1989). Family, race and poverty in the eighties. *Journal of Women in Culture and Society, 14*(4), 856–874.

Bakhtin , M. (1981). *The dialogic imagination*. Austin: University of Texas Press.

Bailey, K. (1987). *The Best of A. B. Simpson*. Camp Hill, PA: Christian Publications.

Barney, G. (1986). *Mormons, Indians and the ghost dance religion of 1890*. Lanham, MD: University Press of America.

Beck, R. (1994.) The ordeal of immigration in Wausau. *Atlantic Monthly, 273(4),* 84–97.

Becker, H. (1970). *Sociological work*. Chicago: Aldine.

Belenky, M., Clinchy, B., Goldberger, N., & Tarule, J. (1986). *Women's ways of knowing: The development of self, voice, and mind*. New York: Basic Books.

Bellah, R. (1987). The quest for the self: Individualism, morality, politics. In P. Rabinow & W. Sullivan (Eds.), *Interpretive social science: A second look* (pp. 365–383). Berkeley: University of California Press.

Bellah, R., Madsen, R., Sullivan, W., Swidler, A., & Tipton, S. (1985). *Habits of the heart: Individualism and commitment in American life*. New York: Harper & Row.

Bellah, R., Madsen, R., Sullivan, W., Swidler, A., & Tipton, S. (1991). *The good society*. New York: Harper & Row.

Berrol, S. (1995). *Growing up American: Immigrant children in America, then and now*. New York: Twayne.

Blumenfeld-Jones, D. (1995). Fidelity as a criterion for practicing and evaluating narrative inquiry. In J. Hatch & R. Wisniewski (Eds.), *Life history and narrative* (pp. 25–35). Bristol, PA: Falmer.

Bok, E. (1922). *The Americanization of Edward Bok*. New York: Scribner's.

Bosma, H., Graafsma, T., Grotevant, H., & de Levita, D. (Eds.). (1994). *Identity and development: An interdisciplinary approach*. Thousand Oaks, CA: Sage.

Bourdieu, P. (1977). Cultural reproduction and social reproduction. In J. Karabel & A. Halsey (Eds.), *Power and ideology in education* (pp. 487–511). New York: Oxford University Press.

Bruner, J. (1985). *Actual minds, possible worlds.* Cambridge: Harvard University Press.

Bruner, J. (1990). *Acts of meaning.* Cambridge: Harvard University Press.

Brunner, D. (1994). *Inquiry and reflection: Framing narrative practice in education.* Albany: State University of New York Press.

Burridge, K. (1991). *In the way: A study of Christian missionary endeavors.* Vancouver, Canada: UBC Press.

Cabeza de Vaca, A. (1527/1964). *The Journey of Alvar Nunez Cabeza de Vaca.* Chicago: The Rio Grande Press.

Capra, F. (1985). *The name above the title.* New York: Vintage.

Carnegie, A. (1920). *The autobiography of Andrew Carnegie.* Boston: Houghton Mifflin.

Casey, K. (1996). The new narrative research in education. In M. Apple (Ed.), *Review of Research in Education, 21* (1995–1996), (pp. 211–253). Washington, DC: AERA.

Chan, S. (Ed.), (1994). *Hmong means free: Life in Laos and America.* Philadelphia: Temple University Press.

Cheung, S. (1995). Millenarianism, Christian movements, and ethnic change among the Miao in southwest China. In W. Harrell (Ed.), *Cultural encounters on China's ethnic frontiers* (pp. 217–247). Seattle: University of Washington Press.

Clandinin, D. E Connelly, F. (1994). Personal experience methods. In N. Denzin & Y. Lincoln (Eds.), *Handbook of qualitative research* (pp. 413–427). Thousand Oaks, CA: Sage.

Clausen, J. (1993). *American lives: Looking back at children of the great depression.* New York: Free Press.

Clifford, J. (1970). *From puzzles to portraits: Problems of a literary biographer.* Chapel Hill: University of North Carolina Press.

Clifford, J. (1988). *The predicament of culture: Twentieth century ethnography, literature, and art.* Cambridge, MA: Harvard University Press.

Clifford, J., & Marcus, G. (Eds.), (1986). *Writing culture: The poetics and politics of ethnography.* Berkeley: The University of California Press.

Cole, W. (1995). Strangers in a strange land. *Time, 146*(15), 50.

Coles, R. (1964). *Children of crisis: A study of courage and fear.* Boston: Little, Brown.

Colon, J. (1975). *A Puerto Rican in New York and other sketches.* New York: Arno Press.

Conquergood, D. (1989). *I am a shaman: A Hmong life story with ethnographic commentary* (Occasional Paper No. 8). Minneapolis: University of Minnesota, Southeast Asian Refugee Studies Project.

Coontz, S. (1988). *The social origins of private life: A history of American families, 1600–1900.* New York: Verso.

Cooper, R. (1986). The Hmong of Laos: Economic factors in the refugee exodus and return. In G. Hendricks, B. Downing, & A. Deinard (Eds.), *The Hmong in transition* (pp. 23–40). New York: The Center for Migration Studies.

Covello, L. (1958). *The heart is the teacher.* New York: McGraw-Hill.

Cowles, H., & Foster, K. (1993). *Prayer voices: A popular theology of prayer.* Camp Hill, PA: Christian Publications.

Crapanzano, V. (1980). *Tuhami: Portrait of a Moroccan.* Chicago: University of Chicago Press.

Crawford, J. (1989). *Bilingual education: History, politics, theory, and practice.* Trenton, NJ: Crane Publishing Co.

Crawford, J. (1992). *Hold your tongue: Bilingualism and the politics of "English only."* Reading, MA: Addison Wesley.

Cremin, L. (1988). *American education: The metropolitan experience, 1876-1980.* New York: Harper & Row.

Cubberley, E. (1934). *Public education in the United States: A study and interpretation of American educational history.* Boston: Houghton Mifflin.

Delpit, L. (1987). Power and pedagogy in educating other people's children. *Harvard Educational Review, 58*(3), 280-298.

Denzin, N. (1989). *Interpretative interactionism.* Beverly Hills, CA: Sage.

Denzin, N. (1994). The art and politics of interpretation. In N. Denzin & Y. Lincoln (Eds.), *Handbook of qualitative research* (pp. 500-515). Thousand Oaks, CA: Sage.

Denzin, N. & Lincoln, Y. (1994). Introduction: Entering the field of qualitative research. In N. Denzin & Y. Lincoln (Eds.), *Handbook of qualitative research* (pp. 1-18). Thousand Oaks, CA: Sage.

Dewey, J. (1897). *My pedagogic creed.* Washington, DC: Progressive Education Association.

Dewey, J. (1900). *The school and society.* Chicago: University of Chicago Press.

Di Leonardo, M. (1984). The varieties of ethnic experience: Kinship, class, and gender among California Italian-Americans. Ithaca: Cornell University Press.

Dollard, J. (1935). *Criteria for the life history.* New Haven: Yale University Press.

Donnelly, N. (1994). *Changing lives of refugee Hmong women.* Seattle: University of Washington Press.

Duenas Gonzalez, R., Schott, A., & Vasquez, V. (1988). The English language amendment: Examining myths. *English Journal, 77*(3), 24-30.

Dunnigan, T. (1986). Processes of identity maintenance in Hmong society. In G. Hendricks, B. Downing, & A. Deinard (Eds.), *The Hmong in transition* (pp. 41-54). New York: The Center for Migration Studies.

Erickson, F. (1992). Ethnographic microanalysis of interaction. In M. LeCompte, W. Millroy, & J. Preissle (Eds.), *The handbook of qualitative research in education* (pp. 201-225). San Diego: Academic Press.

Erikson, E. (1950). *Childhood and society.* New York: Norton.

Erikson, E. (1959a). *Identity and the life cycle.* New York: Norton.

Erikson, E. (1962). *Young man Luther: A study in psychoanalysis and history.* New York: Norton.

Fine, E. (1984). *The folklore text: From performance to print.* Bloomington: Indiana University Press.

Florio-Ruane, S., & DeTar, J. (1995). Conflict and consensus in teacher candidates' discussion of ethnic autobiography. *English Education, 27*(1), 11-39.

Foucault, M. (1979). *Discipline and punish: The birth of the prison.* New York: Vintage Books.

Fraser, J. (1985). *Pedagogue for God's kingdom: Lyman Beecher and the second great awakening.* Lanham, MD: University Press of America.

Freeman, M. (1993). *Rewriting the self: History, memory, narrative.* New York: Routledge.

Freire, P. (1968). *Pedagogy of the oppressed.* New York: Herder and Herder.

Fuchs, L. (1990). *The American kaleidoscope: Race, ethnicity, and the civic culture.* Hanover, NH: Wesleyan University Press.

Galarza, E. (1971). *Barrio boy.* South Bend: University of Notre Dame Press.

Galindo, R., & Olguin, M. (1996). Reclaiming bilingual educators' cultural resources: An autobiographical approach. *Urban Education, 31*(1), 29–56.

Gardner, H. (1993). *Creating minds: An anatomy of creativity seen through the lives of freud, Einstein, Picasso, Stravinsky, Eliot, Graham, and Gandhi.* New York: Basic Books.

Gee, J. (1990). *Social linguistics and literacies: Ideology in discourses.* Philadelphia: Falmer Press.

Geertz, C. (1983). *Local knowledge: Further essays in interpretive anthropology.* New York: Basic Books.

Geertz, C. (1987). Notes on a Balinese cockfight. In P. Rabinow & W. Sullivan (Eds.), *Interpretive social science: A second look* (pp. 195–240). Berkeley: University of California Press.

Gergen, K., & Gergen, M. (1991). Toward reflexive methodologies. In N. Steier (Ed.), *Research and reflexivity* (pp. 76–95). Newbury Park, CA: Sage.

Gibson, M. (1988). *Adaptation without assimilation: Sikh immigrants in an American high school.* Ithaca, NY: Cornell University Press.

Gilligan, C., (Ed.). (1988). *Mapping the moral domain: A contribution of women's thinking to psychological theory and education.* Cambridge, MA: Harvard University Press.

Giroux, H. (1988). Critical theory and the politics of culture and voice: Rethinking the discourse of educational research. In P. Sherman & S. Webb (Eds.), *Qualitative research in education: Focus and methods* (pp. 190–210). New York: Falmer.

Glaser, B., & Strauss, A. (1967). *The discovery of grounded theory: Strategies for qualitative research.* New York: Aldine de Gruyter.

Gleason, P. (1983). Identifying identity: A semantic history. *The Journal of American History, 69*(4), 910–931.

Glenn, C. (1988). *The myth of the common school.* Amherst: The University of Massachusetts Press.

Graff, H. (1987). *The legacies of literacy: Continuities and contradictions in western culture and society.* Bloomington: Indiana University Press.

Greene, M. (1996). In search of a critical pedagogy. In P. Leistyna, A. Woodrum, & S. Sherblom (Eds.), *Breaking free: The transformative power of critical pedagogy* (pp. 13–30). Cambridge, MA: Harvard University Press.

Grumet, M. (1991). The politics of personal knowledge. In C. Witherell & N. Noddings, (Eds.), *Stories lives tell: Narrative and dialogue in education* (pp. 67–77). New York: Teachers College Press.

Guba, E., & Lincoln, Y. (1989). *Fourth generation evaluation.* Newbury Park, CA: Sage.

Gutmann, A. (1987). *Democratic education.* Princeton, NJ: Princeton University Press.

Gwaltney, J. (1980). *Drylongso: A portrait of Black America.* New York: Vintage Books.

Hall, E. (1959). *The silent language.* Garden City, NY: Doubleday.

Hall, G. (1911). *Educational problems, II.* New York: D. Appleton.

Hamilton-Merritt, J. (1993). *Tragic mountains: The Hmong, the Americans, and the secret wars for Laos, 1942–1992*. Bloomington: Indiana University Press.

Handlin, O. (1951). *The uprooted: The epic story of the great migrations that made the American people*. Boston: Little, Brown.

Handlin, O. (1982). Education and the European immigrant, 1820–1920. In B. Weiss (Ed.), *American Education and the European Immigrant, 1840–1940*. Urbana: University of Illinois Press.

Harding, S. (1992). The afterlife of stories: Genesis of a man of God. In G. Rosenwald & R. Ochberg, (Eds.), *Storied lives: The cultural politics of self-understanding* (pp. 60–75). New Haven, CT: Yale University Press.

Hatch, J., & Wisniewski, R. (1995). Life history and narrative: Questions, issues and exemplary works. In J. Hatch & R. Wisniewski (Eds.), *Life history and narrative* (pp. 113–135). Bristol, PA: Falmer.

Heath, S. (1983). *Ways with words*. New York: Cambridge University Press.

Hellmuth, J. (Ed.). (1967). *The disadvantaged child*. Seattle: Special Child Publication of the Seattle Seguin School, Inc.

Higham, J. (1971). *Strangers in the land: Patterns of American nativism, 1860–1925*. New York: Atheneum.

Hirsch, E. (1987). *Cultural Literacy: What every American needs to know*. New York: Vintage.

Hoffman, E. (1989). *Lost in translation: A life in a new language*. New York: Dutton.

Holte, J. (1988). *The ethnic I: A sourcebook for ethnic-American autobiography*. New York: Greenwood Press.

Horton, M. (1990). *The long haul*. New York: Doubleday.

Hoskins, M., & Leseho, J. (1996). Changing metaphors of the self: Implications for counseling. *Journal of Counseling and Development, 74* (January/February), 243–252.

Houston, J. (1978). *Beyond Manzanar: Views of Asian-American womanhood*. Santa Barbara, CA: Capra Press.

Howe, I., & Libo, K. (Eds.). (1979). *How we lived: A documentary history of immigrant Jews in America, 1880–1930*. New York: Dutton.

Huberman, M., Thompson, C., & Weiland, S. (1997). Perspectives on the teaching career. In B. Biddle, T. Good, & I. Goodson (Eds.), *International handbook of teachers and teaching* (Vol. 1, pp. 11–77). Dordrecht, Netherlands: Kluwer.

Hudspeth, W. (1937). *Stone gateway and the flowery Miao*. London: Cargate.

Imhoff, G. (1990). The position of U.S. English on bilingual education. *Annals of the American Academy of Political and Social Science, 508*, 48–61.

Jackson, M. (1989). *Paths toward a clearing: Radical empiricism and ethnographic inquiry*. Bloomington: Indiana University Press.

Jenks, R. (1994). *Insurgency and social disorder in Guizhou: The "Miao" rebellion, 1854–1873*. Honolulu: University of Hawaii Press.

Jorgenson, L. (1987). *The state and the non-public school, 1825–1925*. Columbia, MO: University of Missouri Press.

Kaestle, C. (1983). *Pillars of the republic: Common schools and American society, 1780–1860*. New York: Hill and Wang.

Kallen, H. (1924). *Culture and democracy in the United States: Studies in the group psychology of the American peoples*. New York: Boni and Liveright.

Kalmijn, M., & Kraakamp, G. (1996). Race, cultural capital, and schooling: An analysis of trends in the United States. *Sociology of Education*, *69*(1), 22–34.

Kazin, A. (1951). *A walker in the city*. New York: Harcourt.

Kennedy, D. (1996). Can we still afford to be a nation of immigrants? *Atlantic Monthly*, *278*(5), 51–68.

Kincheloe, J., & McLaren, P. (1994). Rethinking critical theory and qualitative research. In N. Denzin & Y. Lincoln (Eds.), *Handbook of Qualitative research* (pp. 138–157). Thousand Oaks, CA: Sage.

Kingston, M. (1976). *The woman warrior: Memoirs of a girlhood among ghosts*. New York: Alfred Knopf.

Kotlowitz, A. (1991). *There are no children here: The story of two boys growing up in the other America*. New York: Anchor.

Kotre, J. (1984). *Outliving the self: Generativity and the interpretation of lives*. Baltimore: The Johns Hopkins University Press.

Kozol, J. (1991). *Savage inequalities: Children in America's schools*. New York: Crown.

Krashen, S., & Terrell, T. (1983). *The natural approach: Language acquisition in the classroom*. Oxford: Pergamon.

Lagemann, E. (Ed.) (1985). *Jane Addams on education*. New York: Teachers College Press.

Lawyers Committee for Human Rights. (1989). *Forced back and forgotten: The human rights of Laotian asylum seekers in Thailand*. New York: Author.

Lee, G. (1986). Culture and adaptation: Hmong refugees in Australia. In G. Hendricks, B. Downing, & A. Deinard (Eds.), *The Hmong in transition* (pp. 55–72). New York: Center for Migration Studies.

Levin, M. (1950/1973). *In search*. New York: Pocket Books.

Lifton, R. (1993). *The protean self: Human resilience in an age of fragmentation*. New York: Basic Books.

Lincoln, Y. (1993). I and thou: Method, voice, and roles in research with the silenced. In D. McLaughlin & W. Tierney (Eds.), *Naming silenced lives: Personal narratives and processes for educational change* (pp. 29–47). New York: Routledge.

Lindquist, B. (1995). Children learn what they live. *Educational Leadership*, *52*(5), 50–51.

Livo, N., & Cha, D. (1991). *Folk stories of the Hmong: Peoples of Laos, Thailand and Vietnam*. Englewood, CO: Libraries Unlimited, Inc.

Long, L. (1993). *Ban Vinai: The refugee camp*. New York: Columbia University Press.

Lyons, J. (1990). The past and future directions of federal bilingual-education policy. *Annals of the American Academy of Political and Social Science*, *508*, 66–80.

Malinowski, B. (1922). *Argonauts of the western Pacific*. London: Routledge and Kegan Paul.

Manual of the Christian and missionary alliance (1995). Colorado Springs, CO: The Christian and Missionary Alliance.

McBeth, S., & Burnett Horne, E. (1996). "I know who I am": The collaborative life history of a Shoshone Indian woman. In G. Etter-Lewis & M. Foster (Eds.), *Unrelated kin: Race and gender in women's personal narratives*. New York: Routledge.

McCoy, A. (1991). *The politics of heroin: CIA complicity in the global drug trade*. Brooklyn, NY: Lawrence Hill Books.

McLaughlin, M., & Heath, S. (1993). Casting the self: Frames for identity and dilemmas for policy. In M. McLaughlin & S. Heath (Eds.), *Identity and inner-city youth: Beyond ethnicity and gender* (pp. 210–239). New York: Teachers College Press.

McLaughlin, D., & Tierney, W. (Eds.) (1993). *Naming silenced lives: Personal narratives and processes for educational change.* New York: Routledge.

Mills, C. W. (1959). *The sociological imagination.* New York: Oxford University Press.

Miller, D. (1996). "I Have a Frog in My Stomach": Mythology and truth in life history. In G. Etter-Lewis & M. Foster (Eds.), *Unrelated kin: Race and gender in women's personal narratives* (pp. 103–121). New York: Routledge.

Moll, L. (1992). Bilingual classroom studies and community analysis: Some recent trends. *Educational Researcher, 3,* 20–24.

Moll, L., & Greenberg, J. (1990). Creating zones of possibilities: Combining social contexts for instruction. In L. Moll (Ed.), *Vygotsky and education: Instructional implications for applications of sociohistorical psychology* (pp. 319–348). New York: Cambridge University Press.

Moore, D. (1989). *Dark sky, dark land: Stories of the Hmong boy scouts of troop 100.* Eden Prairie, MN: Tessera Publishing.

National League of Cities Survey Cites Youth Problems as Critical. (1994). *American City and County,* (1996), *111*(4), p. 64.

Niklaus, R., Sawin, J., &d Stoesz, S. (1986). *All For Jesus: God at work in the Christian and missionary alliance over one hundred years.* Camp Hill, PA: Christian Publications.

Nicklin, J. (1996). Teaching teachers to protect themselves and their students. *The Chronicle of Higher Education, 42*(33), A18–20.

Oakes, J. (1986, October). Keeping track, part 2: Curriculum inequality and school reform. *Phi Delta Kappan,* 148–154.

Ogbu, J. (1982). Cultural discontinuities and schooling. *Anthropology and Education Quarterly, 13*(4), 290–307.

Ogbu, J. (1991). Immigrant and involuntary minorities in comparative perspective. In M. Gibson & J. Ogbu (Eds.), *Minority status and schooling: A comparative study of immigrant and involuntary minorities* (pp. 3–36). New York: Garland.

Okihiro, G. (1994). *Margins and mainstreams: Asians in American history and culture.* Seattle: University of Washington Press.

Olesen, V. (1994). Feminisms and models of qualitative research. In N. Denzin & Y. Lincoln (Eds.), *Handbook of qualitative research* (pp. 158–174). Thousand Oaks, CA: Sage.

Ong, P. (1983). Chinese laundries as an urban occupation in nineteenth century California. In D. Lee (Ed.), *The Annals of the Chinese historical society of the pacific northwest* (pp. 65–81). Seattle: University of Washington Press.

Phelan, P., & Davidson, A. (1994). Looking across borders: Students' investigations of family, peer, and school worlds as cultural therapy. In G. Spindler & L. Spindler (Eds.), *Pathways to cultural awareness: Cultural therapy with teachers and students* (pp. 35–59). Thousand Oaks, CA: Corwin Press.

Phillips, D. (1994). Telling It straight: Issues in assessing narrative research. *Educational Psychologist, 29*(1), 13–21.

Polkinghorne, D. (1995). Narrative configuration in qualitative analysis. In J. Hatch & R. Wisniewski (Eds.), *Life history and narrative* (pp. 5–23). Bristol, PA: Falmer.

Portes, A., & Rumbaut, R. (1990). *Immigrant America: A portrait.* Berkeley: University of California Press.

Putnam, R. (1995). Bowling alone: America's declining social capital. *Journal of Democracy, 6*(1), 65–78.

Rabinow, P. (1977). *Reflections on fieldwork in Morocco.* Berkeley, CA: University of California Press.

Rabinow, P., & Sullivan, W. (Eds.). (1987). *Interpretive social science: A second look.* Berkeley: University of California Press.

Rabinow, P., & Sullivan, W. (1987). The interpretive turn: A second look. In P. Rabinow & W. Sullivan (Eds.), *Interpretive social science: A second look* (pp. 1–30). Berkeley: University of California Press.

Ranard, D. (1989). The last bus. *Atlantic Monthly, 260,* 4, 26–34.

Reason, P. (1994). Three approaches to participative inquiry. In N. Denzin & Y. Lincoln (Eds.), *Handbook of qualitative research* (pp. 324–339). Thousand Oaks, CA: Sage.

Reske, H. (1996). When detentions fail: Fearful teachers try suing disruptive and violent students. *ABA Journal, 82,* 22–23.

Rich, A. (1986). *Blood, bread and poetry: Selected prose, 1979–1985.* New York: Norton.

Richardson, L. (1992). The consequences of poetic representation: Writing the other, rewriting the self. In C. Ellis & M. Flaherty (Eds.), *Investigating subjectivity: Research on lived experience* (pp. 125–140). Newbury Park, CA: Sage.

Ricoeur, P. (1983). *Time and narrative.* Chicago: University of Chicago Press.

Riegel, K. (1976). The dialectics of human development. *American Psychologist, 31*(10), 689–700.

Riis, J. (1901). *The making of an American.* New York: MacMillan.

Rodriguez, R. (1982). *Hunger of memory: The education of Richard Rodriguez.* New York: Bantam.

Rodriguez, R. (1992). *Days of obligation: An argument with my Mexican father.* New York: Viking.

Roop, P., & Roop, C. (1990). *The Hmong in America: We sought refuge here.* Appleton, WI: Appleton Area School District.

Rosaldo, R. (1980). *Ilongot headhunting 1883–1974: A study in society and history.* Stanford, CA: Stanford University Press.

Rubin, S. (1992). The Ghetto and beyond: First-generation American-Jewish autobiography and cultural history. In J. Payne (Ed.), *Multicultural autobiography: American lives* (178–206). Knoxville: University of Tennessee Press.

Rugg, H. (1941). *That men may understand: An American in the long armistice.* New York: Doubleday.

Rushdoony, R. (1963). *The messianic character of American education.* Nutley, NJ: The Craig Press.

Ruth, J., & Oberg, P. (1992). Expressions of aggression in the life stories of aged women. In K. Bjorkquist & P. Neimela (Eds.), *Of mice and women: Aspects of female aggression* (pp. 133–146). San Diego: Academic.

Ryff, C. (1989). Beyond Ponce de Leon and life satisfaction: New directions in quest of successful aging. *International Journal of Behavioral Development, 12*(1), 35–55.

Sabbag, R. (1995). Lost in America. *Rolling Stone, 703,* 56–72.

Santoli, A. (1988). *New Americans: An oral history.* New York: Viking.

Sarris, G. (1993). *Keeping slug woman alive: A holistic approach to American Indian texts*. Berkeley: University of California Press.

Sarris, G. (1994). *Mabel McKay: Weaving the dream*. Berkeley: University of California Press.

Schlesinger, A. (1991). *The disuniting of America*. Knoxville: Whittle Direct Books.

Schutz, A. (1964). *Studies in social theory*. The Hague: Martinus Nijhoff.

Schwandt, T. (1994). Constructivist, interpretivist approaches to human inquiry. In N. Denzin & Y. Lincoln (Eds.), *Handbook of qualitative research* (pp. 118–137). Thousand Oaks, CA: Sage.

Shell, M. (1993). Babel in America; or, the politics of language diversity in the United States. *Critical Inquiry, 20*(1), 103–127.

Sinclair, U. (1906). *The Jungle*. New York: Doubleday.

Smith, L. (1994). Biographical method. In N. Denzin & Y. Lincoln (Eds.), *Handbook of qualitative research* (pp. 286–305). Thousand Oaks, CA: Sage.

Smrekar, C. (1996). *The impact of school choice and community: In the interest of families and schools*. Albany: State University of New York Press.

Soto, L. (1997). *Language, culture, and power: Bilingual families and the struggle for quality education*. Albany, NY: SUNY Press.

Spindler, G., & Spindler, L. (1990). *The American cultural dialogue and its transmission*. New York: Falmer Press.

Spindler, G., & Spindler, L. (1994). What is cultural therapy? In G. Spindler & L. Spindler (Eds.), *Pathways to cultural awareness: Cultural therapy with teachers and students* (pp. 1–33). Thousand Oaks, CA: Corwin Press.

Strauss, A., & Corbin, J. (1994). Grounded theory methodology: An overview. In N. Denzin & Y. Lincoln (Eds.), *Handbook of qualitative research* (pp. 273–285). Thousand Oaks, CA: Sage.

Swadener, B., & Lubeck, S. (Eds.). (1995). *Children and families "at promise": Deconstructing the discourse of risk*. Albany, NY: State University of New York Press.

Swett, J. (1911). *Public education in California ... with personal reminiscences*. New York: American Book Company.

Takaki, R. (1993). *A different mirror: A history of multicultural America*. Boston: Little, Brown.

Tapp, N. (1989a). The impact of missionary Christianity upon marginalized ethnic minorities: The case of the Hmong. *Journal of Southeast Asian Studies, 20*(1), 70–95.

Tapp, N. (1989b). Hmong religion. *Asian Folklore Studies, 48*, 59–94.

Tedlock, D. (1983). *The spoken word and the work of interpretation*. Philadelphia: University of Pennsylvania Press.

Terkel, S. (1972). *Working*. New York: Avon.

Thao, S., & Lee, M. (1995). *Lao Hmong veterans recognition*. Video documentary of the July 4, 1995, recognition ceremonies in Colorado for Hmong veterans. Written by Moua Lee and produced by Su Thao.

Thernstrom, A. (1990). Bilingual miseducation. *Commentary, 89*(2), 44–48.

Timm, J. (1994). Hmong values and American education. *Equity and Excellence in Education, 27*(2), 36–44.

Tollefson, J. (1989). *Alien winds: The reeducation of America's Indochinese refugees*. New York: Praeger.

Toqueville, A. (1945). *Democracy in America*. New York: Alfred A. Knopf.

Trueba, H. (1994). Foreword. In G. Spindler & L. Spindler (Eds.), *Pathways to cultural awareness: Cultural therapy with teachers and students* (pp. vii–xi). Thousand Oaks, CA: Corwin Press.

Trueba, H., Jacobs, L., & Kirton, E. (1990). *Cultural conflict and adaptation: The case of Hmong children in American society*. New York: Falmer Press.

Trueba, H., & Zou, Y. (1994). *Power in education: The case of Miao university students and its significance for American culture*. Washington, DC: Falmer.

Tuchman, G. (1994). Historical social science: Methodologies, methods and meanings. In N. Denzin & Y. Lincoln (Eds.), *Handbook of qualitative research* (pp. 306–323). Thousand Oaks, CA: Sage.

Tyack, D., & Hansot, E. (1982). *Managers of virtue: Public school leadership in America, 1820–1980*. New York: Basic Books.

Ungar, S. (1995). *Fresh blood: The new American immigrants*. New York: Simon and Schuster.

United Hmong Parents/ACORN. (1994). *Making St. Paul's schools work for everyone: An introductory paper regarding the problems facing the Hmong community in the St. Paul public schools*. Minnesota ACORN, 757 Raymond Avenue, Suite 200, St. Paul, MN 55114.

U.S. Department of Education (1993). *Descriptive study of services to limited English proficient students*. Washington, DC: Planning and Evaluation Service.

Vang, C., Yang, G., & Smalley, W. (1990). *The life of Shong Lue Yang: Hmong "Mother of Writing."* Southeast Asian Refugee Studies Occasional Papers Number 9. Minneapolis: Southeast Asian Refugee Studies.

Vang, L., & Lewis, J. (1990). *Grandmother's path, grandfather's way: Oral lore, generation to generation*. Rancho Cordova, CA: Vang and Lewis.

Van Maanen, J. (1988). *Tales from the field: On writing ethnography*. Chicago: University of Chicago Press.

Vargas Llosa, M. (1981). *La Guerra del Fin del Mundo*. Barcelona: Seix Barral.

Vygotsky, L. (1978). *Mind in society: Development of higher psychological processes*. Cambridge: Harvard University Press.

Walker-Moffat, W. (1995). *The other side of the Asian American success story*. San Francisco: Jossey-Bass.

Walkover, B. (1992). The family as an overwrought object of desire. In G. Rosenwald & R. Ochberg (Eds.), *Storied lives: The cultural politics of self-understanding* (pp. 178–191). New Haven, CT: Yale University Press.

Walzer, M. (1990). What does It mean to be an "American"? *Social Research, 57*(3), 591–614.

Walzer, M. (1996, December). For identity. *The New Republic*, 39.

Weiland, S. (in press). From adult learning to adult learners. In S. Weiland, C. Thompson, & M. Huberman, *Education according to biography: Adult learning and the study of lives* (p. 34).

Wells, A., & Serna, I. (1996). The politics of culture: Understanding local political resistance to de-tracking in racially mixed schools. *Harvard Educational Review, 66*(1), 92–117.

White, R. (1952). *Lives in progress*. New York: Dryden.

Whitman, W. (1968). *Leaves of grass: A selection of the poems*. Mount Vernon, NY: Peter Pauper Press.

Wieseltier, L. (1994, November). Against identity: An idea whose time has gone. *The New Republic*, 24.

Witherell, C., & Noddings, N. (Eds.). (1991). *Stories lives tell: Narrative and dialogue in education*. New York: Teachers College Press.

Wong, S. (1992). Autobiography as guided Chinatown tour? Maxine Hong Kingston's *The Woman Warrior* and the Chinese American Autobiographical Controversy. In J. Payne (Ed.), *Multicultural autobiography: American lives* (pp. 248–279). Knoxville: University of Tennessee Press.

Zeichner, K. (1993). *Educating teachers for cultural diversity* (NCRTL Special Report). East Lansing, MI: National Center for Research on Teacher Learning, Michigan State University.

Author Index

Subject Index